Quote from: "Our La ||||||| W9-BSG-564
and found" by Di...

" .. ironically calling it fiction
would make it easier to believe
There are some truths that cannot
be made credible in any other
way."

"Now I see the dividing line between
fact and fiction becomes increasingly
unclear the harder you search for
it. The same, I must note, has
been said of searching for faith,
searching for God."

OTHER BOOKS BY BRIAN D. MCLAREN

A New Kind of Christian

o

The Church on the Other Side:
Doing Ministry in the Postmodern Matrix

Finding Faith

More Ready Than You Realize

A Is for Abductive (with Dr. Leonard Sweet and Jerry Haselmeyer)

Adventures in Missing the Point (with Dr. Anthony Campolo)

THE STORY WE FIND OURSELVES IN

THE STORY WE FIND OURSELVES IN

Further Adventures
of a New Kind of Christian

Brian D. McLaren

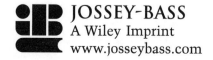

JOSSEY-BASS
A Wiley Imprint
www.josseybass.com

Published by Jossey-Bass
A Wiley Imprint
989 Market Street, San Francisco, CA 94103-1741   www.josseybass.com

This story is a work of fiction; all characters are creations of the author.
Any resemblance to any real person, living or dead, is purely coincidental
and unintended.

All scripture quotations, unless otherwise noted, are from the *New International Version.*

Jossey-Bass books and products are available through most bookstores.
To contact Jossey-Bass directly call our Customer Care Department within
the U.S. at 800-956-7739, outside the U.S. at 317-572-3986 or fax 317-
572-4002.

Jossey-Bass also publishes its books in a variety of electronic formats. Some
content that appears in print may not be available in electronic books.

Library of Congress Cataloging-in-Publication Data

McLaren, Brian D., date
The story we find ourselves in: further adventures of a new kind
of Christian / Brian D. McLaren.—1st ed.
        p. cm.
    Includes bibliographical references.
    ISBN 0–7879–6387–9
    I. Title.
PS3613.C569S76 2003
813'.6—dc21   2002013072

Printed in the United States of America

FIRST EDITION
HB Printing   10 9 8 7 6 5 4 3 2 1

CONTENTS

PREFACE

I STARTED GETTING NERVOUS when *A New Kind of Christian* was released. I'm not temperamentally a controversialist, not polemical, not a
fighter. I don't like arguments, especially religious ones. (Among other
things, in religious argument I find myself becoming a worse kind of Christian.) As the release date neared, I became more and more afraid that the
book would stir up contention and plunge me into a mode of discourse
(self-defense) that I do not want, need, or have time for. I knew that the
book might frustrate some people, but hoped (naively, no doubt) that those
people wouldn't read it. Instead, I hoped that the book would quietly find
its way into other hands where its main effect would be to inspire hope
rather than stir contention. I suspected that there are a lot of "Dan Pooles"
out there—people who love and seek God but feel that something in the
way we're "doing Christianity" is not working.

Although the book has been criticized (with, occasionally, something
like vehemence), people predisposed to disagree with the book generally
have been gracious, feeling, I suspect, that new explorations for better
ways of articulating and living our faith are needed, so efforts such as *A
New Kind of Christian,* though flawed, at least deserve a chance.

Discouraging words, then, have been heard far less often than encouraging ones. I receive a steady stream of affirming e-mails about the book—
thank-yous and requests for further dialogue written with such intensity
and openness that I feel deeply honored and humbled. One sits at the keyboard late at night, banging away at characters—m's, r's, e's,)'s, ?'s, ;'s—
trying to wrestle into symbols one's own questions, neuroses, hunches,
hopes, and intuitions. Often the very pleasure of writing is reward enough.
Then, beyond that satisfaction, to have these sincere and enthusiastic responses come in . . . well, sometimes it's too much to contain.

Along with their thanks, people have responded to the book by asking
for *more*—more information, more dialogue, more exploration. "I didn't
want the book to end," many people have said. ("It gave me a headache!"
said others.) *The Story We Find Ourselves In* seeks to fulfill that request
for the conversation to continue, and to do so with as few headaches as I
could manage (brace yourself for a couple, though).

By way of clarification for readers of *A New Kind of Christian:* No, Neo was not based on one real person, nor was Dan Poole or any of the other characters. All are fictional, but nearly all their conversations were drawn from the many real-life conversations I have participated in over recent years. For readers unfamiliar with *A New Kind of Christian:* I've worked hard to make sure that this book stands alone and doesn't require you to read its prequel. (As you'll realize when you reach the last page, this pair of books may become a trilogy, with each book enriching but not requiring the reading of the others.)

Much of *A New Kind of Christian* explored the issue of postmodernity: what it is, why it matters, and what challenges and opportunities it presents for the Christian faith. Many of us, not least those who are writing and speaking on the subject, vacillate between enthusiasm about the usefulness of the term *postmodern* and feeling sick to death of it. Yes, we believe that postmodernity (a cultural shift still in its embryonic forms) must be understood, grappled with, and engaged, but we also know that in the process, the concept can launch a kind of fad with attendant slogans, jargon, insider-outsider or us-them sociology, and other unpleasant side effects.

With all my ambivalence about the term *postmodern,* I have always been clear that my confidence was in the Christian gospel (appropriately understood), not in any cultural framework, whether modern, pre-, or post-. The more I have written about postmodernity (and so on), the more I have wanted to get to the point where it no longer needed to be written about so much. I wanted to start writing more directly about the Christian gospel itself, from a vantage point within the emerging culture, without always having to describe, validate, and defend the vantage point. *The Story We Find Ourselves In* marks a turn in my work from mapping a new vantage point to describing the scenery from it.

Of course, the preceding paragraph could easily be critiqued. Someone might argue that one's goal as a Christian should not be to describe the gospel from the vantage point of a cultural matrix, but rather to describe one's cultural matrix from the vantage point of the gospel. To do justice to that critique, however, would force me back into the old territory of a conversation that I am trying to extend into new territory. So I'll have to leave that conversation for readers to imagine on their own, indulging myself only in this short bit of wisdom from Lesslie Newbigin: "We must start with the basic fact that there is no such thing as a pure gospel if by that is meant something which is not embodied in a culture. . . . Every interpretation of the gospel is embodied in some cultural form" (*The Gospel in a Pluralist Society,* 1989).

Three real-life conversations deserve to be recounted as background for the imaginary ones found in *The Story We Find Ourselves In.*

1. A few years ago, I was invited to team-teach a course with Dr. John Franke (coauthor, with Dr. Stanley Grenz, of *Beyond Foundationalism* [Westminster John Knox, 2001]) at Biblical Theological Seminary in Hatfield, Pennsylvania. After class one day, John and I took a long walk around the neighborhood of the seminary. We were talking about what might come next theologically—beyond the reigning systematic theologies that took shape in the modern world (from, say, 1500 to 1950)—to answer modern questions and to suit modern tastes. We agreed that new theologies probably would be less analytical in structure and more rooted in the biblical narrative, less about filling in the subpoints of an outline (hamartiology, soteriology, ecclesiology, eschatology, and so on) and more about finding and celebrating meaning from our story.

Then John shared with me his thumbnail summary of the biblical story. I had been working on a similar outline (also relying heavily on alliteration on the letter *c*), and found the similarity of our approaches very encouraging. Although I borrowed and learned much from John's outline that day, no one should blame John (or his seminary) for the ways I have chosen to tell the story a bit differently than he (or they) might.

2. Sometime after that, a perceptive reader of *A New Kind of Christian* remarked to me, "I know you are uncomfortable calling the book *fiction,* so I think I have a category to describe it: *creative nonfiction.*" Thus I was given the term I needed for that book and, now, its sequel. I might slightly adjust his suggestion to *creative essay* or *dialogical essay* (in the tradition of Galileo), having in mind there the meaning "an attempt" for the word "essay." Both these books are attempts to tell our Christian story with whatever creativity I could muster. I hope that the fictional elements will help you engage with the message of the book. Most readers tell me that was the case with *A New Kind of Christian.*

3. A few months ago, I took a once-in-a-lifetime vacation to the Galápagos Islands (all the more memorable because I was accompanied by my eighteen-year-old son, Trevor). The Galápagos serve as the setting for some chapters of this book. I wrote those chapters before visiting the Galápagos, and then made some revisions based on my firsthand experience. (Readers knowledgeable about the Galápagos nevertheless will find at least two small inaccuracies remaining, and will, I hope, forgive them as creative license.) We toured the islands on the *Sea Man,* an ecotourist yacht. Most of our fellow passengers were European, and late one night under the equatorial stars, I enjoyed a charming conversation with a German couple. They are nonreligious spiritual seekers, very much like Kerry, Kincaid, Femke, and Pieter in this book (and like Alice in *More Ready Than You Realize* [Zondervan, 2002]). Talking with them, I realized afresh how distant and irrelevant the Christian message (as we have been

telling it) seems to so many educated and thoughtful people today around the world, and yet how much they need to find a larger story in which the stories of their lives can be located.

With my European friends in mind, I hope that this book will help "nonreligious-but-spiritual" people, discover how their lives and world might look in the context of this new-old story, while helping modern Christians reimagine our story beyond the grid of its modern telling.

Readers will notice that the all too real events of September 11, 2001, find their way into this fictional tale. Since that tragic day, Americans like myself realize more intensely how our whole planet shares a frightening vulnerability: to horrific violence ("theirs" and "ours"); to the poverty and despair and desperation in which violence ferments; to biological and chemical weapons that seem to spread like a gas or a virus from our nightmares into our newspapers; to racial, ethnic, and religious hatred that separates nation from nation, neighbor from neighbor; to a powerful global economy (including an entertainment industry with too little conscience) that reduces every sacred thing into a profane commodity, and every sacred person into a materialistic consumer (and thereby threatens to remove the sacred from our lives more effectively than scientific naturalism ever could). A few Americans like myself also are beginning to realize how superpower status has its downside, and how much is expected from those to whom much is given.

With these new realizations, in these dangerous times, our whole planet now needs more than ever a good story to live in and to live by. There are a number of stories competing for the hearts and imaginations of humanity as we emerge together into this new century and millennium: the regressive stories of fundamentalist Islam and fundamentalist Christianity, or the progressive stories of secular "scientism" or American consumerism, for example. Once taken to the heart of human culture, each of these stories will produce its own kind of world. If the story explored in this book (or something like it) wins enough hearts, yet another kind of world will emerge. The story we believe and live in today has a lot to do with the world we create for our children, our grandchildren, and our descendents one hundred thousand years from now (if?).

As with *A New Kind of Christian*, this book has plenty to turn some readers into critics. If you think that you might be such a reader, please know that I'd rather not disturb you. My preference would be for you to return the book unread to the store where you bought it for a full refund. Neo and friends raise and ponder what may seem to you dangerous questions and dangerous answers in the pages that follow. Please do not assume that their answers are always mine; you may, however, safely assume that I think that all their questions and answers deserve consideration. If you are dissatisfied with some of the answers you find here (as I am), there's a good chance you're right. So I hope that you'll use your dissatisfaction constructively and attempt to articulate better answers yourself. I'll continue to try to do the same thing. Let's be respectful colleagues, not critical adversaries.

Just today, a reader of *A New Kind of Christian* told me, "For the last few years, I have felt like I'm swinging on a trapeze that I can't hold onto much longer. I finally let go of the old trapeze, and found myself flying through the air, hoping and praying I'll stay up long enough for a new trapeze to appear, but afraid it won't and I'll crash down to the ground. Your book came along at just the right time. I feel like another trapeze is coming."

I hope that this sequel will give that reader, and many others, something to reach for.

Laurel, Maryland
January 2003

BRIAN D. MCLAREN

This book is dedicated to Rachel, Brett, Trevor, and Jodi McLaren, whose father I am unspeakably proud to be. What an honor to be part of your stories, and to watch them unfold, as you each find your place in this mysterious, wonderful, meaningful story we find ourselves in.

ACKNOWLEDGMENTS

FIRST, I THANK THE PEOPLE of Cedar Ridge Community Church (www. crcc.org), among whom I serve as a pastor. Much of the material presented in this book first appeared in a series of sermons given there, and many of the fictional conversations in this book were inspired by actual ones in this vibrant, courageous, and innovative community of faith. I know that for them, it's difficult at times having me as a pastor: my ideas are at times a bit unconventional, I travel quite a bit, and my theological preoccupations can make me seem distant or inaccessible sometimes (like I'm on another planet or something). Thanks for your flexibility, patience, love, collaboration, tolerance, understanding, and prayers.

Second, I wish to mention several writings that helped to inspire this book. Daniel Quinn's *Ishmael* (Bantam, 1995), Orson Scott Card's *Pastwatch* (Tor, 1997), and Alan Dershowitz's *The Genesis of Justice* (Warner, 2001) stimulated new and fertile (if unorthodox) ways of reading the book of Genesis in the Bible. The poetry of Wendell Berry (especially *The Timbered Choir* [Counterpoint, 1999] and *Selected Poems* [Counterpoint, 1999]) celebrated a way of seeing creation that I hope I was able to follow in a few of these pages. Dallas Willard's *Divine Conspiracy* (Harper-SanFrancisco, 1998) encouraged me to think more deeply about the kingdom of God image in the teachings of Jesus, along with an apprenticeship model of Christianity.

David Quammen's *The Song of the Dodo* (Touchstone, 1997) is a wonderful and heartbreaking introduction to extinction and evolution from a scientific standpoint, and beautifully written too. John Haught's *God after Darwin* (Westview, 2001) offers Christian theological reflection on the theory of evolution, integrated with process theology, the new Trinitarianism, and eschatological realism. Quite a potent combination! Steven Johnson's *Emergence* (Scribner, 2001) adds richness to the concept of creation presented by Haught.

In addition, the writings and speaking of Nancey Murphy (especially *Beyond Liberalism and Fundamentalism* [Trinity, 1996]), Stanley Grenz and John Franke (especially *Beyond Foundationalism* [Westminster John Knox], 2000), Leonard Sweet and Lesslie Newbigin (too many to mention), David

Bosch (especially *The Transforming Mission* [Orbis, 1991]), Michael Polanyi (*Personal Knowledge* [University of Chicago Press, 1958]), Alan Roxburgh, and N. T. Wright have helped me in my own theological musings. Bob Buford's *Halftime* inspired the halftime imagery in Chapter Thirty.

The people of Jossey-Bass and Leadership Network again have been a pleasure to work with.

Finally, special thanks go to the *emergent* community, "a growing, generative friendship among missional Christian leaders" (www.emergentvillage.com). If it takes a village to raise a child, then it also takes a village to create a book. A person who writes is simply one spokesperson for conversations shared among many friends. The friends should never be blamed for the mistakes or shortcomings of the spokesperson, of course, but they should be credited for whatever success the spokesperson achieves.

B.D.M.

THE STORY WE FIND OURSELVES IN

TEARS ON MY NECK

To: danpoole@backspring.com
From: kellison@cdrc.ec
Date: August 5, 2001
Subject: Request for help, urgent

Dear Dan, It;s terrible after you havent heard from me for so long for me to finzlly email you aking a favr. This is rude of me inded but this is a favor th doing of which will also be a favor to you Im sure.

A good friend of mine is coming to the DC area. It appears she has a rare form of cancer (relapse) that the National Institutes of Health is interested in trying tp treat. I wonder if you can vist her she has no friends in the area there.

I told her about you an Carol and your three wonderful kids. Having NIH interested in your disease is not a good sign. She need some friends and probably doesnt have much time to make them (you understand, cancer very serious) You are one of the b3st I could offer. The fact that you are a m8nister of the gospel is no small advantage at a time like this in her life. (I could presume on Fr. Scott too but he has just retired and moved back to his hometown, Minnsota * think?)

I kn0w you are busy, too many duties and demands already, but if I were in hos[ital with a bad prognosis I know you would be there for me, and if you visit this dear friend, I will consider it more precious to me than if I were the one being blessed by your com-any and suppor.

Her name is Kerry Ellison. from Australia but she lived in California for many years and is a U.S. citixen. Shell be arrive tomorrow. Shell foll you in about me and my current situati0n including why you havent hear from me in so long. I hope to come up and visit her and you to as soon as possle. I wanted to accompany her on the flight but as shell explain myown condition doesnt permit right now (not to worry).

It extremely hard to get internet time here in the islands so Ill close with the assurance that you are in my prayers Daniel as is you family. No need respond as I m using Kerry's account just this once and wont be able to check for you rreply.—Neo (Phil 1722)

P.S. She arrives BWI American #1776 from Miami at 1122 p.m. Monday night and will take cab to hotel near NIH. She mets her doctors at NCI 9 am on Tuesday.

It was a Sunday night, the evening air still warm and moist after a hazy, brutally hot, and humid Mid-Atlantic day. I was tired. For some reason though, I felt that I should check my e-mail before going to bed, something I normally avoid doing because it often keeps me up too late, and most things can be handled better the next morning anyway. I had just returned from leading the evening service at Potomac Community Church, where I serve as pastor.

Those of you who have read the first account of my friendship with Dr. Neil Edward Oliver (whose friends always address him by his nickname, Neo, derived from his initials) can imagine how my eyes widened and my heart began to race as I realized who had sent me this e-mail. I remember slowly lifting my hands from the keyboard as I read, as if I were being arrested or held up.

I hadn't heard from Neo since he left for a 'round-the-world voyage some eighteen months earlier, and had worried about him (and prayed for him) more and more as each month passed. Now, reading this message from him, I began asking myself a dozen questions about his whereabouts and well-being. (His reference to his "condition" was disconcerting—I reread it several times. Also, Neo normally was as meticulous in his spelling and grammar as he was in his dress, so the flood of typos in the message told me that he was writing in extraordinary circumstances.) The references to Miami and the islands made me think of the Bahamas, or some other Caribbean islands, and then (of course!), Jamaica—Neo's place of birth.

By the time I ran downstairs to tell my wife, Carol, about this long-awaited contact from our friend, I had leapt from a hunch to a certainty: "Carol, Carol, wake up," I said, "I just got an e-mail from Neo in Jamaica."

Carol is one of those Southern-born people who sounds sweet and acts civil even when she's being torn from sleep. "Neo . . . an e-mail? Let me see, Dan!" She hopped out of bed, grabbed a robe, and beat me upstairs to my attic office.

"There's nothing about Jamaica here that I can see," she began, leaning toward the computer screen, "but we'll have to set up the guest room for his friend. I reckon she must be terrified. Of course you'll pick her up at the airport, right?" Neo hadn't expected us to put up his friend, but of course we would.

After a night of little sleep for either Carol or me, and after a Monday that seemed even longer than most, I arrived at the airport at 11:00 P.M., only to read "Delayed" on the screens that report the status of flights. At the American counter, I learned that the delay was due to tropical storm Chantal, twirling out in the Caribbean. The woman at the counter gave me my first doubt about my Jamaica theory as she explained that Flight 1776 was a continuing flight from Quito, Ecuador, with a stop in Miami. Ecuador? I remembered wondering what "ec" stood for in the return address of Neo's e-mail, and now at least I knew that piece of the puzzle.

If you fly a lot, you know how these things go. It was 2:46 A.M. when Flight 1776 finally arrived. The last person off the plane was Kerry, being pushed in a wheelchair down the jetway and through the gate.

Three things struck me immediately about Kerry. First, she was strikingly attractive. With her blue eyes, suntanned skin, and graying hair pulled back in a youthful ponytail, she reminded me of a woman whose name I couldn't remember, someone I'd seen in a *National Geographic*, that woman who worked with chimpanzees. (Later, I remembered the name, Jane Goodall, and the resemblance was stronger the more I thought about it, though Kerry was a bit taller.)

Second, I could see on her face a dull tiredness or pain, even as she managed a smile at the attendant who was helping her to her feet and helping her get a bag over one shoulder and a cane into the other hand. She'd smile, and then wince, and then smile again—then another wince as she assured the attendant that yes, she could walk, yes, she was fine, thank you for your help.

Third, as she stood, I noticed—there's no delicate way to say this—that she had no breasts. She wore jeans and a black T-shirt that revealed a chest as flat as any boy's, and before I could fully process what that meant, I was shaking her hand and introducing myself. As she dropped her cane and threw her arms around my neck, I could feel her ribs pressing against my chest. She started to cry.

I felt her tears on my neck as she hugged me. "Neo told me you might be here," she said, "but I didn't want to get my hopes up. Thank you so much for . . ." For some reason, I started crying, too.

Then came a flood of apologies that the plane was so late, and more thanks for picking her up, and questions about a good hotel, and assurances from me that Carol and I insisted she stay with us and consider our home her new home. She had no baggage beyond the carry-on bag that kept slipping off her shoulder. I took it and slung it over my shoulder. The attendant was watching all this from a few yards away, and he now returned and invited Kerry to sit back on the wheelchair, and she accepted. We left the gate, proceeded down the long concourse, past security, through the automatic doors, and out onto the sidewalk, where the attendant again helped Kerry to her feet and said goodbye. The two of us slowly walked across the road to the parking garage, and we were home by 3:45. She mentioned our mutual friend briefly on the way home. "I promised Neo I'd give you a full report on how he's been doing, Dan, but we'll need a few hours for that. A few days would be more like it!"

Carol was still awake when we arrived, and she and Kerry met with a warm embrace. There was no question of any further conversation; we needed to get Kerry to bed as soon as possible and save all talk for the next morning.

But that wasn't to be. The next morning, we faced the pressure of fighting Maryland traffic to get our new friend to Bethesda for her intake at the National Cancer Institute at 9:00 A.M. In fact, it wasn't until that evening that Carol and I got a chance to talk with Kerry at length.

That day, the kids needed Carol's help with their usual stuff (soccer practices, shopping), so I drove Kerry and then stayed at the hospital all day, waiting, reading magazines, doing a little work on my laptop, making a few calls on my mobile phone, visiting the candy machine a couple times in lieu of lunch. Carol joined me in the waiting room later in the afternoon. Kerry was almost finished with her tests, a nurse told us, and would be settled in her room by seven o'clock. Carol and I caught dinner in the cafeteria, and then cautiously entered Room 516. Kerry, sitting up in bed, eating her hospital dinner, welcomed us in.

"Quite a day," she said, as we settled in the squeaky vinyl seats at the foot of her bed.

"I can't imagine," Carol said. And with that, the conversation began and flowed until visiting hours ended at nine o'clock. It was kind of strange, but kind of natural too—as if we were already long-time friends, even though we hardly knew each other. We had immediate trust and warmth; now all we needed was the facts, which Kerry offered.

She was fifty-one, a biologist employed at the Charles Darwin Research Center in the Galápagos Islands, six hundred miles west of Ecuador. She had first been diagnosed with breast cancer five years earlier, back in California. She had undergone a bilateral radical mastectomy, along with an experimental form of chemotherapy, and had been free of cancer ever since—or so she thought until a few days earlier. Her first symptom of relapse had been a slight but nagging pain in her left leg, and then a few days later, while snorkeling in the ocean, she felt something erupt inside her armpit. "It was as if a golf ball suddenly popped through my muscle and bulged beneath my skin," she said. "I couldn't put my arm down normally, and right away, I knew I was in deep trouble."

She paused to glance at the IV tube hooked to her left forearm. "We immediately flew to Quito for some tests," she went on, leaving me wondering what kind of "we" she and Neo constituted. "The doctors in Quito talked to my oncologist in California, and they agreed that I needed care that I couldn't receive in Ecuador. Then my oncologist contacted NCI, and because my cancer is a very rare one, they agreed that I should come here, and Neo contacted you, and so . . . here I am."

In the back of my mind, I wanted to ask more about Neo, but with Kerry sitting there in her hospital gown, an IV dripping into her arm, it hardly seemed right to talk about anything else but her and her condition. She told us about the first day's tests, and what she had been told to expect in the next several days. (She'd be getting some strong chemo, and her hair would be gone within a week, for starters.)

She was pleasant, and her accent was charming, and her eyes were sparkling and alive, but I kept noticing those subtle winces. And the tiredness in her face was unmistakable. When it was nearing nine o'clock and I suggested we let her get some sleep, she didn't quarrel. She just said, "Well, after that tardy flight last night, you must be wiped out too. I'm fine, and I'll never forget your kindness to me. You couldn't have been kinder. I feel bless——. . . uh, fortunate indeed."

Her stumbling over the word "blessed" caught my attention—we pastors notice such things. Carol told her we'd be back the next day. And we were. In fact, either Carol or I or both of us visited almost every day for the next few weeks, not because we had to, but because we wanted to.

Soon enough, Kerry began telling us about her friendship with Neo, and the story that brought her to that bed in that room in that hospital that first evening. The chapters that follow recount her story. When Neo arrived some weeks later, and when I, later still, met many of their mutual friends, I was able to supplement Kerry's recollections with those from her wider circle of friends and fill out the narrative in much more detail. Her story, and theirs, became entwined in the fabric of an even larger story into which my own life and yours too are also woven.

2

ON THE FLOOR OF THE SHOWER

DURING OUR VISITS over the next week or so, between Kerry's IV changes and vital signs checks by the nurses, over hospital meals on white Styrofoam trays, often interrupted by ringing phones and hospital voices on the intercom, Kerry shared her story, and Carol and I made a new friend. There were still sermons to preach and appointments to keep and soccer games to attend and crises to solve at church and at home, not to mention traffic to endure between all of the above, but somehow we managed, and Carol and I look back over those weeks as a rich time, full of wonderful memories.

Kerry Ellison—Dr. Kerry Ellison—had always dreamed of being a biologist. She grew up in Alice Springs, a hot desert town in the outback, populated by poisonous snakes and bizarre lizards like the thorny devil, the bearded dragon, and the huge perenti monitor. It seemed unusual for a pretty girl like Kerry to develop a love for reptiles, but then again, not that many girls grow up in a place like Alice Springs.

Kerry's father had been a minister in a denomination called the Uniting Church, a coming together of various Methodist and Presbyterian denominations in Australia. Like many a pastor's kid—like my own three children, Jess, Corey, and Trent—Kerry's childhood was marked by the rhythms of Sunday school, youth retreats, summer camp, and mission trips. "I never doubted God," she said, "and in fact I think I had an extraordinary love for God, up through my last year of secondary school."

That year, her youth group was assigned a new leader, the old one having returned to Sydney. This handsome young fellow, aptly named Steve Young, came from a more zealous religious background than the Uniting Church—Baptist or Pentecostal, she thought. His spirituality was more fervent and intense than that of anyone she had ever met. She was quite taken with him.

"He believed that my father was too loose in his biblical interpretation, and that our whole denomination was too 'lukewarm.' So he wanted to reassert the biblical truth as he saw it, starting with us kids," she explained. That fall term (starting in March down under), he led them through a study of "creation versus evolution," something quite popular back in the 50s and 60s.

"I suppose, like most public school kids, I never doubted evolution as my teachers presented it, but under Steve's influence, I became a fervent creationist," she said. "I even got permission from my high school science teacher to present a class on creationism at school. I was his prize student, and I think it pained him terribly to see me going off into something that seemed horribly antiscientific to him. Steve coached me on the presentation for weeks, and the whole youth group was praying for me. I didn't convert anybody, but I at least sowed doubts about evolution in some of my classmates' minds. And I managed to alienate my teacher too; he never regained the respect for me that he had before."

Kerry's spiritual intensity began to flag during her freshman year of college as she began to realize that her form of faith was mockingly labeled "fundamentalism" by her professors. In Sydney, exposed to a welter of religious and nonreligious viewpoints, she began to feel that the faith Steve had inspired was slipping through her fingers. "You can't have it both ways," Steve had always said. "It's either God's wisdom or man's. It's either God's authoritative Word or man's autonomous word. It's either creation or evolution."

This either-or dichotomy gnawed at her until one bright fall morning in November of her sophomore year. That day something snapped inside her; something gave way in her mind and heart. She was studying for a taxonomy exam, sitting on a bench at the University of Australia, identifying lists of plants and animals by "kingdom, phylum, class, order, family, genus, species." Suddenly, the beauty of the pattern of speciation overwhelmed her. The pattern seemed so clearly in sync with the theory of evolution, exactly what one would expect if evolution were true in its broad outlines. In an instant, her faith seemed to disappear, to evaporate, and she was left with nothing.

Nothing, that is, but a mixture of fear and elation. The fear ran along these lines: *Does this mean I'm going to hell? What will my father think?* The elation ran along these lines: *Finally, finally I don't have to hide from the facts. Finally, finally I don't have to defend something that I was never really convinced of anyway.*

Kerry wasn't the kind to pretend. That Easter break, she visited her family in Alice Springs and told them everything. Her father tried to be stoical and mature, but his quivering lip betrayed the calm and measured tone of his voice. Her mother got angry and blamed the "extremism" of "that Steve Young." But they weren't ugly or harsh about her loss of faith, and she never felt that their love for her was threatened by her rejection of almost everything they stood for.

The following years were spent in a whirlwind of studies and degrees: a B.S. in biology-herpetology (University of Australia at Sydney, 1972), an M.S. in reptile ethology and conservation (UCLA, 1974), and a Ph.D. that focused on island biogeography, extinction, and the recovery of endangered species (also UCLA, 1980). She married a fellow graduate student, a Californian, and their only child, Kincaid (named for her father), was born about a year later.

Both Kerry and her husband taught at the University of California at Santa Barbara during the 80s. Kerry knew that the marriage was shaky, and she suspected that Alvin might be getting emotionally involved with one of his graduate students. But even so, she was totally unprepared for his declaration one fall morning in 1990: the student was pregnant with Alvin's child, and he would be leaving her and Kincaid that very afternoon. They divorced shortly after that.

That was the second-worst day of her life, she told me one evening as we sat in her hospital room, the TV on but the sound muted. She stared at the silent TV for a long time, and I offered, "I'd hate to think there could be a worse day than that."

The worst day, she explained, came several years later. It was a Tuesday morning. She got a phone call from Kincaid's high school. He had been caught selling pot to a fellow student. She needed to go to the school immediately because Kincaid was being expelled. Stunned, she walked across the hall to her ex-husband's office to ask him to cover her afternoon class so she could go to the school. He refused; he had to go with his wife for their second baby's eighteen-month checkup.

Her head was pounding. She hastily scribbled a note canceling class and posted it on the door of the appropriate classroom. She went to the school and took Kincaid straight to a counselor recommended by the school. Kincaid began crying as soon as they got into her car, crying and cursing and threatening suicide. "To watch your fifteen-year-old son crying like a baby isn't a pretty sight," she said, "but to hear him say, 'I'm going to kill myself, I'm going to kill myself,' through his tears is even more devastating."

That night, after a long talk with Kincaid, she dragged herself into the shower. As she stood there, naked in the hot water, rubbing her chest with a bar of soap, she felt a lump, a large lump, in her right breast, an intrusion that would change—and shorten—her life. *How could I have missed this before?* was her first thought. Then she slumped to the floor of the shower, and it was her turn to cry, sitting naked in the shower, until the water turned cold and she started shaking uncontrollably, sobbing, "I'm going to die, I'm going to die. What will happen to 'Caid?"

Her mother flew in from Sydney as soon as she could, and a few months later, her dad retired early and joined them. The older Kincaid was a huge help to the younger, and, thank goodness, Kincaid was readmitted to school and there were no more incidents. After bilateral radical mastectomy—"a different kind of boob job," she said with a wink—plus chemotherapy, plus radiation, plus three additional years of monitoring, Kerry was pronounced "one of the lucky ones," and she counted herself a survivor in more ways than one.

By 1999, Kincaid himself was enrolled at UCSB and doing well, and Kerry was back to teaching. She applied for and received a year-long grant for a special study she had been dreaming of for years: she would join the staff of the Charles Darwin Research Center (CDRC) in the Galápagos Islands, and perform a DNA analysis of marine iguana populations on the various islands, trying to determine the genetic relationships between isolated groups of animals.

At the end of the study, CDRC offered her a long-term position on their research staff, and she accepted. She continued her work with marine iguanas and also joined the team that was redeveloping "species survival plans" for the tortoise species from which the islands received their name.

She loved her work, but welcomed the annual eight-week leave that was part of her contract, during which she visited Kincaid in the States and her family in Australia for a month each. In 2000, her father died suddenly. In July of 2001, she was introduced to a charming Jamaican fellow whom everyone called Neo.

Early in 2001, Neo had arrived on Santa Cruz, the most developed island of the archipelago. He had come, as thousands do every year, to tour the islands on a specially outfitted yacht. The seven-day cruise in the Galápagos was to be the last stop on a year-long voyage Neo had begun after the death of his parents, funded by the inheritance they had left him. Unfortunately, the government-certified guide, an essential crew member for voyages of this type, had been on an alcoholic binge between voyages, and by the end of the first day, it was clear that he was too unstable psychologically to serve the group in any meaningful way. In fact, he made a few inappropriate advances toward the teenaged daughter of one of the adult passengers, and as a result, the captain ejected him. That threw the whole tour into uncertainty: would the trip have to be canceled? None of the rest of the local crew, except the captain, spoke more than a few words of

English, the language of all the guests. At this point, Neo approached the captain and offered to fill in as guide. His background as a high school science teacher, plus his lifelong interest in Darwin, evolution, and the Galápagos ecosystems, perfectly prepared him for the role. He exceeded the ecotourists' expectations to such a degree that, when they landed in Santa Cruz at the end of the voyage, the owner of the yacht was waiting to meet Neo at the dock. Having been informed by the captain of Neo's skill as guide, the owner took Neo out for dinner, refunded his money, gave him an extra $200, and offered him a job. Neo thanked him but politely turned him down. The owner insisted that he stay another week at his expense and reconsider. The charm of the islands won his heart, and he agreed to stay.

Kerry didn't know how they got Neo officially certified for the role (which is strictly controlled by the Ecuadorian government), but by the time she met him some months later, he was considered a veteran guide, and he seemed completely at home in the islands—not surprising, she supposed, since he was a Jamaican. "He was picking up Spanish with gusto, bad Spanish though it was, with a kind of Jamaican lilt to it. When someone would correct him about some huge error of grammar or vocabulary, he would put his head back and laugh like a bloody kookaburra," Kerry said. "The Galápagos Islanders loved him. His size and skin color, not to mention his irrepressible laugh, made him stand out in every crowd there. He became something of a celebrity, a big fish in that small pond of Puerto Ayora. Also, Ecuadorians love anyone who loves *fútbol,* and Neo was an absolutely rabid fan."

Neo's schedule required him to be aboard ship Tuesday afternoon through Sunday afternoon, leaving him free on land Sunday and Monday nights. I remarked to Kerry that working on Sunday mornings wouldn't have been easy for him, as he felt that church attendance was not an option or a matter of convenience for a committed Christian like himself. Kerry asked me to guess what he did to remedy the situation. I guessed that he would offer an optional service on board the ship for the tourists. Kerry winked and said, "Almost. He couldn't do it on Sunday morning, because that was part of the tour. The captain let him use the ship on Sunday nights though, after the tourists had left. Almost every week, some of them came back for the service. But mostly, he attracted an odd mix of us who lived on the Islands."

I noted Kerry's use of the word "us," and asked if she had returned to her faith at some point. My question made her uncomfortable. "I don't know how to answer that," she said. "But no, I hadn't returned to my faith or the church. The reason I showed up one Sunday night was because, well, an Ecuadorian girlfriend of mine from the Research Center was trying to fix me up with Neo. You know, matchmaking. Neo was about my age, single, spoke English, and she knew that my dad had been a pastor. So with Neo's reputation for doing the little church service on the ship, she thought this was a match made in heaven. The racial thing is no big deal in Ecuador, where mestizos are common. Maricel was the type to say, 'God told me this,' and she was sure that God told her Neo and I would be together. Of course, I thought she was loopy about all that, but all she told me made me curious about this fellow. And there's not a lot of night life in Puerto Ayora."

One night, after leaving the hospital, after hearing this much of the story from Kerry, I thought, *I still don't know if Kerry and Neo are . . . is 'dating' the right word?* When I got home, I looked at Neo's e-mail again for any clue about the nature of their relationship, but I couldn't find anything overtly romantic.

But when I reread Neo's e-mail late that night, I noticed something at the bottom of the page that I had overlooked previously: "Phil 1722." It looked like a biblical reference with some missing punctuation. Did Neo mean Philippians 1:7–22? Philippians 17:22? Philippians 1:7, 22? I got out my Bible and considered all the options, but none of them made sense. I gave up and went to bed. Carol was already asleep. I was just falling asleep when a thought hit me: *Wait, maybe it's not Philippians; maybe it's Philemon.* I quietly ran upstairs and looked up Philemon (which only has one chapter), verses 17 and 22, which read, "So if you consider me a partner, welcome him as you would welcome me. . . . And one thing more: Prepare a guest room for me, because I hope to be restored to you in answer to your prayers."

A perfect fit (except in this case, the "him" was a "her"). Carol awoke when I crawled back into bed. "What's going on, darling?" she asked.

"Sorry to wake you, hon'," I answered. "I think Neo's hoping to stay with us when he comes back to the States."

"That's nice," she mumbled, and was asleep again.

3

LA CENA SANTA

WHEN KERRY CALLED one Friday afternoon in the middle of August, said she had a two-day pass, and asked if could she invite herself over, we were thrilled. On the spur of the moment we planned a cookout and pool party, and we invited a few other friends from church who had heard about Kerry and were praying for her. I drove to Bethesda while Carol finished the arrangements.

Kerry was quite a sight. By this time, just nine days into her treatment, she was completely bald. Even her eyebrows and eyelashes had disappeared. Because her chemo protocol included huge doses of steroids, her formerly thin face had filled out a bit and her skin had a strangely healthy glow. To look at her, you couldn't help but think of a baby with baby fat. Although she still used the cane to walk, her movements seemed more fluid, with fewer winces, which I hopefully interpreted as meaning she was in less pain. Clad in blue jeans, a denim shirt, and a red bandana, she was waiting for me on the green bench outside the hospital entrance, sitting next to an older and obese woman whose eyes (I couldn't help but notice) didn't look in the same direction.

Kerry limped up to my little pickup truck, cane in hand, and leaned in the window instead of opening the door. "Dan," she whispered, "I hope you don't mind. I invited my roommate to join us. She's had brain surgery and isn't . . . well, she isn't all there. I hope you didn't mind, mate, but I felt wicked leaving her alone in the hospital."

I didn't mind, but I wondered aloud how the three of us would fit in the cab of the truck. Maybe if I had a bench seat . . . "No worries," Kerry said. "I'd love to ride in the back of the truck. I don't have to fear the wind messing my hair, you know?"

And so off we went, with Mildred sitting up front and Kerry, with an overnight bag for her and Mildred, in the back. Mildred's speech wasn't always intelligible, but she tried to talk and I tried to understand as best as we both could manage. Once home, we went out back, and to my surprise, Mildred excused herself and returned a few minutes later in a huge, bright orange bathing suit and made herself at home in the pool, where she looked as happy as one could imagine her being. Except for joining us at the picnic table for meals, and coming inside to sleep, Mildred never left the pool all Friday night or all day Saturday. "I had a feeling that bringing her along would cheer the old gal up," Kerry said. "She seemed a wee bit depressed in the hospital the last few days, but I haven't seen her stop smiling since we got here."

After dinner, Kerry changed into her bathing suit—a pair of shorts with a T-shirt over it. When we convinced her to join us—and Mildred—for a swim, she said, "OK. I hope you don't mind if I go in Australian style," and with that, she whipped off her T-shirt. "It's bloody murder to find a top to fit a figure like mine, you know?" And there she stood, half naked and completely unashamed, with two slight depressions where her breasts would have been, her chest looking for all the world like a container of vanilla ice cream with two shallow scoops missing, scars angling up on each side of her breastbone. When she jumped in and Mildred got a closer look at her, Mildred smiled even more than before. It was quite a night.

Our friends left at about ten o'clock. After we got Mildred settled in bed (and in her huge set of adult diapers—which wasn't easy), Kerry joined us (fully clothed now in a Galápagos sweatshirt and shorts) back by the pool at the picnic table. We lit some candles, poured some drinks (just fruit juice—normally we don't have alcohol around the house), and settled in to talk.

"You've been wondering about my relationship with Neo, I reckon," Kerry said, her Aussie "reckon" sounding completely different from Carol's Atlanta version of the same word. "Well, let me calm your suspicions. We're just mates—in the *Australian* sense of the word. Let me tell you our whole story."

Kerry's Ecuadorian friend Maricel from Charles Darwin Research Center was bright, enthusiastic, a hard-working lab technician, and completely unselfconscious about her "Pentecostale" faith. If she successfully completed a difficult challenge in the lab—say, preparing a set of microscope slides for a scientist's research project—the scientist, regardless of religious background (or more likely, lack thereof), would hear a cheerful "Gloria a Dios!" If Maricel was deep in concentration, she would begin humming a religious song, and sometimes her humming would break out into full-fledged singing about Jesus, Dios, or Espíritu Santo. Once, a few of the English-speaking scientists threw some money in a baseball cap and brought it to her as a joke: "You made us feel like we were in church today," they said, "so we had to make an offering."

"She was expressive, but she wasn't the least bit pushy or obnoxious about it," Kerry explained. "She was so completely sincere and so completely herself that you just accepted her singing and enthusiasm as part of who she was, like her brown skin or black hair or big smile. Somehow, she could be so . . . 'religious' doesn't seem like the right word . . . she could be so *happy* without expecting anybody else to be. And that made everyone love her."

Maricel had begun attending Neo's Sunday night services, which they at first called "reuniones en la Aventura," because the ship on which they were held had the name *La Aventura*. Gradually, the name for the meetings was shortened to "Aventura," so they would just say, "Let's go to Aventura," which had a nice ring to it.

When Maricel told Kerry about the meetings—and especially about how charming and nice Neo was ("Creo que el es perfecto para ti," she said)—Kerry remembered feeling two things: first, that it was sweet of Maricel to be watching out for her, and second, that saying no to the invitation would be a big mistake. Both thoughts surprised her, because normally, she would be irritated by anyone trying to play matchmaker for her, and a church service had held no interest for her for many years.

So she went. *La Aventura* had a spacious front cabin, air-conditioned and furnished with comfortable chairs and tables, enough for about thirty passengers and crew, and was fronted with huge windows, so that passengers could enjoy the views as they sailed among the islands. It was a beautiful setting for their meetings. The *reunion* began with food, a kind of mini-potluck of fruit, coffee, and maybe some *platacones* (like potato chips, but made of Ecuadorian *platanos*) and salsa. Then Neo prayed in English, and Humberto (an Ecuadorian who owned a little convenience store in Puerto Ayora) translated into Spanish. The crowd of about twenty-five was two-thirds Spanish-speaking, and the rest spoke some Spanish. Neo's Spanish was probably the weakest of all, but everyone was impressed by how hard he tried and how fast he was learning. If you were a Spanish-speaker, you would have understood one hundred percent of what was said; if you spoke English only, then maybe sixty percent would have been translated for you.

After the prayer, Neo had them read a passage of the Bible. He read it aloud once in English, with the English-speakers reading aloud in unison, and then did the same in Spanish. Then Neo asked them two questions: What did you notice? What struck you? The discussion that followed went on for about twenty minutes, with everyone participating except

Kerry, who was intrigued to hear this odd mix of people—shop owners and tourists, educated and uneducated, religious and less so—sharing their insights and reactions to the text they had read together.

Then Neo asked another question: <u>How does this relate to your life?</u> And again, the discussion flowed—bouncing back and forth between English and Spanish—and the honesty of the people was both attractive and unnerving to Kerry. "They were talking about their divorces and alcohol problems and debt, things people don't normally talk about except with their closest friends. Even the tourists, who knew nobody except for one another and Neo, began joining in. It was like . . . instant intimacy or something. I was gobsmacked by the whole thing, really."

She was even more shocked by what happened next. Neo opened a bottle of wine and placed a loaf of fresh-baked Ecuadorian *pan* on the table. He said a few words about the meaning of taking what he kept calling "the holy supper" (which Humberto translated as "la cena santa"), and invited everyone to sit in silence and pray until they wanted to come forward. "<u>And be sure to listen too</u>," Neo encouraged them, "<u>because God's Spirit may be saying something deep inside you.</u>" Then Alvaro began playing his guitar, and he and Maricel began singing some beautiful songs in Spanish, and one by one, people would come forward and kneel in front of the table. They would then take a sip of the wine and a piece of the bread, and then remain kneeling for a few minutes before returning to their seats. The tourists first watched the others, and Kerry watched as one by one each of them came forward too. And most of them were crying as they did so.

Kerry began crying too. She wasn't sure why. But she wouldn't go forward. "You must remember," she said, "that I didn't—and still don't, really—buy any of it: not God, Jesus, the Holy Spirit, the Bible, heaven, and certainly not hell. So there I sat. I couldn't go forward and be one of the faithful, but I couldn't stop crying either."

Eventually the singing ended, and Humberto said a long and beautiful prayer in Spanish, and everyone stood and began giving hugs to one another. Kerry would have felt terribly self-conscious about her red eyes and tear-stained face, but everyone else had them too. "The hugging thing was a bit weird though," she said, patting her breastbone. "You know, the chest-to-chest bit can be a bit of a shock to people when they whack into my sternum and there's no . . . padding."

She went right up to Neo and, after receiving a hug ("He was a huge fellow, especially compared to all the small Ecuadorians"), went right to the point. "I'm a scientist, Mr. . . . Dr. Oliver. I'm not disposed to this sort of thing. But something happened to me tonight. I was crying like a . . . like a child or something. I hear that you're a scientist too. Maybe you can explain this. What's going on?"

Neo told her about his initials being his preferred name, and then surprised her by answering her question with a question. "Are you working tomorrow?" She said yes, but asked why he wanted to know. "Because," he said, "to give a good answer to your question, I'd need to learn a lot more about you."

She smiled and slapped him on the arm. "That's either the smoothest pickup line I've ever heard, or that's an invitation I can't refuse."

Neo held out his hands and laughed. "Take it either way. Can you get free? I have Mondays off."

Kerry worked on her own projects, so she was free to take off whenever she wanted, but she had some work that needed attention. She made a counterproposal. "How about this: how about you join me tomorrow? I have to do some work on Pinta. It's quite a long boat ride, and I really should have some company anyway."

Neo loved the idea, especially because Pinta, closed to tourism, was one of the islands he had never seen. They made arrangements to meet at 5:00 A.M., just a few docks over, where the CDRC kept its small fleet of boats.

"And that became my weekly schedule," Kerry told us (pronouncing "schedule" as "shed-yule," Australian style). "I'd go to Aventura nearly every Sunday night, and then Neo would join me in my work nearly every Monday."

4

A MATE FOR LONESOME GEORGE?

KERRY LOOKED DOWN, SMILING, placed her palms flat on our picnic table, and sighed. There was a period of silence, and then she said, "They were some of the happiest days of my life, those Mondays. A thousand pities they've come . . ."

Carol reached over in the candlelight and put her two hands on Kerry's. "Nobody's giving up hope yet, right?"

Kerry smiled and said, "That's why I like Mildred so much. The cancer killed the part of her brain that would make her afraid of what's coming, so she's just living each day until she . . . until she dies. I'd better figure out how to do the same."

Carol and I have been in pastoral ministry and around death and dying long enough to know that the best thing to do at times like this is not offer assurances, but just listen. "I'm sure you'll be just fine" is intended to cheer up the person in pain, but it also gives the unintended message "You're not allowed to talk about death." Dying is hard enough, but dying and not being able to talk about it—if you want to and need to talk—is harder still. So we just listened to see if she wanted to say any more.

"Too bad I have to use up so much of my last days of life sleeping!" she joked. "Well, at least my dreams better be exciting!" And with that, we blew out the candles and helped her get settled in her room. A few minutes later she returned to the kitchen to get a glass of water for the baggie full of pills she needed to take.

After she took her pills, she came and gave both of us a hug. "Thanks," she said. "Tomorrow I want to tell you about our Monday conversations."

We slept in that Saturday morning. When we finally got up, Mildred was already in her orange bathing suit, floating on her back in the pool with a big grin on her face, looking straight up into the blue as if she were listening to a conversation among the few early morning clouds. We managed to get her to come out and dry off long enough for breakfast, and then, after we helped her to get some sunscreen on, she was back in the pool again.

Kerry asked if we could take a short walk around the neighborhood. "With my cane, I'll be a bit slow, but I'd like to keep up my exercise. I've been going batty locked up in the hospital." Carol offered to stay and keep an eye on Mildred, so Kerry and I set off walking in my suburban neighborhood. After exchanging remarks about the nicely kept lawns and gardens, we were silent for a while, and then I asked her about that first Monday she spent with Neo.

"It was odd," she said. "All morning, I think he hardly said more than a few dozen words. Mostly he asked questions and then listened to me. But a person can say a lot by listening, you know?"

On that first Monday, Kerry said, she and Neo met at the docks well before dawn (which comes just after 5:30 there on the equator). The twelve-hour equatorial days mean that you don't want to waste daylight when you have a lot of outdoors work, Kerry said. Neo was learning a lot about boats during his time on *La Aventura,* and so he helped get the gear stowed (including an extra tank full of gas) and then got the motor started on the Center's fastest *panga,* a kind of inflatable boat used by the researchers for landings on hard-to-access islands.

Kerry was in the middle of an interesting project. There are several distinct species of tortoise still surviving on the islands, she explained, but one species, a saddle-backed race from Pinta, was all but extinct. Only one old male survived, now held in captivity at CDRC and named "Lonesome George" by the staff. Every captive tortoise in every zoo in the world had been checked for genetic compatibility to Lonesome George, but no matches were found. So every few years when funds and personnel were available, staff would mount expeditions to Pinta to see if a female could be found. That kind of search was difficult because of the island's thick, nearly impenetrable vegetation, mostly cactus and saltbush and thorns. Recently, a visiting research vessel equipped with an onboard helicopter had visited the islands. Kerry convinced them to take her up in the helicopter, and from the air she had detected on the southeast end of the island some semi-open areas that seemed to have the kinds of trails through which tortoises move. Unfortunately, because of the strong winds and dense vegetation, they had been unable to find any place safe for the helicopter to land that day. So Kerry had been eager to check out those areas on foot.

But the boat ride to Pinta took nearly four hours if the water was smooth, and more otherwise, and landing a boat on the island could be a dangerous challenge under the best of conditions. The coast was rocky and the surf often violent. It could be done though, and Neo was eager to help Kerry find a suitable opening in the rocks. They studied the maps and aerial photos for several minutes, and then they embarked. Over the growl of the Johnson motor, Neo shouted, "Well, Kerry, tell me your story." With Neo at the stern manning the throttle (and wearing a shabby old red baseball cap, she recalled—odd, because he usually dressed so carefully), and with Kerry on the seat in front of him facing backwards and leaning toward him so they could talk over the motor's roar, she began telling him the story she had shared with us over the previous days.

Always the scientist, Neo was especially interested in all the details of her cancer. She was impressed with his knowledge of chemotherapy and radiation therapy. After hearing all the medical facts that she recounted, he shook his head. "You're blessed to be alive," he said.

"That's the closest he got to preaching to me all morning," she recalled.

Unfortunately, none of their attempts to gain access to Pinta were successful. The surf was too wild and the sharp volcanic rocks too hazardous. Even the thick rubber of the inflatable boat had limits, so after several hours of looking for a suitable point of entry, they headed back to Puerta Ayora just past midday. "Well, I guess Lonesome George will stay lonesome," Kerry said sadly.

On their way back, Kerry suggested they stop and check on a population of land iguanas she had been following on North Seymour, an island with much easier access. This they did, and while they walked the rough terrain, Kerry asked Neo to share his story. "He spent a long time telling me about you, Dan," she said.

On their way back to the boat, Neo slipped on some loose gravel and fell forward onto the sharp, black volcanic rock that juts out so pervasively on the islands, badly bloodying his shins and knees. Even worse, in his attempt to break his fall, his hands landed on an opuntia cactus pad, and he had six or eight long spines embedded in the heels of his hands. No bones were broken though. Kerry couldn't imagine how she could have gotten him back to the boat, large man that he was, if he'd broken a leg.

It was after dark when they motored into the harbor at Puerto Ayora. Back aboard *La Aventura,* she cleaned his wounds and bandaged his shins, and then they set out to extract the cactus spines. "It was a romantic end to our first date," she said, "with Neo and I sitting across a table by candlelight, the boat gently rocking, the Pacific breezes blowing into the cabin through the open windows, his hands in mine . . . except that mine were holding a razor blade and a pair of tweezers, trying to extract those nasty cactus spines, and blood was dripping down our forearms!"

By the end of the evening, Neo wasn't as good as new, but he was better off for Kerry's first aid, and Kerry had heard Neo's personal and spiritual story. "He was so like and unlike my father," she said. "I couldn't help making comparisons. Like my father, he was sincerely and utterly devoted to God. Unlike my father, he was so open and human and . . . not real *religious* about his spirituality. I remember thinking, *It's as if this chap has discovered a whole new way of being a Christian.*" I smiled at this and told her I agreed one hundred percent.

Neo walked her back to the Center by lantern light, his brown hands and knees bandaged in white gauze and tape, like a little boy who had had a bicycle accident. As he said goodbye, he said, "Kerry, any Monday you'll have me, I'd be honored to be your field assistant. Just let me know. I'll see you next Sunday night."

And without thinking, she said, "Great. See you then." He waved a bandaged hand, and then he turned back toward the marina, his lantern swaying in the darkness. As she walked to her room, she thought, *Crikey! I just agreed to go to church two weeks in a row!*

All week, she thought about what a great listener Neo had been, and when it was his turn to speak, how open he had been. Like Maricel, he seemed comfortable with his faith; it wasn't something to prove or something to hide—just part of who he is. And while he hadn't preached to her, he had gotten her thinking about things she hadn't thought about since college. "Even during my first bout with cancer," she said, "it was all about science and odds and medical technique, not about faith or prayer or preparing for life after . . . death."

All that week, she thought of questions she wanted to ask Neo the next time they talked, theological questions of many kinds, but they all boiled down to this: *How could he, an obviously intelligent man, and a man of science no less, believe all that stuff?* ("Stuff" isn't exactly the word Kerry used.)

Kerry and I had circled my block and were just returning to my backyard when Carol ran out and told me I had a phone call waiting. She escorted Kerry to the backyard, and by the time I got off the phone, they were escaping the late-morning August heat in the pool. My kids were in the water too, throwing a Frisbee with Mildred. Mildred's eyes looked wild, and she didn't make all the catches, but she kept laughing and mumbling in an odd, jubilant way. I noticed how Jess, my oldest, was especially kind to Mildred. Corey and Trent seemed a bit frightened of her, but they seemed intrigued by an adult who never tired of playing in the pool.

After lunch, Kerry, Carol, Jess, and I sat in lounge chairs in the shade. (Mildred, freshly covered in sunscreen, returned to the pool, accompanied by Corey and Trent, who were getting more used to her by now.) Kerry returned to her story. She had attended Aventura the Sunday following Neo's fall, and again found herself crying by the end of the service. She checked Neo's hands and legs afterwards, and he seemed to be healing fine. When he asked about helping her the next day, she told him she'd be glad to have him. She had another long boat ride scheduled.

Their second Monday was to be spent counting tortoises and observing their behavior on the slopes of the southern volcano on Isabella Island. They again left Puerto Ayora before dawn, again taking the Center's fastest *panga,* because the trip would take a few hours. As they cruised toward Isabella, with the sun rising between morning clouds, Kerry started listing all of her theological questions. "I figured I'd get them all out on the table, and then he could sort through as to where to start," she said. "I had to speak so loudly over the motor that I think I must have sounded a bit angry. But I wasn't angry. I was . . . serious." After they'd beached the *panga* on a strip of sand at the end of a rocky cove, Neo said, "Kerry, rather than answering your questions, could I tell you a story?"

"Sure," she said.

He hauled their backpacks out of the boat and said, "Let's call it 'The Story We Find Ourselves In.' I think it will either answer your questions or help you live with them a little more comfortably."

5

HONKING AND THUDDING

NEO AND KERRY LEFT THE SHORE and began to ascend the volcano's lower slope. In the Galápagos Islands, the lower elevations are arid; the higher you go, the more rain falls, often in the form of *garua*—a fine mist. For North Americans trained to expect lush greenery at low elevations near the coast, with arid and rocky mountain tops high above, the ecosystems of the Galápagos seem upside down.

They quickly ascended through the gravelly region of treelike opuntia cactus (which Neo avoided carefully), carpeted in patches with a beautiful reddish ground cover that Kerry called *sesuvium*. Neo noticed how nearly every plant in that region—except *sesuvium*—had formidable thorns, including a bramble of nearly leafless branches that Kerry identified as *Parkinsonia,* which they stopped to observe because it carried, along with huge thorns and tiny rows of leaves, beautiful yellow flowers bursting out of green buds. The land was dotted with small trees called *palo santo*— "holy stick" in English—whose white bark and leafless branches gave them a ghostly quality. They had leaves only in the wet season, January through April, Kerry explained. Neo commented on the irony of the name. "Holy sticks should be vibrant and green and fruitful," he said, "not bare and gray. Holiness is beautiful and vigorous, not ugly and barren."

"Maybe so," Kerry responded after a pause, "but maybe there's something holy about having a beautiful end." She explained, "They're called 'holy' because they give off a pleasant aroma when they're burned, and so the priests used to use them as incense in churches on the mainland. They give a gift as they turn to ashes. Maybe there's a special kind of holiness in that."

Neo looked at her and smiled. "Good point."

Gradually, they left the arid zone below them and the land became greener. Here and there were the first tree ferns, and more of the ground was covered with grass and other ground ferns. As they came over a small rise, Kerry shot out one hand to halt Neo and covered her mouth with her index finger from the other hand to signal him to be quiet.

Before them stretched out what looked like a large rolling lawn, scraggly with weeds, dotted with a few *scalesia* trees and pocked with a few muddy potholes. In each pothole rose the huge domes of the giant tortoises—eleven in one hole, two in another, three in another. Off in the distance, two tortoises walked into a thicket in single file, at a brisk pace for a tortoise. Closer, between them and the first pothole, a single huge tortoise lumbered with a steady gate—step, step, step, then bending its neck down to bite a tuft of grass, then step, step, step, step, with its head held high, then another dropping of its head to feed.

Kerry and Neo slowly sat down, cross-legged on the grass, almost in reverence. "Amazing," Neo said, and they sat in silence for several minutes. Kerry pulled out a notebook and jotted down some field observations.

Then Kerry recommended that they follow the pair that had disappeared into the thicket a little farther up the slope. "That looked like a male pursuing a female," she said. "Could be a chance to observe a bit of tortoise romance."

They circled around the tortoises wallowing in the potholes, and then they came to the thicket. Kerry crouched down, and they half-walked, half-crawled forward. Then Kerry motioned for Neo to drop down onto his belly, as she had done, and move forward, almost commando style.

After a few minutes, they were lying on their bellies, partially hidden under the drooping fronds of a tree fern, soft moss and lichen beneath their bellies and hips, the rising equatorial sun beating down on the backs of their legs, which stretched out beyond the scant shade of the bush.

Honk-ah . . . honk-ah, honk . . . honk-ugh. The deep, bellowing grunt was one of the most unearthly sounds Neo had ever heard. Primeval, he called it. It was a more familiar sound to Kerry, but it still never ceased to silence her and fill her with awe. Neo and Kerry traded back and forth a pair of binoculars for a closer look.

From under the branches of the bush, they watched as, just ten or twelve meters ahead of them, a huge male tortoise mounted a smaller female. His indented lower shell, the plastron, cupped the rear dome of the female's upper shell, the carapace. His front legs barely reached the top of her dome, and his rear legs held him partially erect. With the binoculars, they could see his huge tail slip under the female's shell, probing, probing, dripping with mucous. The male's neck craned over her dome and arched downward. With each grunt, his mouth gaped and his moist black eyes blinked. *Honk-ah . . . honk-ugh.*

"This could be two hundred million years ago," Kerry said. "This drama of courting and copulating has been playing for at least that long."

Neo put the binoculars down and responded, "In that story I was saying I was going to tell, the first episode is called 'Creation,' which is just what those two over there are doing." His voice low and his pace slow, his upper body propped up on his elbows, Neo started talking. He was making this up as he went along, but he sounded like he was reciting poetry.

"Before the beginning," he went on, "before galaxies began their slow spin or planets whirled in their circular dances, before the original singularity banged into existence in an explosion of energy that seems too momentous and substantial to be called light, there was a Being we humans like to call God. The real God, the One beyond our words and concepts . . . I mean the Being who really is . . . is, of course, far more wonderful, mysterious, and great than our minds can conceive, certainly more so than any human concept of God could possibly contain.

"Think about it, Kerry. How can we imagine a God whose power, love, whimsy, and wisdom imagined, calibrated, and created a universe like ours—including those massive gray-black creatures over there? How can we comprehend such a God? After all, as you well know, we humans are little more than hairless primates, a small twig on a small branch of the tree of life, hunks of living meat with three-pound brains suspended on bone and packaged in skin, born naked and crying and afraid and often dying much the same, and in between, self-impressed beyond all reason, only on occasion slightly awake to our smallness and frailty and dignity and wonder."

Kerry took the binoculars and watched the tortoises in silence for a few moments. Then she spoke over the grunts of the male and the deep, hollow sound of shell thudding against shell. "That's really quite poetic, Neo, but if your poetry is true, if there really is a Creator, what makes you think we could ever make contact with him or her or it or them? Wouldn't the Creator be as far beyond our comprehension as . . . as we are beyond a virus? So why even bother thinking about such lofty and impenetrable mysteries?"

"Well, that's where the story comes in, Kerry. I believe we are connected to the Creator, irrevocably, by a story, a true story that begins with the words 'In the beginning, God created the heavens and the earth,' a story that ends with 'Behold, I make all things new.' This story that begins and ends with creation is all about creation in between its beginning and end, this story we find ourselves in. True, it's not the only story that tries to explain where we are, who we are, and why. There are other stories, similar in many ways but profoundly different too."

Kerry interjected, "Well, I'm glad you acknowledge that your story isn't the only one, the only way, if you know what I mean. Because I think we're way beyond anybody claiming to have the only truth."

"Actually," Neo replied, taking his turn with the binoculars, observing the honking and thudding still ongoing in front of them, "if you get a feel for this story we find ourselves in, I think you'll come to realize that it has room for all the other stories too. It doesn't exclude them, or mock them, or despise them. I believe it's the story in which all other stories can find themselves too."

Suddenly, the male tortoise slid off the female, and the two creatures sat side by side in the sunlight, motionless except for their blinking, and the slight movement of their front limbs and the soft skin under their necks as they breathed in, out, in, out. Kerry leaned over on her side and asked Neo how that could be. How could his story make room for the others? Didn't Christians believe that it was an either-or thing—either their story was right or one of the other stories was?

Before he had a chance to answer, she asked another question. "Forget about the other stories. What about all the different versions of your story? How do you deal with all the differing versions of this one supposedly true story?"

Neo was still speaking softly, but he was growing more animated. His Jamaican lilt started to come through. "You're right, Kerry—even if we concern ourselves only with this story, we discover that there are many versions of it, many variations on it. And you're also right that the versions and variations are filled with minor discrepancies in the details. But the broad outline, the general plot, the flow, the current, the trajectory common to nearly all its varied versions is, in my mind, a masterpiece in the truest sense of the word."

It was hot now, and Neo pulled off his red cap and wiped his forehead. A mischievous look crept over his face, and he asked, "Hey Kerry, can I preach a bit?"

Not sure what he meant, she said, "Sure, mate. Why not? Whatever you fancy."

Then Neo started "playing preacher"—as I had seen him do, once, a couple years earlier. He half-whispered and half-sang, "This story is the best one around, sistah. It has the truest news, the deepest views, the highest theme, the most inspiring dream, the plot most full of meaning and magic, vigor and rigor, startle and sparkle, emotion and motion. As my students used to say, it rocks! If you give it a fair hearing, I think you'll agree. Can I get a witness-ah? Can somebody say 'Amen'?"

Kerry laughed and shouted, "Amen!" She gave Neo a high-five, and then he held out his arms and managed a small bow in their cramped quarters. She couldn't tell, however, whether his preaching was fully playful or partly serious.

6

BEING GIVING BEING TO BEINGS

THE TORTOISES WERE PLODDING out of sight now, back down the hill toward the potholes. Neo and Kerry pulled themselves out from under the bush and continued climbing farther up the volcano's slope. She made notes each time they sighted a tortoise. When tortoise sightings became less frequent, Kerry began explaining the volcanic origin of the islands. After a few minutes, she interrupted herself. "I'm sorry, Neo," she said. "I think I distracted you. Go ahead with the story."

"It's OK," he replied. "The geological story you're telling me is part of the theological one I'm telling you. It's all connected. But let's rewind the tape. Back five hundred years, to the birth of the modern age, and back another thousand, to the beginnings of the medieval world. Back another three thousand, to the first written records of human culture. Back another thirty-five thousand, to our ancestors who painted on cave walls in Europe, and back a hundred thousand, to our first Paleolithic human ancestors in Africa, and back a million, to prehominid primates, and back sixty million, to the age of the dinosaurs, and back four or five billion, to the first complex proteins and then the first primitive cells, and back eight billion, to the formation of the earth, and back eleven to fifteen billion years, to the beginning—as we understand it—of all that exists in our universe.

"Imagine going backwards through time—the whole universe shrinking back, reversing the 'big bang,' contracting in a big suck into a tiny singularity, a shrinking point of unimaginable density and unimaginable potential. And imagine that point blinking out to . . . nothing. Don't imagine just empty space. That's not nothing enough. Imagine empty space, and then imagine the matrix of space itself contracting into nothing and time as we know it folding in on itself until it too disappears."

Kerry interrupted, "If my brain were a computer, Neo, I think it would be saying, 'Illegal operation: must shut down.'"

"I know, Kerry. Try as we might, I don't think we can imagine nothing. Someone tried to define it as what dead rocks think about when they no longer exist. For us living beings, as soon as we try to think about nothing, nothing becomes a something that we think about existing somewhere at some time, and at that moment we've stopped thinking about nothing. It's probably beyond our understanding, and maybe for good reason. Maybe nothing is impossible. Because even if you suck the universe of time and space into a singularity and blink the singularity away, even if you are left with nothing, you still don't have nothing, exactly. You have a something—according to this story I'm telling you—that would be better referred to as a Someone.

"Subtract the cosmos, and you have nothing left, except for"—Neo winked—"one small detail: God, a being, a life, a mind, a heart, an intelligence, a creative personality, an essential goodness, an inexpressible beauty, a light beyond all seeing, an infinite song that by its very being gives meaning to meaning, gives glory to glory, gives life to life, a pure consciousness—pure in every sense of the word."

Kerry paused, trying to process all this. Then she noticed and drew Neo's attention to a small lizard basking on the top of a lichen-covered rock. "There's one of your Deity's creations over there," she said. They both recognized it as a lava lizard—a female, according to its coloration. "I don't expect to find any tortoises in this next section of the volcano, because it's really steep, but quite often I find some at the rim of the crater, so do you mind if we push for the top now?" Of course, Neo didn't mind.

As they started climbing again, Kerry asked, "Here's a question I've always wanted to ask since I was a little girl in Sunday school: Before the beginning, what was God doing?"

"Who knows?" Neo responded. "We can't imagine. Or better said, we can only imagine. We can only imagine a God in whom love can exist and be shared without being selfish love. We can imagine a God who communicates within a community of one that is not solitary, capable of communicating without simply talking to himself—and I apologize for having to use that masculine pronoun, but what can we do, stuck in language as we are? Anyway, you can imagine God living and loving in perfect solitude that is also perfect companionship, alone and all-one without ever being lonely. We can imagine a goodness so full, so complete, so absolute that the goodness is its own perfect, unending good company and satisfaction. We can begin to imagine. . . ."

Kerry interrupted, "OK, OK, OK! Maybe the question 'What was God doing?' isn't the best way to put it. Perhaps a better question would be

'What was God being?' But I guess even that fades into silliness. It's like asking, 'What was Being being?' This talking about God isn't easy, you know?"

"Right," Neo replied. "It's like a lot of things in science. Language is the best tool we have, but it keeps getting in the way. So in science, we revert to mathematics. And in theology, we revert to poetry. Mathematics and imagination are two ways of talking about things beyond normal language."

"Math and poetry," Kerry said. "I never thought of them that way."

To Kerry's surprise, they did find tortoises on the steep slope, and all of them were moving upwards toward the rim. "This is the kind of thing we're trying to figure out. Why would they be migrating now? There's so much we don't know."

Neo was winded, but he remained focused on his subject. "Sometimes, when your imagination takes you to these lofty, dizzying dimensions, this realization can climb up your spine and surprise you so that you physically shiver: *Not only could such a Being exist, but such a Being could generate a universe with a creature like me in it, a creature like me, capable of thinking thoughts and imagining images . . . like these, right now.*"

Neo seemed to be really short of breath now, so Kerry stopped and motioned for him to sit beside her on a rock. Looking back from this height, they could begin to see the ocean that surrounded them. "Keep going," she said. "You're having trouble keeping up with me physically, but I'm barely keeping up with you intellec——. . . well, *spiritually.*"

"OK," Neo replied. "This is important. Imagine this majestic Being considering the possibility of creating other beings that really, really exist. Not just imaginary beings. Not just projections of God's own thoughts. Not just puppets, actors, dream images, and not just possibilities or scenarios or simulations, but beings that are given the gift that is most absolute, a gift that only Being can give: the gift of being, of existing, of standing out of nothingness into reality . . . the reality of being created and acknowledged by the Being who is all that ever was. If this story is in any way true, then something like this must have happened—something like this, but surely beyond this too. And this Being decides to become something that this Being has never before been: a Creator of a universe like this—*the* Creator of *this* universe."

Kerry picked up on his last remark. "Neo, do you think there were other universes before this—others in a different space and time, or perhaps others that operate in a matrix other than space and time? Do you think there could be parallel universes even now? Whenever I think about God, which isn't all that often, I think about parallel universes for some reason."

Neo was staring out over the ocean far below them. "Well . . . God knows. That may simply be none of our business. But here we are on this particular rock, on this particular island, in this specific ocean, on this specific planet, in this particular solar system, on the edge of this particular galaxy—and we got here somehow, and this story offers one possible explanation: *Being* decided to create beings."

"Sounds pretty simple," Kerry said. "Too simple for me."

"Ah," Neo said, turning to her. "But it really isn't that simple. It's not easy—I know it sounds strange to say it this way—it's not easy being Being and deciding to create other beings. It's not easy if you want them to really exist, again, not just as ideas in your imagination, so to speak, but as real beings in . . . in a place outside your imagination. And so that's God's first challenge, to create an outside—because up to now in our story, there is no outside, there is only God. So God must begin by creating a not-God, an outside, a place for beings to exist."

"But Neo," Kerry asked, "can there really be an *outside?* I mean, if God exists, wouldn't God be everywhere?"

"Well, yes . . . or I mean, no . . . or, well, that's part of our problem with words like 'inside' and 'outside' and 'everywhere,' isn't it? We're using words from our experience to describe something so far beyond our experience (I think we'll just have to live with that frustration) but I see your point, and I think you see mine: God is making beings that really can *be,* not just imaginary beings in God's imagination. And when I say 'beings,' I'm not talking just about beings like Maricel or Humberto or Adam and Eve. Sure, we can include them later, but right now, when I say 'beings,' I just mean 'things that be' . . . things that exist, like hydrogen atoms and quarks and gravity and light—whatever these things are! I'm talking about viruses and rotifers and blue-green algae and yellow pond lilies. I'm talking about wood ducks and platypuses and parrotfish—and Galápagos tortoises, like that pair we just saw or like poor old Lonesome George.

"Because surely, they're all part of the delight that the Being imagines giving being. The Being wants the quarks and gluons and muons and electrons to really be *out there,* not just *in here,* in God's imagination, just as I wanted the words I just spoke to be there, outside, someplace, out in the air and then in your ear and in your mind, not just *in here,* in my head. So the Being, in becoming the Creator, begins by making the creative medium, like the air for the sound waves I'm making right now, the paper or screen or canvas for the artist to create on. God creates the matrix of space and time so that beings can be, so that the beings imagined by the Being can be expressed in an *outside,* in a *somewhere* . . . in a place and time."

Neo had caught his breath, and so they continued their climb. Every ten or fifteen minutes, they'd come upon another tortoise also climbing the steep slope toward the rim. Neo continued, "And so, in the beginning, God created space and time—'the heavens and the earth,' Genesis says— and in that moment, Being became Creator. Perhaps I should say, "*our* Creator," because, again, as you said, the possibility is surely there that the Being had created other universes before or elsewhere—again, assuming that words like 'before' and 'elsewhere' make any sense at all in this context."

Neo was silent for a few minutes, and then continued. "Isn't it fascinating that the ancient Jews who told and retold the ancient poem of Creation had an instinct—God-given, I think—that the universe didn't always exist? They lived in a world abounding in sacred creation narratives."

"I remember reading the *Gilgamesh Epic* in college," Kerry said. "Is that the sort of thing you have in mind?"

"Exactly," Neo said, "and many of them, like *Gilgamesh,* are still available to us today, preserved for thousands of years, first by oral tradition and then in writing. But interestingly, in the alternative stories, matter generally comes from preexisting matter. For the Jews, there is this very different conviction that matter comes not out of some preexisting stuff, on the one hand, and not, strictly speaking, from nothing, on the other hand, but rather, all matter comes from meaning. Does that make sense? That matter comes from an idea in the mind of God, an idea that is expressed in a meaning-making word, *Let there BE . . .* ?"

7

A STORY OF EMERGENCE

AT THIS POINT, Kerry interrupted Neo again. She told him about her youth group leader, Steve, and his either-or ultimatum about God and evolution. It didn't sound like Neo was a biblical literalist. How did he reconcile God and evolution?

Neo laughed. "Kerry, believe me, I've been in a lot of debates about all of this back in my career as a teacher. Back in the early 90s . . . well, that's another story for another time. Let me just answer your question. I think that the literalism of many of my fellow believers is silly. I don't mean them any offense, and I'm sure many of my opinions are no less silly than theirs. But still . . ."

Kerry replied, "Well, to me, believing in God at all seems pretty silly sometimes. Why does their literalism seem sillier to you than your own belief?"

This section of the climb just below the rim was the steepest yet. Neo needed another rest. Finding a chair-sized rock, black, porous, obviously volcanic, Neo sat, beads of sweat forming on his coffee-brown forehead, and leaned forward with his elbows on his knees. He took a couple of deep breaths and continued talking. "All my own silliness aside, do they imagine God literally saying, 'Let there be light'? In what language? Hebrew? Latin or Arabic maybe? Or maybe English, but if so, which accent—American, English, Aussie, or Jamaican? And where did the air come from to propagate the sound waves for God's literal words; and for that matter, where did the vocal cords come from for God to say those words? And as for the business of the six days, assuming that you're not a flat-earther, you have to acknowledge that when it's day on one side of the globe, it's night on the other. So when Genesis says that the first day begins and ends, from whose vantage point does it mean—Sydney, Australia, or Greenwich, England?"

Kerry laughed and said, "You're being very wicked."

Neo replied, "Actually, St. Augustine raised some of these kinds of questions long before I did. He too was bugged by Christians who seemed to be know-it-alls. But please don't misunderstand, Kerry. Like the staunchest literalist, I believe in the story of Genesis, but I think I believe it more in the way that ancient Semitic nomads huddled in their blankets around a winter fire would have believed it, as they told it and retold it, generation to generation, feeling the poetic rhythms—'and there was evening and there was morning, a second day, a third day, a fourth day . . .' I believe in it as a story that gives us something so much more important than textbook-style so-called objective facts and newspaper-style information—two things that we moderns value far more highly than our ancestors did. For me, it is a story that gives us *in-formation* . . . a story that *forms* us inwardly with truth and meaning—something that we moderns seem to value far less highly than our ancestors did."

"So, Neo," Kerry interjected, "you see it as a myth, right? It's just another creation myth."

Neo replied, "No, no, no. I didn't say that. In fact, the more I interact with the story, the less I want to carve it down to fit in any modern categories, whether 'myth' or 'fact.' And I certainly don't want to reduce it with a *just* into anything less than fact. No, Kerry, to me, it's far more than 'just myth' or 'just fact.' To me, it's the beginning of the story we find ourselves in, right here and right now." As he said those last words, with one hand he patted the rock he was sitting on, and he lifted the other hand in a sweeping gesture. Kerry shook her head, whether in disagreement or frustration or just from being overwhelmed, neither she nor Neo could tell for sure.

Kerry and Neo continued climbing, and soon they reached the edge of the crater. They savored the view: down into the black crater, with its plume of smoke and its gray ash showing deep scars of erosion, and then across the crater to the green foliage spilling in over the rim, and beyond it to the Pacific, stretching blue, blue, blue out to the horizon to the northwest. Kerry unpacked lunch, and they talked more about the amazing process of how these islands were formed, and the fate they might face in the distant future. Meanwhile, they enjoyed cheese and tomato sandwiches, raw carrots, and fresh mangoes.

"It's hard to believe that a tortoise could make it up that last bit there," Neo said. "So steep." But along the rim, several tortoises were visible, grazing on grass and leaves. And all around them, huge tortoise droppings in various stages of decomposition dotted the landscape.

Kerry explained, "Some of their migrations we understand very well, but some we haven't figured out yet."

After lunch, as they walked west along the crater's rim, Neo got back to the story. "Isn't it fascinating that the ancient Jews, whose poem this is, somehow knew that all that exists came from formlessness, emptiness, darkness—that the world as we know it arose out of nothingness, kind of like the way this island arose out of the chaos of the ocean? I'm thinking about how the poem continues: 'Now the earth was formless and empty, and darkness was over the surface of the deep.' The story they found themselves in was not the descent of a better, more highly evolved or highly ordered world into the turbulent world we experience. And it wasn't the nonstory of stasis, either, the story of an eternally unchanging perfect state that was ruined and so devolved into a story. No, the story they understood to be our human story was from the first sentence a story of . . . emergence, evolution, development, order arising from chaos, life being coaxed from the waters. I guess that's why I make such a big deal about evolution—not because I worship Darwin or anything, but because I feel that somehow we Christians have confused ourselves, and everyone else too, about our own story. Sure, there are crises and complications and tragedies and dangers along the way, as there would be in any story. But overall, to me, it's a story of emergence."

"Maybe that's the word you should use, then, instead of 'evolution.'" Kerry said. "Emergence. But you do believe that the universe has gone bad, right?"

"Well, yes, in a way," Neo said, "but I think it would be better to say that I believe that we *human beings* have gone bad, both as individuals and as cultures. No denying that. But that doesn't mean that the story of humanity is irrevocably ruined. The story is being saved, and that saving involves a kind of new and ongoing creation that's like the original creation; it's all about God bringing life and balance out of sickness and disintegration, just like order coming from chaos in the first verses of Genesis. 'The Spirit of God was hovering over the waters,' the poem says, inviting order and life to emerge from disorder and barrenness. Spirit was being coaxed from clay, into clay, like this island emerging from unseen sources beneath the mysterious deep blue Pacific out there." With both arms extended now, he turned and gestured around the whole circle of the rim.

"It's like this volcano," he went on. "When it erupted, everything around us was blackness and death, very literal sulfur and flames, you know? But look at the life that's returning here, gradually, over time. Amazing."

At this, Kerry laughed again. "You're quite a teacher," she offered. "And a poet too. Anyway, I've got to write down a few notes. While you've been talking, I've been mentally counting male and female tortoises, and I don't want to forget my count: two males, eight females." As Kerry pulled out her notebook, Neo pulled out a water bottle and shared it with her. They were both sweating, the sun was hot, and their journey down would be a bit longer than their journey up.

A few hundred meters down the slope, Neo said, "You know, Kerry, our views of the rim behind us and the ocean below us have constantly been changing. As our journey progresses, our perspective on everything changes. I think that's worth keeping in mind in our story too. I think that's the beauty of the first few chapters of Genesis in the Bible. Are you aware that Genesis has two creation stories, told from two different perspectives? Of course, they're both told from an earthbound, prescientific perspective, because that's where the storytellers lived. But each story is unique."

"Well," Kerry said, "I could wish that the whole book of Genesis had been told in a bit more of a scientific way."

"Maybe that's our job—to translate," Neo said. "But any perspective we use, even a scientific one, will still be to some degree earthbound and limited, right? If some super-advanced *Star Trek* alien species or even our own descendants in a thousand years were to read the latest *Scientific American,* they'd get a good laugh, don't you think? I'm sure they'd just howl about our most advanced notions of up-quarks and neutrons and electrons and TOE theories, just as we might feel snobbish toward the prescientific language of Genesis. The point is that we don't need to know about our story from the perspective of some super-advanced *Star Trek* alien species that may see us as a planet to be assimilated, or perhaps as a delicacy to be consumed, right? But we do need to know our story from exactly the two perspectives given to us in Genesis: from the Creator's perspective, which we get in the first creation story, beginning in Genesis 1:1, and from our own human perspective, which we get in the second story, beginning in Genesis 2:2."

Just then, Kerry slipped on some loose gravel, and Neo helped her get her footing. "I've never heard about this two-story perspective business," she said. "Keep going."

Neo said, "From the Creator's perspective in the first story, creation is a meaningful idea, a 'let there be,' expressing a pattern of meaning into a space and time so that it can become real beyond words. It's as if God said, 'Let $E=MC^2$,' and there was light, you know? To me, the story is about Being giving beings the good gift of being. How could being be otherwise, deriving from God? No wonder the poem has the refrain . . ."

Kerry finished the sentence for him. "And God saw that it was good."

"Exactly. Exactly!" Neo replied. "The second creation narrative is told much more from a male human perspective, men who till the ground asking, 'Where did animals come from, and where did *women* come from, and what went wrong and got us to this point?' At least that's how I read it."

"That," Kerry answered, "is the other thing that has always bothered me—first, the nonscientific business, and second, that male human perspective business. It's caused us women a lot of pain, you know. I wish that perspective had been left out."

"Yes, yes . . . sadly, bad readings of the Bible have brought a lot of grief to you women—and to my people too!" Neo replied. "We've got a lot in common on that one. But that's getting ahead of ourselves. That's more from the next episode of the story, really. But give this second perspective another chance. How about this: we see these ancient men reminding themselves through this story that the animals and women around them came from God; along with this added understanding: in some real sense, the creatures that surround a man in a man's world—plants and animals and female humans—are given by God for man to enjoy as good company. They're not to be used, exploited, hated, or feared; they are his God-given companions, especially the woman at his side. They're to be noticed and named, so that the one not-so-good thing in this creation—being alone— could be remedied. Man would live in a network of relationships, with the soil, the trees, the sun and seasons, the animals, and his own kind, male and female. How does that sound?"

"That's a beautiful picture, Neo. Way better than painting women as the origin of all evil," Kerry said. "The way you read this story, it almost sounds like a different story. It's so different from what I, and I guess what most people, grew up with."

They didn't need to pause as often on the way down, but they did pause at one point to enjoy the afternoon sun sparkling on the Pacific to the west. "Here's perspective again," Neo said. "From this perspective, we see the light playing on the water, but from down at the beach, it might not be so beautiful at all."

"But down there, we'd see something else," Kerry replied. "There would be some other beauty shining." Neo smiled, and they continued their downward trek. He noticed that he wasn't so out of breath as they descended, but his thigh muscles began to burn.

A while later, Neo picked up the conversation again. "There's one other surprising thing that the second creation story in Genesis suggests to me. It's something shocking, maybe put best when it's put in a way that borders on heresy: *God is not enough,* the story says. That has nothing to do with any deficiency in God; it has to do with the storyline God had in mind for us. God doesn't want to be the only reality in our lives, the only relationship in our network, the only message on our screen. In the story we find ourselves in, God wants us to name the giraffe, and laugh as it reaches the tall, tall branches; name the zebra, and smile as it gallops across the plain; name the fruit bat and name the dragonfly, and wonder as they fly above us—and enjoy them all. Like that lava lizard you showed me on that rock, or the tortoises copulating down there. Noticing and naming and enjoying our fellow creatures, as we're doing today, is part of why we're here."

"I can say amen to *that!*" Kerry said, with a slightly mischievous smile.

They were returning by a different path, one less steep. Kerry explained that steep paths are easier to climb than they are to descend, and with Neo's fall on North Seymour fresh in their minds, it made sense to take a longer but safer path back. Eventually they reached another grassy area with potholes filled with tortoises, similar to the habitat they found on their ascent. They sat in the grass on a rise from which they could look up to the rim and down a short distance to the beach. At the opposite edge of the grassy area, another pair of tortoises was mating, and their odd honking and thudding mixed with the melodies of finches and mockingbirds.

With that soundtrack in the background, it was natural for them to continue talking about how the story positioned men and women in relation to one another, how it could be interpreted from both chauvinist and feminist perspectives. Neo's tone grew a bit more tender, and Kerry wondered, later, if he had meant for her to read anything in between the lines as he continued. "Kerry, I think the story tells us that the Creator wants man and woman to find each other, as a lost part of themselves. And so in the story we have the man and the women, naked, together, both innocent and passionate, not ashamed to see and be seen, to know and be known, to need and be needed, to want and enjoy another being, given by the Being."

A long pause lingered. Then Kerry, feeling a bit uncomfortable, shifted the mood and said, "I guess, in the presence of all these other created beings, it can make sense to call the first Being the Supreme Being, even though that title seems a little . . . a little cold and technical."

Neo said, "Yes, but which name does the job perfectly?"

Kerry replied, "No wonder there are so many."

Neo went back to his thought about God not being enough. "This is the story we find ourselves in, isn't it? Caught between two dangers: a hyperspiritual danger that says, 'It is good enough for human beings to be alone, so all they need is God,' and a hypersecular danger that says, 'It is good enough for human beings to be with the other created beings; forget about the Supreme Being from whom all being and blessing flow.' Neither of those options is good enough. The only viable option in our story is for us human beings to enjoy the company both of our Creator and of our fellow creatures: our brother sun and sister moon, our brother fox and sister fruit bat, and especially of our mates—either sexual mates or mates in your Australian sense of the term, our friends—in whom we find a lost part of ourselves restored to us again."

"I never thought of that," said Kerry, squinting as if to bring back memories from her childhood in Sunday school. "What a crazy thing! In the Genesis story, the rib is taken out of Adam—by God! God seems to want Adam to feel incomplete on purpose. God nicks a part of him on purpose! That means that Adam is—meaning we are too—incomplete by God's design! I must have heard this story a dozen times, but I never thought of . . ."

"It's wonderful, isn't it?" Neo urged. "The story is telling us that we were designed to be incomplete and unfulfilled in ourselves as monads, as isolated individuals. We feel an ache in our side, like some part of us is missing, so that we'll always be looking outside ourselves for belonging and connection, for it is not good for a person to be alone—not in this story! And so in this story we live in a garden, with all the creatures around us, and we walk with God in the cool of the day."

This can cause us to behave in odd ways.

That's how that Monday felt for Kerry—as if she and Neo were Eve and Adam, walking on the paradise of this wonderful, primeval island, surrounded by creatures full of intrigue and delight.

If someone had asked her, even a few weeks before, whether she was lonely, she would have said no, not at all. She had her work, her son and her mother (with whom she kept in close touch by e-mail and visits), her friends at the Center, her colleagues. Busy, yes, but lonely, no.

But that afternoon, walking down that volcano with Neo, she felt so *accompanied,* so befriended, so not alone, that she began to see how lonely she really had been without even realizing it.

And more. She felt a certain other feeling. She had been on these islands for years now, but on this day, she felt something new. She didn't want to call it God, but it seemed to be something real and *there.* "Nonsense," she'd say to herself when she began to acknowledge it. She'd push the feeling away. But it would resurface again, and again, almost following her, or waiting for her around every turn.

As she and Neo angled down on that sloping switchback trail toward the spot where their boat waited on the beach, Kerry asked Neo to keep talking. "This is really good for me," she said. "You were right. This story of yours is just what I needed."

"It's not just my story," he said. "It's everybody's."

8

A SIGNED WORK OF ART

THEY DESCENDED THROUGH A ROCKY AREA, weaving between the black volcanic boulders typical of the islands. Farther along, Kerry pointed out some lava formations that resembled mounds of coal-black cake batter emerging from gray sand and reddish gravel. They appeared to ooze out like oily goo, but to the touch, each surface was hard and mercilessly sharp, as if embedded with tiny shards of glass. The terrain began to level off after a while, and they gradually reentered the more arid zone of cactus and *palo santo* that stretched to the shore. Blue-footed boobies nested in this area, and Neo and Kerry knelt in the sparse shade of an opuntia tree to watch a mother tending her fluffy white chick. The nest was composed of pebbles and sticks and cactus thorns, a sparse circle on the rocky ground. "Such tenderness amidst all the severity of the landscape," Kerry said.

Neo noted the starkness of the colors too: dull black rock, white downy chick, blue feet and blue bill of the brownish mother bird, her yellow-brown eyes, mild green of the cactus pads and bright yellow of the opuntia flowers, all under the gloriously blue sky. "Amazing, just amazing," he repeated.

As they left the boobies behind, Neo continued speaking, but more softly than usual now, as if a special feeling of peace or awe had come over him in the nesting area. "This first episode of the story has profound meaning to me, to me personally, as a scientist, as a follower of Christ, as a human being. It seems to me that we have to start here to begin to understand who we are: part of a larger creation and connected to it, but also given a unique status—created in 'our image,' says God. We find ourselves carrying this special endowment of *the breath of life,* which may suggest our intelligence, our consciousness, or our conscience—I'm not sure. We find in our souls and in the story a resonant need for connection with God, with creation, and in particular with the rest of humanity. We have this God-given sexual identity that is good and very good. We feel an inescapable responsibility to be stewards of the rest of creation—just as a gardener cares for a garden, the story tells us. We aren't an accident. We aren't orphans. We aren't on our own. We aren't in charge. It's not our world, to do with whatever we want. We may be at the top of the food chain in many places—although don't the little microbes beat us all in the end?—but we aren't at the top of the chain of Being. We have a place, and we have a mission as gardeners and as namers and as companions to God and one another. And if we take seriously the phrase 'in the image of God,' we can understand our mission as something so profound and so . . . *awe-inspiring*: we are here to be God's junior partners in creation. It's as if God is the master artist and the world is a studio, and God creates us in it to be God's young apprentices, God's students, learning to create too."

"It's like the mother booby back there, really," Kerry said. "She has life and the power to give life, and gives her chick life and the power to give life too. That's a feminine picture of God, I guess, and a great way to read the story. But I can't stop thinking that that's not the way it's been interpreted in our culture." Kerry shook her head. "Neo, I so wish people had seen it your way, but I think too many of us have read the story to say it gives European white males carte blanche to play God over creation; so 'having dominion' gives them a license to pollute and exploit. You know, the whole Industrial Revolution thing."

"Yes," Neo said, "that's one of the great tragedies of our whole human history: the failure of everyone, not just white European males, to feel the majestic sacredness of the poetry that begins our story. As you say, chapter one is not a license to kill or pollute or exploit—no way. It's the opposite: an invitation to cocreate, to learn the sacred art of living life and giving life creatively, as apprentice artists in the Master's studio."

Kerry was nodding her head now, in understanding if not yet in full agreement. For a while, the only sound was the crunching of their shoes on gravel. Then Neo said, "So here we are—you, a European nonmale white, and I, a non-European male nonwhite, trying to get the story from our unique perspectives."

"I like the way you put it a minute ago," Kerry said, "about being apprentice artists."

Neo replied, "Yes, it's perhaps the most profound way in which we humans bear the Creator's image. We're capable of giving being to new things, babies—to be sure, a dimension of the image of God given to all living things—but more: ideas, languages, poems, songs, homes, cities, civilizations, even religions. The parallel is awesome: ideas, languages, poems, civilizations, religions, and so on don't self-create. They are utterly dependent on us, their creators, for being, just as our universe didn't self-create and can't endure without being sustained by the Creator. So we're given this most amazing gift, not just the gift of being, as wonderful as that is, but also the gift of creating, of helping add things-that-be—ideas, poems, homes, religions, and so on—to the universe."

"Wow," Kerry said. "I wondered what you meant earlier when you said that even other religions have a place in the story. So you see other religions as . . . as part of creation, because they are creations created by creative creatures."

Neo chuckled and said, "That's a bit better than I said it, really."

They reached a cliff overlooking the cove where their trek had begun. There was nowhere to sit, so they took off their packs and stood for a few minutes, facing south and west, watching huge swirling flocks of small swallowlike birds that rose and fell like fog in the wind currents along the cliff. They traded Kerry's binoculars back and forth, trying to follow the soaring and diving of individual birds, but the birds' acrobatics defied their attempts, and eventually the patterns of the whole flocks in choreographed motion, seen without binoculars, fascinated them even more than the acrobatic movements of individuals. Kerry identified the species: "*Oceanodroma gracilis* . . . storm petrels. Aren't they magnificent?"

"Arcs laid on the air, as soon as made, not there," Neo said.

"What's that?" Kerry asked.

"It's a line from a Wendell Berry poem," he answered.

As they resumed their descent, Kerry asked Neo how he would contrast his Christian version of the creation story with the alternatives presented in other religions. "Hmmm," he said, pausing to think for a moment. "There's a very popular story that says the universe came into being by itself, and that everything that has happened has happened by accident. In this story, which arose most forcefully in modern Western civilization, there is no God, no Being beyond our beings, no Creator. In this story, we can be at the top of the food chain and every other chain; no one is around—as far as we know—to challenge our claim to being the Supreme Beings. There is much in this story to flatter our pride, and this story probably has fueled technological advancements more than any other. It explains so much. In fact, you could say that this story seems to explain everything about everything except one small detail."

"Which is?" Kerry asked.

"Which is human experience—joy, sorrow, outrage, grief, hope, longing, wonder, love—the awareness that you're alive and that you're going to die and that both of those facts matter to you and mean something to you. And certainly you'd have to include overtly *spiritual* human experiences as well. So, even though it explains so much, this secular story marginalizes so much of human experience, and in the end, I think that this secular version can become a dangerous *perversion* of the true story. But again, it does take seriously how . . . how *real* creation is. And as a result, people who follow this story have excelled in seeking to understand creation, to learn its language and discover its deep structures and potentials for development."

"You've nailed it," Kerry said. "That's the version of the story I've always found myself in, and you've nailed both the strong and weak spots in my story. It's just as you said. Sometimes the weak spots bother me, and sometimes they don't, I guess. Got another competing version?"

"Sure. There's another story that says this universe is all an illusion, that Being didn't actually create beings, but that Being simply dreams or imagines beings. In this version of the story, when beings realize their true situation—they aren't beings at all, but dreams or emanations of Being, that they don't actually exist *outside* God's mind at all, but rather are illusions or thoughts *inside* the mind of Being—they achieve enlightenment by releasing their distinctiveness as beings into the fullness of Being."

"I can't believe I actually followed your explanation there," Kerry said with a laugh. "That's the Hindu version, right?"

"Yes, more or less," Neo answered. "There's a lot about this ancient Eastern story that we need to hear. These days, it often serves as a correction to the previous modern Western story, I think, by saying the very opposite: the previous story says there is no God or spirit, and this one says there is nothing *but* God and spirit. If I were to make a mistake, I'd rather make the latter than the former, because the former story, that God does not exist, never was true, but the latter story, that nothing but God exists, at least *used to* be true. In other words, according to the ancient Jewish story, it was true before God created anything. This Eastern version reminds us that we beings cannot exist apart from Being, that we are ultimately connected to God and to all that exists in profound ways, ways that are easy to forget in our modern Western world, where the first story often predominates. This Eastern version of the story is, I believe, one of humanity's most lofty creations."

The path split into four paths at this point, one heading east, one west, and two continuing south, and Kerry chose the most direct southward route to the rocky shore. The beach, where their boat was now visible on the sand, lay a few hundred meters east of them, to their left. This trail was strenuous and a bit dangerous, and required them to use both hands and feet. At the bottom, along a section of shore covered in black cobbles smoothed by rolling in the surf, they sat down for a few minutes before going to the boat. Kerry picked up a round black stone and tossed it gently in her hand. "So," Kerry said, "you don't believe that Hindu story, at least not like you believe the Jewish story, but yet you find value in it, meaning in it."

"Sure. And I *believe in* all the value and meaning I find in it. For me, the ancient Jewish story lies in between the other two, or maybe it arches over both, you know? This ancient Middle Eastern story embraces both the modern Western story and the ancient Eastern story. It acknowledges the modern Western assertion that this universe is real. That rock you're holding really exists; it's not just an illusion or dream—nor are we. It acknowledges the modern Western belief that the universe operates on many levels according to patterns we call 'laws of nature'—a better metaphor than 'laws' would be 'language of creation' or 'music of creation,' I think. This story celebrates a kind of enlightenment—celebrated in a period in history we call the Enlightenment—that comes from treating the stuff of the universe as real stuff, and studying it, analyzing it scientifically, and doing amazing things with it."

Kerry looked down at the black cobble in her hand as Neo continued. "And the ancient Middle Eastern story also acknowledges the ancient Eastern assertion that this universe is not independent, that it depends on the Creator so it can come into existence and stay in existence. It also acknowledges that because of our common connection to the Creator, all that exists is interconnected, related, interwoven. It agrees with the Eastern belief that the universe pulsates with meaning, as one would expect of any universe that was spoken by Being into being. It celebrates a different kind of enlightenment—not scientific, but mystical—that comes from seeing the universe as an expression of the mind and heart of God, in which God's breath breathes, and God's language sings, and God's fingerprints are detected and felt, and God's signature is read."

After a few moments, Kerry said, "You know, Neo, sitting here, feeling the weight of this rock in my hand, looking out at the waves, watching those sea lions sleeping peacefully on the boulders over there, it really does feel like we're part of a story or maybe a signed work of art. What I feel now, I've felt several other times in my life, but the feeling is so fleeting. I wish it would stay." She lobbed her cobble out into the water, and it sank with a *plunk*.

Neo smiled at her and said nothing. Without a word, they walked over to the boat and pushed it out from the little arc of sand at the end of the cove. This time, Kerry pulled the cord and revved up the motor, and Neo sat facing her as she piloted them back toward Puerto Ayora. She said, "So, mate, if you're right, here we find ourselves, in a grand story of creation. I'm not saying I believe it. But I'm saying I can imagine believing it."

"That's a great start, Kerry," Neo said, raising his voice over the roar of the motor. "But remember: it's not only about creation way back whenever. This creation keeps unfolding, every breeze bringing something new into being. Even us here today . . . through our friendship we're being created. We're growing, changing, becoming. We're masterpieces in progress, so creation is continuing in us. Right now!"

"Wait a minute," Kerry said, wiping some salt spray from her face. "I thought the story said that God rested on the seventh day. Wouldn't that mean that God stopped creating long ago?"

"Well," Neo said, "God wouldn't exactly need to keep creating directly. After all, God just created this really cool universe that has been given the ability to keep generating new creative possibilities, right? God creates a creation that keeps bringing new creative creations into being. But at the same time, you have to acknowledge that it's all God's work of art, right? The old theologians talked of *creatio originalis, creatio continua,* and *creatio nova:* original creation, continual creation, and new creation—which I think we'll talk about some more, later on in the story. But it's all about creation, from beginning to ending. How else could it go, with a Creator as wonderful as this? Pretty cool, wouldn't you say?"

"Pretty cool, Neo." Kerry felt that she was riding a swell of creative possibilities as real as the rollers that bore them homeward. She twisted her wrist, and the engine roared even louder, and they veered toward Santa Cruz. It became too hard to talk over the sounds of the boat surging over waves and the motor at full throttle, so they both settled into a comfortable silence. It was after dark when they reached the marina. The stars were especially bright that night, and after tying up the boat and gathering their gear, they sat on the dock, dangling their feet over the falling tide and enjoying the clear sky for a long time. It was well after midnight when Neo returned to *La Aventura.*

9

TORQUING NORMAL MODES
OF THINKING

THE FOLLOWING MONDAY BEGAN with mist and fog. For a while, it looked like the sun would break through some ragged gray clouds, but then the winds picked up. Rain fell off and on for the rest of the day. Neo showed up at the Charles Darwin Research Center at about ten o'clock. "I figured this wasn't much of a day for field work," he said.

Kerry invited him in and fixed him a mug of strong Ecuadorian coffee. She introduced him to some of the others at the Center. Maricel wasn't there. She was picking up a visiting scientist at the airport over on Baltra. Between rain showers, Kerry took Neo out back to the pens where baby tortoises were being raised. A thirtyish American strolled out with them, a Ph.D. in ornithology named Glenn. Glenn wore the khaki uniform of the Center, and Neo noticed how his hair was of the same light brown color. He sported a scraggly beard, small but thick glasses, and a big smile. He had a gold front tooth, which seemed to evoke a corresponding twinkle in his eye when he smiled, which he did often.

"Maricel tells me you're a man of God," Glenn said, almost mocking, but not quite. "Every Sunday she invites me to *La Aventura*. She says you're a tour guide by day, and a spiritual guide by night. She says you can give me a guided tour of God."

Neo smiled. "There's a certain crossover of skills, I suppose. But the way I see it, you're already doing God's work yourself. You just might not realize it."

"Heck, no, I don't think so. I certainly wasn't doing God's work last night," he said, laughing. "I bought me a bottle of tequila down at the Havana Bar, and a young *chica* from town helped me finish it. I think we did a little of the devil's work last night."

"No, no," said Neo, "I was referring to your work here at the Center. Saving the flora and fauna of the islands, especially the Galápagos hawks, right? Protecting some of God's most fascinating creatures sounds like pretty holy work to me."

That launched them into a long conversation about the captive breeding program for tortoises there at CDRC, along with the status of several endemic bird species, as they walked among the tortoise pens and back toward the main building. They came to a small round table under a veranda, and the three of them got a second cup of coffee each, and sat down together.

Realizing that Glenn wasn't leaving them any time soon, Kerry said, "Glenn, Neo promised to tell me the second installment of the story of the universe today." She was joking, but serious too. "You're welcome to eavesdrop."

"I love eavesdropping," Glenn said. "It's not every day you get the inside scoop on the story of the universe. Fire away, your Eminence." Then he genuflected and crossed himself three or four times and began raising his hands and bowing toward Neo, again mocking, but somewhat good-naturedly. *Trying to keep things light,* Kerry imagined.

Neo smiled at Kerry and turned to Glenn. "Last week, Kerry and I talked about creation. For me, that's episode one of the story, a most important episode for us to understand these days, especially here in these islands. It's an episode that never really ends. But episode two kind of invades it or hijacks it."

"What do you call it? Episode two, I mean. 'The Hijack'?" Glenn asked.

"Maybe you can help me name it after you hear it," Neo said.

"Let's hear it then. We need the word of God around here in this evil temple of Darwinism," Glenn said, gesturing comically with his hands and accidentally spilling his coffee, which took a few moments to clean up.

When the coffee was mopped up, Neo said, "For starters, you have to remember that, according to this story anyway, the universe that God created is a real one. It isn't a fantasy universe, a simulation universe, a test universe, or a dream universe. It's real, and what happens here is real."

"Sounds pretty obvious. That spilled coffee made an undeniably real mess," Glenn said.

"Not so quick, amigo," Kerry cut in. "Last week, Neo was telling me that it's not such an easy thing for God to create something 'outside' himself . . . or herself, or Godself, or whatever. I think he's trying to say that the idea of creation involves the kind of world that we scientists like: something real, predictable, substantial, measurable—that sort of thing."

"Yes," Neo said, "and that's essential for the next episodes to make any sense. So let's go back in the story to the human community living as hunter-gatherers—"

"But just a minute," Glenn interrupted. "What about miracles? I mean, if the universe is real, the kind of universe we scientists like, how can you have miracles?"

"Miracles," Neo said, "probably are overrated."

Kerry and Glenn responded in unison, "Huh?"

"What do you mean by that, Neo?" Kerry asked. "I wouldn't expect you to say such a thing."

Neo replied, "OK, here's a little thought experiment. God creates this universe with something we call gravity, whatever that is—we really don't have a clue, you know? And gravity means that if you slip from one of those volcanic cliffs along the Pacific, you'll experience a nasty fall and terrible injury. Let's imagine that on your way down, you cry out to God in that most eloquent of prayers—*Help!*—and ask for a miracle, and let's say that God answers, damping gravity for a moment so that you float back up to safety. And let's say that every time you fell or experienced any corollary danger, you similarly prayed and were similarly granted a miracle. You can imagine what would happen."

"Yeah," Glenn said. "You'd become a daredevil—pardon the pun. You'd try anything, because really, the danger of any risk could be averted. Risk would disappear, which would be really boring, come to think of it, and—"

"I never thought of that," Kerry interrupted. "And along with that, people would lose all sense of . . . of responsibility, of limits. It would create a planet full of indulgent, irresponsible children and spoiled brats, really. Especially because if God granted miracles on demand for one person, he . . . or she, or whatever . . . would be required to do the same for everybody, just to be fair, right? And it wouldn't be very *real* either, I imagine."

Neo replied, "That's right. What might seem like paradise would pretty quickly become a boring or surrealistic nightmare, which becomes less attractive the more you think about it."

Glenn cupped his coffee mug in both hands: "Well, you're torquing my normal modes of thinking. So, Neo, are you a Christian who doesn't believe in miracles?"

Neo answered, "No. Of course I believe that miracles are possible. In fact, I've experienced a few myself, or at least I think I have. But as I said, I think that miracles are a lot more problematic than most people realize. If God grants one, we expect two, and if two, two million. So miracles would need to be pretty carefully dispensed, which is generally what you find in the Bible, actually. Miracles aren't all that common, but we talk about them a lot, so they seem more common than they really are—like shark attacks or tornados that keep getting broadcast on TV, just because they're so rare, giving us the impression that they occur far more often than they actually do. But that's just the tip of the iceberg, really."

Kerry asked what he meant, and Neo continued, "Try this on. This whole idea of dividing the world up into two categories, the natural and the supernatural, the normal and the miraculous—have you ever wondered if that's the only way, the right way, to categorize things?" Glenn and Kerry both made faces that said they had no idea what he meant, so he continued. "OK. You've heard about the miracle of Jesus turning water into wine, right?" They both nodded.

"Grape vines turn water and soil into grape juice all the time—a pretty amazing transformation—and we don't call that miraculous. And then yeast cells ferment the sugars of the grape juice into wine, and we don't call that miraculous. But it's just that in one case, we understand the mechanisms—photosynthesis, fermentation—and in the case of miracles, we don't. What if there are explanations—and I'm sure there must be—for any legitimate miracle? The Bible itself suggests this at times. For example, the crossing of the sea during the exodus from Egypt is definitely seen as a miracle, but also it has a natural explanation: a wind blew back the waters. For the ancient Jewish people, it wasn't either the wind, which is a natural explanation, or a miracle, which is a supernatural explanation. It was, in a sense, a perfectly natural supernatural event, exactly the kind of thing you might expect in a universe created by a God of the type we're imagining."

Kerry and Glenn still looked puzzled. "I'm sorry," Neo continued, "this probably sounds like nonsense. Let me try a different approach. Would you agree that, for us as scientists, the world is ultimately mechanistic? In other words, it's like a closed system of causes and effects, completely impersonal, in the end only the outworking of physics and mechanisms?"

Glenn responded, "Yeah, sure. Kind of like a really big cosmic pool table, where somebody racked up the balls and took the first shot, and everything is still happening, balls rolling over here and there and everywhere." Glenn almost knocked over his coffee again with his gesticulations.

"Right," Neo responded. "I think that in the modern era, religious people bought into that mechanistic model of the universe right along with the scientists. So they had to keep bringing God in to interfere, to flip a switch . . . stop a ball rolling over there and redirect it into another ball over here." Neo was drawing imaginary lines on the table to illustrate.

"So the things that would have happened anyway, we call natural. And the interferences we call supernatural."

Neo stopped and looked first at Kerry, and then at Glenn, as if his point had been made perfectly clearly. But their blank stares made it clear that he wasn't even close.

Kerry spoke first. "So you're saying that really, since God created the pool table and started the balls rolling to begin with, the *whole thing is supernatural.*"

"No," Glenn, answered, "I think he's saying that since God really, really exists, just as much as the pool table—at least as Neo sees it—then for God to pick up a pool cue and be a player in the equation is natural. So the *whole thing is natural.*" They both looked at Neo.

Neo said, "Actually, I think you've both made my point, sort of. My point is that the universe didn't come equipped with these categories of 'natural' and 'supernatural.' They're human constructions, modern constructions, arising out of our Western intellectual history. And I guess I'm saying that before we dig into episode two of the story we find ourselves in, it would be good to try to dislodge those categories, and try to see the universe from a different perspective, not just the narrow little perspective of modern Western Ph.D.'s like . . . well, like the three of us."

"Touché," said Glenn. "We Ph.D.'s can be a pretty pigheaded and arrogant phylum! So go on, Neo. It's my fault that we got on that major tangent into mechanism and miracles and playing pool. I have a feeling I know what's coming. You're going to tell us about Adam and Eve and the apple, right?"

TOO SMART, TOO POWERFUL
FOR THEIR OWN GOOD

NEO SMILED AT GLENN and said, "I think I might surprise you." Glenn made a beckoning motion with his hands that seemed to say, *Come on, let me have it,* so Neo continued. "I think something unfortunate happened in Western theology a long time ago. Can I take us on one more tangent before we dive into episode two?"

Kerry nodded, and Glenn said, "Sure, Neo."

Neo said, "One of the toughest decisions the earliest Christians had to make was how they would respond to Greek philosophy, which was a powerful cultural force in their day. There were a number of competing schools—Stoic, Epicurean, Platonic, and the like—so it certainly wasn't a monolithic force. But it was a force to be reckoned with. I suppose the early Christians could have ghettoized themselves and refused to engage with it, but they did engage, and courageously so. I think they had to, because Jesus had sent them into all the world, to all the different nations. They couldn't just ghettoize."

"Yeah. And so?" Glenn asked.

"In engaging with Greek philosophy," Neo resumed, "those Christians had to adopt Greek terminology, and terms can be kind of like Trojan horses, bringing in foreign ways of thinking that aren't native to the story."

"Kind of like introduced species here on the island," Glenn said, "that don't really fit and then disrupt the natural system."

"I never thought of theology as being similar to an ecosystem." Kerry said. "Interesting analogy, Glenn."

Neo agreed, and continued. "Well, one of those introduced species is the idea that there are two worlds, like our two categories of natural and supernatural. For the Greeks, there was the ideal world—we might call it the spiritual world—which was the real world. Then there was the material world, the physical world—and this is counterintuitive for scientists like us—which was the less real world."

"In a way, that's actually not so different," Glenn said. "For us, the real world is the invisible world of mathematical equations, and the physical phenomena that we interact with are just examples of the universal theories or equations that everything runs on . . . you know, Newtonian mechanics, quantum mechanics, that sort of thing."

"There are parallels, you're right," Neo said, "but for many of the Greeks, there was a moral superiority to the ideal world, and a moral inferiority—and for some, moral evil—to the physical world. So you have this huge gulf, two different realities: the higher one more real and noble than the other, the lesser one subject to change and decay. And here's the connection to where I want us to go in episode two: I think that we tend to use Greek lenses to read the book of Genesis, which introduces the first three episodes of what I'm calling 'The Story We Find Ourselves In.' Christian theologians even created a kind of Trojan-horse term to enfranchise this Greek grid. Have you heard of Christians talking about *the fall?*"

Kerry jumped in. "My dad used to talk about that all the time. 'It's because of the fall,' he'd often say when something bad happened. Are you saying that that's a Greek concept, and not a truly Christian one?"

"It's not quite that simple," Neo replied. "But I am saying that when you take episode one seriously, you realize that for the ancient Jewish people, there was one world, not two. And God was in that world, very naturally. The poetic language in the story speaks of God walking with Adam and Eve in the cool of the day, for example."

"I always liked the part about them being naked," Glenn interrupted. "That's my idea of paradise. I wouldn't mind going natural right now!" Glenn made a show of taking off his shirt, and Kerry said, "Oh, stop. Grow up, Glenn."

Neo shook his head with a smile and continued. "So it's one world, one universe, a universe with matter and life and God, not chopped up between real-ideal versus illusory-material, between spiritual and physical, supernatural and natural. It's one, beautiful, integrated world. And human beings are part of it. The world is their garden, their home. That's another way, I think, of saying that they're hunter-gatherers, humanity in its most primal state, living in a day-by-day dependence on the world, to find fruits and nuts and leaves and whatever else they ate."

"Are you saying they were vegetarians?" Kerry seemed intrigued, because she was a vegetarian herself.

"Maybe," Neo replied, "but I don't think that matters. Don't the anthropologists tell us that primitive humans were insectivores?"

At this, Kerry and Glenn gave one another a disgusted look, and Neo chuckled and continued. "Anyway, whatever their diet, they are living in this world, primitive by our standards, but then again, they're living in harmony with the rest of creation, without pollution or terrorism or bio-chemical warfare or nuclear weapons, so their way of life had some ad-vantages."

"No kidding," Glenn said. "So where does the big fall fit in?"

"In the modern telling of the story, there is one cataclysmic event in which the first humans descend—or fall, if you will—from their ideal, per-fect state into the material, imperfect story of history," Neo said.

"But the story you told me last week said that the world was perfect, and then it became polluted by evil. Isn't that the same thing as saying that it's fallen?" Kerry asked.

"Well, maybe this is a tangent we should just forget about, but . . . OK. The Jewish story says the world as created was good, even very good. But it didn't say *perfect*. Perfect is more of a Greek concept. Can you see that? Perfect has all the baggage of Greek idealism: ideal, unchanging, complete, fully formed, all that stuff. But that's not the universe that God creates, as I read the story, especially in light of science, and even more, in light of a later part of the story that is more eschatalogical."

"Whoa!" Glenn interrupted: "I know what *scatological* means, but *es-chatological?*"

"Let's save that for later, Glenn," Neo said. "My point here is that by importing the Greek idea of a fall from a perfect, unchanging, ideal, com-plete, harmonious, fully formed world into a world of change, challenge, conflict, and all the rest, the story is distorted. Because for ancient Jewish people, who originally gave us this story, and on whose terms we need to take it, this distortion or this invasion of the story by introduced species—as you put it—disrupts the ecosystems of both episode one and episode two, and everything that follows, really. Remember: there's just one world for the Jews: this good world, God's world, our world, where what we call matter and spirit, or natural and supernatural, or physical and meta-physical are all part of the same big, good, wonderful world. The God-given goodness in creation isn't lost because of what happens in episode two. God's creative fingerprint or signature is still there, always and for-ever. The evil of humanity doesn't eradicate the goodness of God's cre-ation, even though it puts all that goodness at risk."

"Sounds like pollution," Glenn said.

"So, Neo, if you don't believe in the fall in those terms, what is episode two about then?" Kerry asked.

"Here's how I think of it. With all due credit to Darwin, and perhaps even more deservingly, to Alfred Wallace, let's accept that evolution is more or less true, that God creates a world that in a sense must go on creating itself so that its story isn't God's forced story, God's imposed story, but instead, its own real story, a story of emergence."

"OK, OK, now this is coming together," Glenn said, now every bit as earnest as he had been mocking earlier. "That's why you were making that big deal about the story being real and good, not ideal and perfect. Because a *perfect* world in the Greek sense has to be fully formed, finished, complete. In the Greek sense, it can't be developing and growing and changing, because that would imply that it had been imperfect, or less than fully formed, when it began, and that would be unworthy of God. But for you, Hebrew *good* is better than Greek *perfect*, because good has the potential of developing even more goodness, but perfection just sits there in a kind of static sterility. Good is dynamic, creative, fruitful, robust. What a wild thought, that good is better than perfect. Is that what you're saying?"

"Exactly. In fact, to get around this problem with perfection, some Greek thinkers posited that the material world was created by a lesser god, an evil god. But that's another tangent. Getting back to *this* story, it's God's ongoing creative process; it's not a mechanistic process taking place apart from God, and it's not a simulation being run in the mind of God. We're dealing with a good world in the Jewish sense, not a perfect one in the Greek sense—one world, one reality, one universe in which what we call matter and spirit are integrated. I have to keep emphasizing this, because it's so hard for us. We're so indoctrinated by modern Western thought, which is so indoctrinated by Greek dualism—you know, the idea that the universe is divided into two inherent categories."

"I just want to get on to the next episode." Kerry said, "So keep going, Neo."

"OK. Human beings are developing, living as hunter-gatherers. Their brain capacity is increasing, as we would expect it to. They are living more or less harmoniously and dependently in the world. Then they begin to develop language. Language makes possible all kinds of other innovations and social arrangements. And then things start going wrong."

"Now you're coming to the apple and snake business, right?" Glenn asked.

"Not so fast, Glenn. Try to see this in a fresh way. Try to stick with the story as it is preserved for us in Genesis, without all the overlays and interpretations. When I read Genesis without preconceived Greek notions like a fall from the ideal to the real world, I don't see just one crisis. I see an avalanche of crises. And they all relate to a disintegration of the pri-mal harmony and innocence of creation. In a sense, they all involve hu-man beings gaining levels of intellectual and technological development that surpass their moral development—people becoming too smart, too powerful for their own good."

"Sounds like me last night with Maria and the tequila—*powerful!*" Glenn said, striking a weightlifter pose and expecting a laugh that didn't come.

Neo continued, ignoring Glenn's interruption. "So what do Adam and Eve do? They say, 'We don't want to have to answer to anybody. We want to be at the top of the food chain. We want to be like gods ourselves.' And they go beyond the limits that they know they should keep. That's what taking the fruit is about. It's about experiencing evil, tasting evil, which means disrupting the balance, going beyond their proper limits as crea-tures, as part of creation. And as soon as they do, they lose trust in one another. They feel shame, fear. Because human trust is based on respect for limits—boundaries, we often call them—respect for differentness, re-spect for uniqueness. And so sexually, Adam and Eve want to cover their differentness, because sexual trust is gone. And then—"

"Then," Kerry interrupted, "as I recall, their sons fight with each other. So trust between brothers is broken, and Cain, I think it was, crosses the boundary and kills Abel."

"Yes," Neo said, "and that one is so interesting. Do you remember what their argument was about?"

"Religion," Glenn said. "Typical. Religious hatred in the Middle East goes way back."

"Yes, but I think it's more profound than that. Abel, the story says, brought a sacrifice of an animal to God. I think this suggests that Abel has gone beyond his ancestors, who were hunter-gatherers, like Adam and Eve in the garden. Now Abel has become a pastoralist, a herder of sheep or goats or cattle. That's the next step up in the scale of development. You have a little more freedom than hunter-gatherers have, because your herds can eat stuff—grass—that you can't. But you're still quite dependent, quite humble, right? You're nomadic, because you have to move to where the grass is greener as your herds defoliate one area after another. Are you with me? OK. Now, remember what Cain brought as his expression of worship?"

There was a moment of thoughtful silence, and then another moment. "Oh, I see where you're going!" Kerry said. "I can't believe I never thought about this. He brings crops. So he's moved beyond being a primitive hunter-gather and beyond being a pastoralist to being a sophisticated agriculturalist."

"Ah," Glenn said, "and that's the root of all evil! Because when you plant crops, you gain independence. You have more control over your situation. You don't have to keep moving on when the goats eat all the grass. And so you can settle down. And . . . wow! . . . when you settle down, you can accumulate stuff. You don't have to travel so light. So ownership becomes a big deal. And when you can own and accumulate, you have stuff to protect, because others might steal it. And not only that, but other people might want to steal your land."

"Or," Neo said, "you might want to lay claim to the land that your hunter-gatherer and pastoralist neighbors traditionally have used. You need it for your fields and crops. And if those comparatively primitive nomads come through with their herds, you call it trespassing and—"

"And if they trespass, you kill them." Kerry cut in. "Stunning!"

"Do you remember where Cain killed Abel?" Neo asked.

"Oh, my God!" Kerry said. "I do remember. Wasn't it in a field? The scene of the crime is the source of their conflict. Simply stunning."

THE GLOBAL AND
THE PERSONAL

THERE WAS A LONG MOMENT of silence. Glenn broke it. "This is amazing, most reverend Neo. I mean, I've always made fun of those stories before, but now, listening to you, I realize what a philistine I've been. They're . . . awesome."

"Awesome, yes, and tragic too, don't you think?" Neo said. "Things get worse. Human beings leave their identity, their life, their story as creatures in God's creation. Their intelligence has developed beyond their moral wisdom and self-restraint."

Glenn was into it all now, and spoke excitedly. "And as they become more independent, they lose their connection to God, their sense of dependence, I mean. That reminds me of that old story about the guy who walks into a bar and—"

"Keep going, Neo," Kerry cut in, reaching over and putting her hands gently up to Glenn's mouth. "Ignore him. This is good."

"OK," said Neo. "So they experience alienation from God, and they feel internal shame, and the alienation disrupts their sexual relationships, and . . ."

Glenn obviously wanted again to offer a funny line here, but Kerry reached over and restrained him a second time, and Neo continued, ". . . and the agriculturalists kill their pastoralist brothers. And eventually, the subsistence agriculturalists create surpluses, and they acquire greater and greater wealth, and primitive economies develop. And with economies come first towns and then cities. And with cities, people begin to feel even more independent, as you said, Glenn. Cities are little self-contained social worlds for people. If you live in a city, you don't feel much need for God at all. You can do whatever you want. And so what comes next in the story? The first megacity: the Tower of Babel. It's interesting, because the ancient text says that Babel became possible because of technological advancement. The high-tech innovation back then was the brick. If you can make bricks, you're no longer dependent on God-given stones, which are hard to shape and stack. Now you can mass-produce uniformly sized bricks, so your buildings can be really tall and impressive.

"But, even though you can build bigger cities and taller physical structures, the whole social structure eventually collapses, because the people can't get along. Each language group—then, as now—considers itself superior, and the conflict drives the people apart. So there's this self-sabotaging dimension to human achievement. Human achievements are impressive, like the Tower of Babel, but tragic too, because we keep fouling things up and we can't get along."

"I'm no expert," Kerry broke in, "but I think you forgot something. What about Noah?"

"Oops. You're right, Kerry," Neo said. "I completely forgot. And I shouldn't forget that story here, of all places. In the story of Noah, humans are grappling, I think, with the realization that our evil has the capacity to unleash a flood of complete chaos and destruction. So human beings become *horribly* evil. In Genesis, God is pictured as feeling brokenhearted for creating us humans, because of our evil and violence. So, from living peacefully as hunter-gatherers in gardens, we advanced—that might be the wrong word—to the level of ancient civilizations full of oppression and social and personal evil. And so the ancient Jewish storytellers pick up a story that is preserved in many cultures: the story of a primal, catastrophic flood."

"You're bringing back my college ancient history class. Gilgamesh, right?" Glenn asked.

"As I told Kerry last week, there are a number of ancient versions of the story. I think it reflects one of the greatest fears of ancient people. You move from being hunter-gathers and animal herders to farmers who gather around cities, and where do you settle? In the fertile, flat river valleys, where the best farmland is. And when floods come, your whole world is destroyed. Water seems to represent a kind of archetypal chaos, and the ancient Jews seem to realize that if we live apart from our true story as creatures in God's creation, creatures who are free to learn and grow and advance but always need to respect their limits as creatures in God's creation, if we disconnect from our story and promote ourselves to autonomous, godlike status so we can write our own story in our own way, apart from God, apart from moral limits, then a flood of chaos overtakes us."

Kerry said, "It's a little bit like Glenn's coffee a while ago. When it's in the cup, it's good, it's OK. But when it spills out of its limits, we have a mess. And so human beings get out of control. We get out of our story. I think I have a name for episode two."

"What is it? 'Spillage'? 'Mess'? 'It's All Glenn's Fault'?" Glenn offered.

"'Crisis.' Because humanity's advancement creates a crisis. And it strikes me"—here she turned to Neo—"that just as you said that episode one is ongoing, so is episode two. We're still living in the same crisis. There used to be one world, one story. But now, we've separated ourselves. We've moved out of that world and that story and struck off on our own. We've broken the robust dynamic harmony of goodness, so men and women struggle in conflicted relationships, like Adam and Eve. New economies arise and compete, often with lethal results, like Cain and Abel. Languages and cultures strive for dominance, as at the Tower of Babel, and civilizations develop in the flood plain of complete chaos and self-destruction. We've mucked up the story. That's the crisis, *the crisis we find ourselves in.*"

There was another silence. Glenn took another shot at being funny, asking, "Is this the place where the organ plays and you pass the offering basket and we give you all our money?" But Kerry and Neo were both deep enough in thought that they didn't respond.

The rain had let up again, and for a few minutes the sun was shining hot and strong. Mist was rising from every exposed surface, and the humidity was thick. The three left their now empty coffee cups on the table and walked out from the veranda into the full sun, which had brought all the tortoises out from their hiding places. One of the Center's workers was dumping food into the pens—a mix of vegetables and fruit sprinkled with white powder, which, Kerry explained, was a mineral supplement with a lot of calcium in it.

Glenn returned to the previous conversation. "So that's why you see our whole struggle here at CDRC—against extinction, against destruction of the environment—as God's work, as holy work. I thought you were joking before."

Neo responded, "I was completely serious. Glenn, I know that you're a bird expert, not a herpetologist like Kerry, but are you familiar with the theory of how these giant tortoises evolved?"

"I guess so," Glenn said. "The story I heard is that some regular-sized tortoises floated out here on mats of vegetation and colonized the islands, and then evolved into the massive sizes we see here."

Neo replied, "That's the old theory. That's what most people think, including most scientists. Kerry, do you want to tell him the newer theory?"

"It's not a theory, really," Kerry said. "The fact is, giant tortoises once were found on all the continents, even in North America, some much bigger than these, according to the fossil records. There is still a giant tortoise in sub-Saharan Africa, *geochelone sulcata*, which reaches about two hundred pounds. And there's still one left in Asia, *manouria emys*, which reaches maybe one hundred pounds or more. So there's no reason to believe that these tortoises were anything less than giants when they drifted out here to the islands, sometime after the islands were formed by volcanic activity, arising from the grinding together of two tectonic plates about three million years ago. What's striking about these tortoises, then, is not that they're giants, but that they're still alive."

"What happened to all the others, like the ones in South America, I guess the ancestors of these guys?" Glenn asked.

Neo answered, "That's where the new theory comes in. What happened to them? *Us.* We happened to them. Big tortoises are easy to catch and good to eat. So wherever we humans found them, we decimated them. The reason that the really big ones survive on these islands, and also on Aldabra Atoll in the Indian Ocean, is that these places were inaccessible to humans . . . until very recently. And what happens when humans arrive here? We slaughter tortoises by the thousands. And we introduce feral goats and rats and cats that threaten to eradicate them entirely. Wherever we go, we fail to respect the limits, the boundaries, the balance and harmony, and so we keep expanding episode two—chaos, or crisis, or whatever you want to call it."

Glenn pretended to hit his forehead with his hand. "Wow. I never thought religion . . . or whatever you call this . . . I never thought all this talk about God or the Bible could have anything to do with me and my life's work. This is . . . amazing. And kind of disturbing too."

"Why do you say disturbing, amigo?" Kerry asked.

"I don't know," Glenn answered. "It's just that I've been pretty successful at keeping all this stuff relegated to . . . you know . . . fairy tales, myths, superstitions, ignorance. But in this light, I feel kind of ignorant myself. Note the date and time, my friends. This doesn't happen often."

For several minutes they watched a group of juvenile tortoises, their gray-black shells highly domed and about the size of basketballs, their skin elephant gray and wrinkled, their huge, teary, black eyes blinking in the bright equatorial sun. The tortoises foraged through the pile of food, picking out pieces of watermelon and banana (skins and all), which seemed to be their favorite parts of the salad.

Glenn continued. "You know, I've never really thought much about this stuff before. I mean, I always saw religion as a bunch of doctrines that people argue about, or rituals that they use to keep themselves from feeling lonely or small in the big bad universe, or dogmas and scare tactics that they use to keep the unruly masses in line. I never . . . I *never* thought of religion as a story of the universe before. And I certainly never considered whether it could be the true . . . uh, I mean, *a* true one." Then, turning to Neo, with a big smile, he said, "Thanks, Neo. You've messed up my whole life." And then he surprised Kerry, because this was most unlike Glenn: he gave Neo a hug.

After the hug, Neo went back to leaning on the fence that surrounded the tortoise pen, his forearms resting on the top plank of weathered wood, looking down at the animals as they ate. Kerry stood a few feet away, also looking down into the pen. Glenn faced the other direction, leaning backwards against the fence and looking out toward the ocean. The sun disappeared behind some clouds, and a few drops of rain fell, but no one moved.

"Mind if I really mess you up a little more, Glenn?" Neo asked. Glenn said he'd had plenty enough for this decade, but go ahead anyway.

"There are global and social dimensions to this thing, you know— humans destroying the environment, causing extinctions, continuing our long legacy of oppression and greed and ethnic hatred. But in some ways, those global and social phenomena are the expressions of a lot of individual, personal choices. I guess the global dimension and the personal dimension create a kind of vicious cycle."

"What do you mean by the personal dimension?" Glenn asked.

"You know, like you and Maria and the tequila last night," Neo said, firmly, but without a lot of emotion.

With that, Glenn stood up straight and walked away. Without a word. They heard the screen door at the rear of the Center squeak open and then slam; a few seconds later, the front screen door squeaked and slammed too.

"That was uncalled for, Neo," Kerry said. And without being exactly sure why, she followed Glenn, leaving Neo staring at the tortoises, listening to the first screen door slam and then, after a longer than expected pause, the second. And then it started to rain hard, and it didn't stop for the rest of the day.

A NEW KIND OF PEOPLE
IN THE WORLD

NEO MUST HAVE FELT TERRIBLE, Kerry imagined, to leave on *La Aventura* the next morning on such tense terms with both her and Glenn. She was mad at him in about the same way she had been mad at her father on a number of occasions when she was younger. Why did he have to push it? Why did he have to add that last little jab? Why couldn't he have just left that unsaid? But all week, in spite of her frustration, the thought never crossed her mind that she wouldn't show up on Sunday night at Aventura, and she looked forward to spending the next Monday with Neo, too.

She was walking along the dock toward *La Aventura* on Sunday evening when she heard a voice calling her from the shore behind her. It was Glenn. She hadn't seen him all week. In fact, when she left Neo so abruptly on Monday, she had hesitated for a minute inside the Center, almost going back to give Neo a piece of her mind. Then she thought better of it, and decided to catch up with Glenn and console him. But by the time she stepped out the front door to find him, he was nowhere to be seen. Their paths hadn't crossed all week, and she had been wondering how he was doing.

Glenn ran down the dock toward her. "Mind if I join you tonight?" he asked.

"Great," she said, while thinking, *What's going on here? Glenn, coming to church?*

They walked down the dock arm in arm, climbed onto the ship, and crouched down to enter the main cabin. Neo's back was turned toward them. He was talking with Maricel, who seemed upset about something. Neo must have seen Maricel's eyes move from his face to beyond his shoulder, and so he turned around and looked—"gobsmacked" was Kerry's word for it—both shocked and happy to see Glenn and Kerry.

Glenn walked over and shook Neo's hand. "No hard feelings, OK, your eminence?" he asked.

Neo looked flustered but relieved. "No hard feelings," he replied. His brow unwrinkled and his whole face broke into a big smile. There was an embrace, first with Glenn, then with Kerry. "I'm so happy you two came, so happy," Neo said. "All week I've . . ." He couldn't finish the sentence because Maricel had taken his arm and resumed talking to him. Neo caught Glenn's eye and mouthed "later," and Glenn gave him a thumbs-up.

Before long, a record crowd had squeezed into the cabin. Bad weather on the mainland had postponed Sunday's flight back to Quito, so almost half of the guests from the previous tour—held over for an extra day at the hotel a few blocks away—had come back for the service. They seemed completely comfortable with Neo; you'd never think they were about to attend a church service. It seemed more like a cocktail party, actually, especially because a few held beers and one was smoking a cigarillo.

Tonight, for some reason, Neo spent more time lecturing than usual. (Later, Kerry learned that he was addressing some questions that two of the guests, both secular Jewish passengers from the week's tour, had asked him.) His lecture was all about Abraham.

Abraham, Neo explained, is called a patriarch, which means the father of a tribe. And in fact, Abraham was in a sense the father of three tribes, Judaism, Christianity, and Islam. In the world of Abraham's day, people assumed that there were many gods, and that these gods were more or less territorial. One ruled a river, another ruled a mountain, another a forest, another a desert.

If you were passing through a desert, you would want to make an offering to the appropriate territorial deity. If you decided to settle in a certain plain and plant crops there, you would want to appease the god of the plain, and maybe the god of the river too, and the god of the nearby mountain just for safety. You wanted to be sure to stay on each god's good side, since each had a capricious, nasty, and unpredictable side too.

But Abraham became possessed by a startling conviction: there was one true and living God, who was the God of all territories, who was, in fact, the maker of heaven and earth, and whose existence relativized all other alleged deities. ("Relativized" was Neo's term, and Kerry didn't know what it meant, and doubted that anyone else did either, but no one interrupted him to ask.) And this one true and living God was not capricious, nasty, or unpredictable; this God could be trusted to be completely good, all the time.

Then Neo opened a Bible to Genesis and set the stage for a story about a quiet moment that took place some four thousand years ago in a remote area in the Tigris-Euphrates valley, in modern-day Iraq, then one of the cradles of what we call civilization. This obscure Semite received a message from this one true and living God:

> The LORD had said to Abram, "Leave your country,
>   your people, and your father's household,
>   and go to the land I will show you.
> I will make you into a great nation,
>   and I will bless you;
> I will make your name great,
>   and you will be a blessing.
> I will bless those who bless you,
>   and whoever curses you I will curse;
>   and all peoples on earth
>   will be blessed through you."
> So Abram left, as the LORD had told him.

"Here we are on *La Aventura*," Neo said, "and when God makes contact with Abraham, God invites him to launch out on an *aventura* too." To leave the Tigris-Euphrates valley, Neo explained, was to leave security of civilization and to enter the unknown. Abraham didn't even know where his journey would lead, and there were no maps to show him the way, so it truly was a journey of faith, a sense, a hunch, a wild dream that there was something out there for him, and that Someone would guide him there . . . although he had little idea who or how or where.

But Abraham did have an idea why. Neo launched into a long explanation of ancient Hebrew poetry, because, he said, God's promise in the story was recorded as a poem. Ancient Hebrew poets loved parallelism: in parallelism, the poet repeats a sentence structure, with slight variations, for various purposes, maybe for restatement, or intensification, or clarification, or elaboration, or contrast. In this context, Neo drew out some of the parallelisms:

I will make you into a great nation . . . I will make your name great. This restatement intensifies the sense that Abraham is being given a wonderful promise and is entering into an inspiring destiny.

I will bless you . . . you will be a blessing. The great status promised to Abraham, however, is not exclusive. He is not blessed to the exclusion of others, but rather, he is blessed *instrumentally* (another word that Neo didn't explain, but that Kerry wished he would have—even though she "got" it—to clarify for those who didn't). In fact, *being blessed* is elaborated on in the second phrase, Neo explained: the kind of blessing that Abraham will receive is the blessing of *being a blessing* to others.

I will bless those who bless you, and whoever curses you I will curse. Oddly, Abraham's blessing won't exempt him from conflict. In fact, the promise suggests that conflict—being cursed at times by others—will be part of the identity of this blessed people.

All peoples on earth will be blessed through you. The English translation here, Neo said, obscures the fact that the same single Hebrew word underlies the different English words "people" and "nation." In that light, God says, "Leave your people. Leave your identification and status as a member of a certain known people. Now, step out into the unknown, from a certified somebody who is a member of a people and step into a journey where you don't know who you are anymore. As you do this, I will give you a great new identity: you will become a new kind of people in the world; you will have a new identity. And that new identity—as a people blessed by the one true and living God—will bring blessing to all the other peoples."

Then Neo launched into a long discussion about the word "election." Kerry was confused by this, thinking he was talking about politics, and then realized that *election* must have been a technical term of some controversy in theology that neither she nor anyone else in the service seemed to understand (or care much about). Eventually, she guessed that by *election*, Neo simply meant being chosen to be blessed in this way. He said that one of the greatest heresies (another word that she wished he had found a synonym for) for both the Jewish people and Christians (and maybe Muslims too, she wondered) is a failure to take seriously these important lines of poetry. When religions assume that their adherents are chosen only *to be blessed,* and forget that they are blessed *to be a blessing,* they distort their identity and they drift from God's calling for them. When they assume that they are blessed *exclusively* rather than *instrumentally,* when they see themselves as blessed to the exclusion of others rather than for the benefit of others, they become part of the problem instead of part of the solution.

Then Neo became very personal. He told the group of people crowded into the cabin of *La Aventura*—Ecuadorians and Americans, Christians and Jews, believers and agnostics, and some atheists too—his own story, how he had once been a pastor, feeling himself called in a special way, like Abraham, to bless others. But he discovered that "being a blessing" was harder than he anticipated, and he had become very discouraged and disillusioned, and eventually left church work. He went back to college for advanced studies in science, and eventually became a teacher, a high school science teacher. But even in that role, he said, he realized that he was no less possessed by this identity, someone whom God had blessed so that he could be a blessing to others.

He told them about the death of his father, and his decision to leave teaching to care for his mother, who was very ill. "It was all the same," he said. "Different jobs, different titles, different cities, but the same calling: to enjoy God's blessing so that I could be a blessing to others, whether to a church, to a classroom, or to my mother. Or to be here on *La Aventura* with all of you tonight."

13

A RESISTANCE MOVEMENT
AGAINST EVIL

THEN ONE OF THE GUESTS from the previous tour, a fifty-something woman with nice jewelry and her hair dyed red, raised her hand and interrupted Neo. "Look, Neo, I'm a Jew, OK? But not a very good one. I mean, I hardly keep any holidays, and to tell you the truth, I wonder if I've really believed any of it for most of my life. It's a cultural thing, a heritage, you know, about not disappointing my mother. Anyway, look, I'm from New York City, Manhattan. You live in the Big Apple and you're trying so hard to stay alive that you don't think much about being a blessing to anybody. I mean, just surviving is tough, you know? You want to do unto others before they do unto you." There was a little laugh from the fluent English-speakers at this.

"But I want to tell you that what you're saying has helped me understand what it means to be a Jew. I mean, this is positively wild—a black . . . uh, African American . . . uh, Jamaican Christian like yourself helping me *get it* more than any of my rabbis ever did. It's wild—not something I expected to take home from this vacation in the Galápagos!"

After that, Neo never really got control of the conversation again. Everyone had something to say, mostly along these lines: if more people understood what it meant to be religious in this way—being blessed to be a blessing to others, not just to be some spiritual elite—then religion would have a better name in the world.

At one point, a young fellow with a British accent, clean-cut and well dressed, asked a question that Kerry also had been thinking about. It had to do with the "curse" part of the poem: Why would anyone want to curse people who had this identity of being a blessing? And why, if it's wrong for them to curse Abraham's people, is it OK for God to curse them? Isn't that kind of vengeful? What does it mean to curse?

Neo's response was long and rather complex, in Kerry's opinion. He talked about the limits of language in talking about God and God's involvement with us. Echoing his conversation with Kerry and Glenn the week before, Neo explained the danger of importing what he called "foreign meanings" from outside the context into the text, comparing (as Glenn had done) those foreign meanings to the invasive species (like goats, rats, dogs, and cats) that were causing so much trouble to the native flora and fauna of the islands. The idea that "curse" here meant "send to hell" is an example of this kind of invasive meaning, since Abraham had no idea of hell. This idea surprised Kerry: Abraham had no idea of hell?

To get a better idea of what "curse" meant, Neo suggested they try to contrast it with blessing. To bless in this context, they agreed, would mean to try to help, to bring resources, to encourage, to believe in, to support, to affirm, to have a high opinion of. Neo suggested, in summary, that it would mean to express love and support.

"God doesn't say, 'I will control you and help you control all the nations of the world,' right?" Neo asked. "It's quite significant, really, that in that era of empires, God doesn't tell them to conquer their neighbors and build a theocratic empire. No, God's promise to bless them, and God's commission of them to be a blessing, suggests something significant, but not coercive, controlling, overbearing." Then he suggested that cursing would mean withholding help, refusing to give resources or encouragement or affirmation. It would express disappointment, disapproval, anger, and resistance. Then he asked if anyone remembered that old Irish blessing about the wind being at your back, and said that the idea of cursing in the poem suggests that any who oppose Abraham's descendants in their cooperation with God would find the wind of God's displeasure in their face.

To her surprise, Kerry found herself speaking up for the first time at Aventura. "So if this whole story is about God creating a good world"— she winked at Neo as she said this—"then Abraham's family is being enrolled as God's helpers or collaborators . . . and the wind will be at their back, so to speak, in cooperating with God in the ongoing creation of good in the world, right?" Neo nodded and she continued, "That would mean that anybody who opposes that general direction of creating good, of helping the world become better not worse, anybody who opposed that would be working against God, kind of unmaking or uncreating the world that God has been making, destroying God's work, right? And of course, God would be against that."

Neo said, "Yes, exactly. And that would also explain why people might want to curse God's collaborators. Let's say that you're determined to exploit the poor or practice violence or rape the environment or break promises, and there are these people who are always telling you that you're wrong, always standing in your way. Naturally, you'd hate those people. You'd curse them."

Kerry replied, "So really, this poem is about God starting a resistance movement to all the evil in the world, right? It's brilliant, really. This is starting to make sense to me. Not that I'm . . . in . . . I mean, not that I'm totally there or anything, but . . ."

Neo broke in. "But you'd rather live with the wind at your back than in your face, and you'd rather be on the side of God's ongoing creation than on the side of destructive human selfishness, right?"

"Yeah, right, I guess so," Kerry mumbled, blushing, feeling embarrassed now for making herself conspicuous by speaking up at all.

"Well, that's probably a pretty good place to finish up our discussion tonight," Neo said, seeming to sense her discomfort. Then, as usual, Alvaro took out his guitar and led in some singing, as Humberto helped Neo prepare the *cena santa*. Kerry noticed that Maricel wasn't singing with Alvaro this week, and although she remembered seeing her before the reunion started, she scanned the cabin and realized that she must have left at some point.

Kerry still didn't feel honest participating in the *cena santa,* and she didn't sing, although she enjoyed listening, but she did remember praying that evening, praying that if God was there, she wanted to be one of the blessed-to-be-a-blessing ones, with God's wind at her back. "If you are there at all . . . " she whispered again at the end of the prayer. She again felt embarrassed, but wasn't sure why.

After the reunion, Kerry and Glenn went out on the deck of the ship because it was so crowded down in the cabin, and the cigarillo smoke made Kerry feel a bit ill. She was interested in finding out Glenn's reaction, but before she could ask, Neo emerged from the cabin. "Good, you haven't left," he said to Kerry. "I needed to ask you about something."

First, though, he asked Glenn how he'd enjoyed the reunion. "Well, it certainly was relaxed and interesting," he said. "And you didn't even take an offering, which I appreciated. And nobody threatened anybody with eternal conscious torment in the sulfuric flames of hell's nether regions, which I also appreciated, although I was worried for a while that all the talk about cursing might take us there. But it didn't. And one of your tourists offered me a gin and tonic, which was a nice touch for a church service. So I'd give the night, overall, a 7.5 or 8 out of 10. If you have dancing next week, I'll go for a 9."

The three of them laughed, and then Kerry asked what Neo wanted to ask her about. "It's about Maricel," he said. "What did you tell her last week?"

Kerry said, "Tell her? We had a long talk after work on Wednesday, no, Thursday. I told her all about our conversations the last few weeks, you know, about 'The Story We Find Ourselves In,' as you call it. Why? Is there something wrong?"

"She was really upset with me," Neo answered. "In fact, she wouldn't even stay for the meeting tonight. She kind of left Alvaro hanging. He doesn't feel confident having to play guitar and sing without her there. Anyway, it's no big deal, but . . ."

"But that doesn't make sense, Neo. Maricel should have been enthusiastic about what I told her. I mean, she's been preaching to me and praying for me ever since we met, you know? And I've been tolerant of her, but I haven't given her the slightest encouragement that I was, you know, moving in her direction faith-wise. So I thought she'd be excited to hear that some of this is at least beginning to make some sense to this hardened Australian skeptic."

"I think I know what happened," Neo said. "Kerry, did you tell her anything about my views on evolution?"

"No. Not specifically. I just kind of retold the story as you told it to me," she answered.

Glenn spoke up: "I can see it coming. Neo's version of the story isn't literal enough for Maricel, right, Neo? I mean, for her, it's either right out of the book, black and white, completely literal, or else it's no good."

"There's that either-or stuff again," Kerry complained.

"Don't be too hard on Maricel," Neo responded. "She's part of another whole story too, a story about liberals and conservatives and modernity and epistemology and foundationalism and . . . but we don't need to get into all that. It's just that for people like Maricel—and she's not alone, believe me—it's not an easy thing to hold on to faith in the modern world. There are all sorts of attacks and insults and challenges. So they hold on to their faith in a sort of embattled way sometimes. And if someone like me comes along and seems to be . . . loosening up . . . it seems like I'm capitulating. And that makes me look like a traitor, I think. Oh man, what a mess."

"So," Glenn said, "you've become a traitor, and Maricel needs to disassociate from you. Sounds like we're ripe for an inquisition or a witch hunt. Here we have it, another religious war, right here on *La Aventura*. That's why I've always wanted to stay away from religion. Close call. I was almost willing to give this another try."

Neo sat down on the deck of the ship, leaning against the cabin wall, one elbow resting on one knee. He put his head back and let out a deep sigh. "I hate this stuff too, Glenn. I really do. I didn't mean . . ."

"It's not your fault she's a closed-minded fundamentalist," Glenn said, also sitting down on the deck.

"Come on, Glenn," Neo said firmly, "You know Maricel. She's your friend, Kerry's friend, my friend too. People like me mess up her world a bit. We don't fit in her categories. That's frustrating to anybody. It's a knack I have, really, frustrating people. I did it to you last week, eh?"

"And you help people too," Kerry responded. "But I see your point. For you to help me, to make sense to someone like me or Glenn, almost guarantees that you'll not be understood by Maricel, whose faith is so simple."

"So simple, yes, and also so genuine and robust and sincere," Neo added. "I'll have to go find her. We'll need to talk this out. Kerry, would you let Alvaro and Humberto know that I had to run? They'll see to it that the doors get locked. I've got my key."

Neo was stepping off *La Aventura.* "Maricel lives right up the hill, right?" he asked Kerry.

She gave him a few landmarks for finding Maricel's place, and as he walked out of the circle of light cast by the deck lanterns, she called out, "Neo, are we still on for tomorrow?"

Neo was standing on the dock. "Sure. I'll be at the Center about seven o'clock, OK?"

Glenn offered to walk Kerry back to her place at the Center. They stopped for a drink on the way back and had a long talk about God, Neo, Maricel, religion, and the improving selection of beers on the islands.

14

CONVERSATION:
GOD AND HUMANITY

"I'M A LITTLE WORRIED that they won't have a horse big enough for you, Neo," Kerry said, as they walked up the gravel path toward the stables the next morning. "These Ecuadorian horses are spunky, but they tend to be small."

It was a quiet morning, amazingly cool for a dry-season morning near the equator. The mist had lifted. The crunch of their steps on the gravel was punctuated by the calls of the island falcons (the object of Glenn's studies and conservation efforts), the quiet chirping of finches, the screech of mockingbirds, and the lyrical songs of yellow warblers.

Kerry's plan for the day was to check on some land iguanas that had been head-started—hatched in captivity and released when they were large enough to avoid predation by their main enemies: the native falcons that circled overhead and the feral cats that hid in the underbrush. Land iguanas once were common on the northwest side of Santa Cruz, but the cats had pushed them to extinction. Back in the 1970s, a group from a neighboring island, deemed closely related to the Santa Cruz population, had been reintroduced. Every year, Kerry would do an informal count to see how they were doing, and especially to check for any signs of successful reproduction in the wild. Later in the year, she would check for nests— pits dug in the widely scattered areas where the soil was suitable. From those nests, eggs would be carefully removed and hatched at the Center for head-starting future generations. The climb was steep, and there were no roads up the west side of the volcano, only paths, so horses were the best mode of transport.

The caretaker at the stable said, "No problema, no te preocupes," when Kerry expressed her anxiety about Neo's size. Sure enough, there was one larger horse. "He a little e-slow, but he *so* e-stronger for you," the care-taker said to Neo, with a big smile and some pride about his English.

Soon they were mounted and moving up the trail. There was twice as much crunch, crunch, crunch as before, but the sway of the horses was pleasant, and Kerry was happy to have company today.

Neo's talk with Maricel the previous night had gone all right. "She can be intense," Neo said.

"That's an understatement," Kerry said with a grin.

"It turns out that she had been storing up a pretty long list of concerns about me," he said. "You know, she was born Catholic, and she was pretty unhappy a few weeks back when I invited the priest from St. Francis Church in Puerto Barquerizo Moreno to speak to our group."

Kerry replied, "That must have been before I started coming. I've heard of him—Padre Raul, right? People say he's a good man."

"He's wonderful," Neo said. "But Maricel strongly resents the Catholic Church for not making the gospel clear enough to her as she grew up. I tried, gently, to tell her that if she understands the gospel now, she shouldn't be holding grudges and she should extend a little grace to him. Of course, I had to ask her to do the same toward me. But I think I'll be walking on eggshells for a while, since I didn't really pass her test."

Kerry asked what the issues were, and Neo explained. "Did I believe that Adam and Eve were actual people? Did I believe that the earth was created in seven twenty-four-hour days? Did I believe that a real snake talked to Eve? You know, that sort of thing."

"Just what we were talking about on Isabela," Kerry said. "Why are those questions so important to Maricel?"

"In the modern world," Neo said, "people thought that the greatest truths were simple and clear, black and white, simple lines, no fuzziness or mystery. Of course, ancient people didn't think that way, but modern people can hardly imagine that. Ancient people lived in a very different world . . . a world where they assumed that more was unknown than known, and that whatever humans see is just a glimpse into the depth of mystery, like holding a candle in the dark. The candle is precious, but it isn't like lighting up the world with stadium lights, you know?"

Kerry didn't understand what Neo meant by "in the modern world." It seemed as though he thought "the modern world" was in the past. She said, "But Maricel doesn't think of herself as a 'modern person.' She just thinks of herself as—"

"As a good Christian," Neo interrupted. "And she is. But she's more hooked into modernity than she realizes."

Putting aside her ongoing uncertainty about what Neo meant by "modernity," Kerry focused on Maricel: "It just doesn't make sense to me. She should be grateful for how you're helping me, not upset with you."

The trail was wide enough for the horses to walk side by side. Neo said, "Really, Kerry, you can understand how Maricel feels, because, in a way, you're both frustrated by the same thing. It's all about certainty. For Maricel, religious uncertainty is dangerous, and for you, religious certainty is equally dangerous."

"Hmmm. Maybe so. Well, anyway, I'm glad you talked to her," Kerry said. "I'd hate to be in the middle of a religious conflict between you and Maricel. It was bad enough when you and Glenn had that run-in."

They were silent for a while. Then Kerry pointed out how the ecosystems—microhabitats, she called them—were changing as they increased in altitude. "It's a bit different here from any of the other islands. Really, each island is unique." Then she asked, "I was hoping that today you could tell me about episode three . . . you know, of the story you've been telling me."

"You mean episode four," Neo said.

"No. We had episode one, 'Creation,' and then episode two, 'Crisis.' That's as far as we've gotten."

"What about last night, Kerry? That *was* episode three. Just to keep the C-thing going, let's entitle it 'Calling.'"

"Last night? Oh . . . of course, I guess that makes sense. Abraham and his descendants are God's episode-three crisis response team, to bring a blessing into a world that had been infected with episode-two evil. So *calling* means God recruiting you to be part of this movement of people who want to bring God's blessing back to the world."

"That's right. It's really the same as our word 'vocation,' derived from Latin. To be called, to hear your calling, or to find your vocation are all ways of saying that you have signed up with this higher purpose or mission in life. You're not just here for your own agenda, or for a company agenda or a national agenda or an economic agenda. You're here for God's agenda. You want to be part of God's ongoing creation of the world—against all the forces that are working against that creative process. You want the world to become the kind of world God dreams for it to be."

"But Neo, that sounds a wee bit dangerous. I mean, isn't that where a lot of terrible things come from . . . from people who are sure they're doing God's work? Isn't it true that a lot of folk have been killed to fulfill what somebody thought was God's will? I guess it's that *dangerous certainty* thing again. That really concerns me."

They rode on for a few minutes, and Kerry wasn't sure Neo had heard her. He looked straight ahead, sitting erect on his horse, holding the reins in both hands, giving no indication of responding to her. Finally, she asked, "What are you thinking?"

He slowly wrinkled his brow and pursed his lips, and then he said, "I'm just thinking that you've introduced one of the central problems of episode four."

"What's that?"

"It's a problem of guidance and communication. God can sign up some people to be part of the team, so to speak, but what does God do when the players who have been recruited keep getting mixed up and playing for the wrong side? They're certain they're right, even when they're wrong."

"Yeah. Major problem. So what do you want to call episode four?"

"Let's call it 'Conversation.' But really, we could call it 'Cycles' too. Because in episode four, Abraham's descendants go through cycle after cycle of following God's calling, and then drifting or rebelling, eventually playing for the wrong side, and then repenting and returning to God's agenda, God's dream, and then they lose their way again, and so on. Through it all, God is their faithful guide and companion. And through it all, the conversation with and about God and humanity intensifies, which is where I get the title for episode four. If you focus on the human tendency to miss the point and wander from the path, episode four is totally depressing. But if you focus on God's constant faithfulness and patience through the deepening conversation, it's just as inspiring."

They crossed the high point on the west slope of the volcano to the north side of the island, and the vegetation quickly thinned to some scrubby bushes and cactus trees as they descended. The heat was so strong, and the shade so scarce, that when they came to a shamble of a tree, they decided to dismount and let the horses rest in the slowly shifting shade. They walked a distance away to another smaller tree with just enough shade for them. Neo offered to give Kerry the high-altitude overview of episode four.

"If you think of it geographically," Neo said, scratching in the gravel with a twig, "think of Palestine as being in the middle here, and think of Egypt to the southwest there, and think of the Tigris-Euphrates Valley—part of modern-day Iraq—to the north, actually the northeast, up here. The story starts with Abraham up here in Iraq about 2000 B.C. Then it moves briefly down here to Palestine, and then all the way down here to Egypt from about 1800 to 1400. Then the action moves back here to Palestine from about 1400 to about 700. Then it moves back up here to Iraq for a couple hundred years, and then back to Palestine around 450. So it's up, middle, down, middle, up, middle. Get it?"

She laughed. "It's easy for you. You know the story. I heard all kinds of Bible stories as a kid, but I have no idea how they fit together—which comes first, that sort of thing. To me, they're just isolated episodes in a larger story I never really understood."

"What a tragedy," Neo said. "What an educational fiasco. But it's all too common. OK, let's imagine you're a kid again. Here's how I'd tell the story. Better get comfortable."

15

PRIESTS AND PROPHETS

KERRY USED HER PACK as a pillow and laid back on the gravel, her elbows up, her hands cradling her head, her legs straight out, her feet crossed. Neo was propped up against the tree trunk.

"Once upon a time," Neo began, "God entered into a special relationship with a man named Abraham, who lived in a land that is now called Iraq. God promised Abraham that his descendants would be a blessing to the whole world if they remained faithful to God, which Abraham promised they would do. God led Abraham out of what is now Iraq to settle in a land to the south called Palestine. After he settled in Palestine, Abraham had a son named Isaac, whose name means 'laughter'—but that's another story—and Isaac had a son named Jacob, who also was called Israel, which means 'God-wrestler'—but that's another story too. Israel had twelve sons. One of them, Joseph, ended up down in Egypt, which is—"

"Another story, right?" Kerry finished. "I think I remember that one."

"Right. And Joseph later invited his brothers to come and live down in Egypt to escape a terrible famine in Palestine. After Joseph died, his descendants were enslaved by the Egyptians, and they lived as slaves for a very long time. Eventually, God inspired a man named Moses to become the liberator of the people. Moses had to stand up to the king of Egypt, called Pharaoh, and persuade him to let the people go. It wasn't easy, but eventually the king relented. The people left Egypt, but wandered around as nomads for forty years before they were ready to reconquer their homeland, which had been resettled during their long absence—"

"Just a minute," Kerry interrupted. "You said they became nomads—again? That's interesting. It reminds me of what you were telling me last week, you know, about the progression from hunter-gatherers to nomadic herders, to agriculturalists, and then to people who live in cities. So they leave Egypt, which I guess is pretty advanced, right? And they get demoted back to being nomads. It strikes me that maybe that will help them become more dependent on the Creator again, right?"

Neo leaned forward and caught her eye. "That's a great insight, Kerry. I never thought of that before. That makes a lot of sense. In fact, they even go farther back than being nomadic herders, because they become gatherers again too, gathering quail that come to them on the wind and manna that falls with the dew. But that's—"

"Another story," Kerry offered, smiling at Neo's compliment.

Neo continued, "As they resettled, they organized themselves under leaders we often call judges. These leaders eventually were replaced by kings, some of whom, like the great King David, were good kings, but many more were bad. Eventually, the kingdom experienced civil war. Some centuries later, the northern kingdom, which was named Israel after their ancient patriarch, was overrun and destroyed by Assyrian marauders from the north, from the Tigris-Euphrates region in modern-day Iraq."

"You mean the same land where Abraham had originally come from?" Kerry asked.

"Yes, basically, although there had been a lot of changes in power over the centuries. At any rate, eventually, another regime from the Tigris-Euphrates region returned to conquer the southern kingdom, which was called Judah. They didn't kill everyone though. They brought many of them to their cities, and there they lived in exile as slaves or servants, first to the Babylonians, and then to the Medo-Persians. Finally, some of them gained permission to return to their homeland and rebuild their capital city of Jerusalem, along with their temple. And that's the basic story line of the Hebrew Bible, which Christians call the Old Testament."

"So that's episode four?" Kerry asked. "I wish somebody had given me that simple overview as a kid."

"Thankfully, it's simple enough on that level. But as you know, nestled within this story are hundreds of other stories. And through it all, something very important is happening."

"What's that?" Kerry asked. Before Neo could answer, the horses started snorting and stomping, seeming to be irritated with one another. Kerry recommended that they get moving again. So Neo and Kerry returned to the horses, remounted, and continued their slow descent toward the north coast of the island.

The trail was narrower here, and they couldn't ride side by side. Neo took the rear, so that Kerry could hear him better, and he picked up the story again. "Through those centuries, basically from about 2000 B.C. through about 450 B.C., roughly fifteen hundred years, the people are being formed as a culture, as a community."

"Those are some more good C-words. Maybe they could be a better title for episode four," Kerry said. The word "conversation" didn't make much sense to her as a title yet.

Neo continued, "Maybe so. You can take your pick. Anyway, the people are gaining a deeply held identity as a special people with a special relationship to God. Sometimes, as I said, they forget that identity. But God always reignites the flame that flickers or burns low."

"How does God do that?" Kerry wondered, turning in her saddle to face Neo for a minute. "Send them telegrams?"

"Not quite. This is where the idea of a conversation comes in: God sends them people—or I guess it would be better to say that God inspires people among them—who will fulfill several important roles to keep the communication flowing between God and God's people," Neo explained. "Look, if it helps you to remember them, think of them as the 'four Ps': priests, prophets, poets, and philosophers."

"Clever," Kerry responded, at least a little ironically. All this alliteration was a little too cute. She was most interested in what Neo would say about ancient Jewish philosophers. It seemed like the Greeks had a monopoly on philosophy. But Neo started with the priests.

He explained that the priests were the day-to-day spiritual educators and guardians of the people. They helped the people sustain and strengthen their faith through the regular rituals of worship, through weekly Sabbaths and annual holy days.

"The prophets," Neo said, "were very different. They were an odd and special breed. The priests had credentials; they all came from the same clan. But the prophets arose unpredictably, and they had no credentials except their own charisma and courage and refusal to be ignored. Modern people usually think of prophets as predictors of the future, but the ancient idea of a prophet was more along the lines of a charismatic leader, a person seized with a passion from God to convey a message from God. Often they confronted the people about their moral and ethical failures— oppressing the poor, forgetting widows and orphans, that sort of thing. The prophets cried for justice and genuineness, and would confront hypocrisy wherever it appeared—including in the powerful.

"Some prophets were rough and unschooled, and others were refined and cultured. Many of them recorded their inspired messages in carefully crafted poetry, so there's some overlap with the poets," he explained. Kerry suddenly was distracted at this point. She dismounted and motioned for Neo to do the same, signaling for him to be quiet.

Soon she was on all fours, crouching behind a boulder. Neo came up behind her. She pointed to a huge pair of land iguanas, barely visible beyond some stands of opuntia cactus. "They're males," she said. "They were probably released here a few years ago; they're almost fully grown now. See the way they're rising up on their front legs and nodding their heads? They're battling for dominance. I wouldn't be surprised if there was a . . . yes, there she is over there, the female they must be fighting over. This is a positive sign. It suggests to me that there will be some reproduction going on in this group later this year. We'll have to keep our eyes open for juveniles from last year. We're so much happier when we see natural reproduction going on. Hopefully, someday soon we can discontinue the head-starting."

After a few minutes, they were back on the horses, heading farther down the gentle northern slope of the volcano. Another half hour passed. They didn't see any more iguanas. Kerry finally said, "We might as well turn back. The iguanas are almost always found among the cactus trees. They basically just sit and wait for the fruits to fall. Not a bad life, really. But I don't see any cactus trees between here and the shore." They turned the horses around and headed back up the trail toward the high point where it crossed the shoulder of the volcano. They could see the silhouettes of *scalesia* trees scattered along the crest of the volcano.

Here in the middle elevations of the north side of the island, the breeze was less strong and the temperature was more severe in the hot sun. They kept ascending, retracing their path. They talked little, except to point out land iguanas. There were more of them visible now on the upward trek toward the crest. As the sun rose higher, more seemed to come out of hiding. Kerry counted twenty-seven, about half the number that had been reintroduced there—an encouraging count. She took notes at each sighting. They didn't see any juveniles though.

16

POETS AND PHILOSOPHERS

WHEN NEO AND KERRY REACHED the high point of the trail and entered the first cooler shadows of the *scalesia* trees, they dismounted and unpacked the lunch Kerry had prepared. They looked back down over the gray-brown northern side of the island and out to the ocean. Several other islands were visible in the distance. Then they could turn and look south across the greener southern side of the island, with more distant islands more faintly visible off toward the horizon. Days this cloudless and clear were rare any time of year in the Galápagos. As they ate and drank, they savored the view, the breeze, the shade, the quiet, while the horses munched nearby on tufts of fresh grass, and a few insects buzzed and chirped in the bushes. After they'd finished eating, Kerry asked about where Neo had left off with the story an hour or so earlier. "You were talking about the 'four Ps.' I forgot what they were though. Let's see— philosophers, prophets . . ."

"Poets and priests," Neo finished. "OK, as I said, the priests were the credentialed clergy, so to speak. The prophets were the charismatic leaders who arose unpredictably through Jewish history. Then there were the poets. They tried to capture the experience and emotion of the people— their laments, hopes, joys, praises, fears, piety, furies, doubts, faith, affections—the whole range of human emotion and experience. They articulated the hearts of the people toward God, and they tried to capture the heart of God for the people too. David is the most famous of the poets, but there were others, like the sons of Asaph."

"I never really thought of the Bible as having poets—you know, artists. I thought that the idea of the Bible being inspired meant . . . well, that God dictated everything to them," Kerry said.

Neo responded, "Yes, unfortunately, a lot of people are given that idea by well-meaning but misguided preachers and pastors. The fact is that no serious theologian holds to what people used to call the 'dictation theory,' that God dictated the words of the Bible to the writers. No, it's clear that their own personalities and styles of writing were expressed, not overridden, in their production of the texts that today make up our Bible. In whatever sense the Bible is God's book, it never stops being a human book either, full of human personality and artistry and culture."

Kerry remarked, "You know, I'm still kind of ambivalent about all this. But if I were a poet, I would describe this view and this breeze and this beautiful day as a sign of God's amazing, utter *friendliness,* you know? It's hard to believe that we can be so . . . so free, and safe, and happy here, and yet right at this exact moment, people are dying, and crimes are being committed, and other horrors are taking place all over the world. If there is a God, I don't know how he—or she, or whatever—balances out all the glory and squalor of this world in the big cosmic equation."

Neo waited a moment, and then said, "You're sounding like the fourth kind of communicator now. There were priests, prophets, poets . . . and philosophers. And the philosophers had an intriguing role."

Kerry seemed curious, maybe skeptical. "My father never talked about philosophers in the Bible. Who are you referring to?"

Neo answered, "Well, I don't mean abstract, academic types. Your father was right—you won't find them in the Bible. Philosophy for the ancient Jews simply meant a way of life characterized by a passionate pursuit of wisdom. So there's the book of Ecclesiastes. We don't know who the writer is, although some—not me though—think it was Solomon. The writer simply calls himself 'the preacher.' And there's the philosopher who wrote the book of Job. That's some serious philosophy. And again there's overlap, because Job is a work of poetry too."

"So you don't think Job was . . ." Kerry was looking for a word.

"Historical?" Neo supplied. "No, not really. Job seems to me more like an ancient work of philosophy. It actually reminds me of an opera more than anything else, a kind of philosophical opera. It's different from Greek philosophy, of course—so much more concrete and down-to-earth. But like Ecclesiastes, it seems to be a genuine attempt by faithful people to grapple with the mysteries and hardships of life."

Kerry's childhood Sunday school knowledge was beginning to come back to her. "I seem to remember Job, Ecclesiastes, and one other book being lumped together . . ."

"Ah, yes," Neo said. "Proverbs. It's a kind of practical philosophy. It seems to me that Proverbs is like grade school. It represents a philosophy of common sense, where life fits together, where life follows predictable rules and patterns. The grade school challenge is to figure out which proverb fits which situation. Then, Ecclesiastes is like college. Now the rules don't apply sometimes. There's chaos and mystery in addition to order. And then with Job, you go to graduate school, and you cope with times in life when reality is the very opposite of what you would expect."

Kerry responded that she was impressed to think of the Bible including philosophy. "My impression, looking back at my childhood, was that the Bible was a kind of anti-intellectual document, you know, primitive and uneducated. But the way you describe it, it's a lot more . . . more sophisticated and multifaceted than that."

"No doubt," Neo said. "You see that same kind of complexity in the poetic sections. In the book of Psalms, for example, we find some poems that describe a world where everything fits together and makes sense. Then it has other poems that agonize over the areas of life that don't seem to make any sense. And then there are psalms that seek to rebuild your faith in the face of all the confusion and chaos."

Kerry replied, "Does that ever bother you, Neo?"

"Bother me? What do you mean?" he asked.

"I don't know. I guess I always thought that the Bible explained all the mysteries and tried to make simple sense of things," she said. "But for you, the Bible seems to explore mystery, not clarify it. For some reason, that's somewhat disappointing to me."

"You're sounding a little bit like Maricel now, Kerry. Anyway, I think that's another false impression that preachers and pastors often give: that the Bible is God's answer book to remove all mysteries and make everything simple and clear. The fact is, the Bible deals with life's absurdities and craziness with pretty amazing honesty. Sometimes, the best the Bible does is to name the agony, you know, just describe it without attempting to resolve it or explain it. Sometimes, I think the Bible is more of a question book than answer book; it raises questions that bring people together for conversation about life's most important issues."

"I don't know whether to be happy about that or sad," she replied. "I guess I *am* like Maricel in that way. Part of me wishes that it *would* offer some easy answers."

Neo was quiet for a minute, and then added, "Yeah, Kerry, I know what you mean. But honest answers seldom are easy ones. I guess you could say that the Bible is a book that doesn't try to tell you *what* to think. Instead, it tries to teach you *how* to think. It stretches your thinking; it challenges you to think bigger and harder than you ever have. At least that's how it works for me. It not only records ancient conversations among human beings and God, but it also stimulates new ones, never failing to create a community for essential conversations that enrich all of life."

"Like this one today," Kerry said with a smile. "Amazing."

They got up, organized their backpacks, mounted their horses, and began their southward descent toward Puerto Ayora. By the midafternoon they were nearly halfway back down the slope to the stable. They reached the stable around dinnertime, left the horses in the care of the chatty stableman, and then walked together back to town. "It's been a good day," Kerry said. Neo wasn't sure whether she was referring to the number of land iguanas they sighted or to their conversation.

As they reached the road that would take Kerry back to the Center, she stopped and faced Neo, and said, "I guess your title, 'Conversation,' makes sense after all. It's a better word than 'control,' which is why I think I've always resisted coming back to any kind of faith. I just can't buy the idea of a controlling God, with people being like chess pieces or something. The way you tell the story, God really is much more a companion, a conversation partner *with* the people, guiding them, but not manipulating them, not robbing them of that gift of freedom. It's kind of like us scientists working with the land iguanas. You know, we want them to survive, to live, and so we try to help. But it's their life. We want them to have their freedom, not to be in a cage."

"That sounds right to me," Neo said.

Kerry continued. "And I really like the idea of a conversation going on between the Creator and humanity—the people talking to God, and God getting a message to the people through other people."

Then Kerry paused and looked Neo in the eye. "Do you think, Neil Edward Oliver, that you are God's messenger to me?"

Neo looked a little surprised by her question. He stuttered a bit, uncharacteristically, and said, "I . . . I . . . I guess . . . I guess that's for you to decide, Kerry. But I certainly hope that could be true." Then Neo reached out and took her hand and held it for a just a minute in both of his—his hands large and brown, hers thin and white. "I'll see you Sunday," he said, and turned quickly and left.

Kerry didn't see that he was biting his lip. And Neo didn't see that she had started limping as she walked back to her apartment near the Center. *Did I strain something in my leg?* she wondered.

17

ONE ARM IN A CAST,
THE OTHER HOOKED TO AN IV

MY WIFE, CAROL, SELDOM CALLS me on my office phone. She generally uses my cell phone. So I was surprised that first Wednesday in September when I picked up the office phone and heard her voice. "Daniel, I've been trying to reach you for an hour!" she said. Sure enough, when I looked down at my cell phone, the stupid battery had gone dead. I forgot to recharge it the night before. I apologized and asked her what was up.

"Dan, Neo's coming. He just called from Quito, Ecuador. He's stopping in Jamaica, and then he'll be here on Friday. Do you want me to call Kerry and tell her?"

"I've got a better idea," I said. "Let's run down to Bethesda and tell her ourselves." Kerry had been pretty sick in recent days. Her chemo had caused her mouth and esophagus to develop small ulcers, and it was hard for her to eat, and equally hard to talk. We hadn't visited her since the previous Friday—our schedules had been so busy. We hadn't talked by phone either, to spare her the pain of talking.

Carol loved the idea, so I finished my work and picked her up, and we crept slowly through the rush hour (an ironic name if there ever was one) to get to NIH by 6:30 P.M. Kerry was watching CNN with a tray of untouched food on her tray table. She smiled when we walked in, but her smile didn't look convincing. She kept swallowing hard and coughing softly.

We gently hugged her and then sat down. We told her about Neo's expected arrival, and she smiled again, more convincingly this time. Then Carol unrolled some crayon-colored pictures that her Sunday school class had created for Kerry the previous Sunday. Carol got some masking tape from the nurse's station, and after Kerry looked at each drawing, Carol taped it on the wall, directly in front of Kerry. "Let me keep this one here," Kerry said hoarsely, holding the last picture.

It was a drawing of an island with a volcano. In the blue water around the island there were fish of all sizes and shapes and colors, even a diamond-shaped fish that Carol said was supposed to be a manta ray (the young artist had told her so). There was a dolphin jumping out of the water, and a whale doing the same. Around them were all kinds of birds, also of all shapes and sizes, some a simple rounded M shape, and others more elaborate, with long tails and brightly colored wings. On the island there was a stick-figure person standing beside a big gray tortoise. And up in one corner was a bright sun, with yellow and orange rays shining out, the yellow rays straight and the orange ones curvy. In the other corner was an airplane. In the bottom corner, below the airplane, there was the name, Aaron, and below the name, a message: GET WELL, KERY. Aaron had left out the second "R."

"I told the kids all about you, Kerry," Carol explained, "and about your work with the animals on the island. Aaron stayed after class to finish this one. He wasn't satisfied until all the air was filled with birds, and all the water was filled with fish."

"The airplane caught my eye," Kerry said. "It will be so good to see Neo again."

We chatted for a while, but left early. Carol and I hardly spoke all the way home. As we pulled in the driveway, Carol said what I had been thinking. "She doesn't look good, Dan. Worse than last week even. I wonder if she's going to make it."

"Her chances weren't good when she arrived," I said.

As I got to the door and pulled out my keys, I heard the phone ringing inside. I managed to get to it by the sixth ring. It was a young man's voice—friendly, a bit shy, southern California accent "Mr. Poole, hey, this is Kincaid Ellison, Kerry's son. I just got off the phone with my mother, and she suggested I call you."

Only tonight had Kerry told her son how serious her relapse was. Up until now, he had been under the impression that she was just having some tests done. He was very concerned, so concerned that he was thinking about withdrawing from classes for the semester so he could be with her. He planned to come for at least a week or so, arriving via a United red-eye flight on Tuesday morning at Dulles, the same airport where Neo would arrive the Friday before. I offered Kincaid a place to stay. At first he politely refused, but eventually I persuaded him to accept.

When I hung up, Carol, who had overheard my part of the conversation, said, "I reckon we can put Neo in the guest room and Kincaid in Trent's room, and Trent will get the couch. Well, Dan, you know how I've always dreamed of opening up a bed and breakfast when the kids grew up—looks like I have my chance, just a little earlier than I expected." Carol's cheerful, flexible, hospitable nature always amazed me. Sadly, my first thought had been less openhearted. As eager as I was to be good to Kerry's son, I was apprehensive that his presence would interrupt the time with Neo that I was looking forward to so much. Things were OK at the church, but I was worried about a few things—primarily some unrest in my lay leadership board—and I hoped to get some advice from Neo about how to deal with it.

The unrest had to do with some ways that Neo's thinking had affected my own. "Dan's going liberal," was how one board member, Gil, had said it to another, Marlin, in my presence, some weeks before—jokingly, but only half-jokingly, I feared.

I worked extra long and hard on Thursday to finish my sermon and get ahead on the next week's work, since Friday and Tuesday would require trips to the airport and time with our incoming guests. On top of the board member's comment, which I couldn't stop thinking about, I had to do all my own administrative work. Some weeks earlier, I had asked my administrative assistant to resign—poor work habits, missing deadlines, surly attitude. Since then, she had been telling all her friends at the church that she had not been adequately trained or supported in her work and had resigned because I was too demanding and difficult to work with. I had gotten several calls and notes (not friendly ones) from her friends, who assumed (of course) that she was right and I was wrong. It's funny how little conflicts like this can drain the joy from even the loftiest work. This stress made the thought of taking some time off to be with Neo even more pleasant.

Neo's flight was scheduled to come in right at dinnertime (5:36 P.M.) at Dulles—a long drive at any time and a nightmare during rush hour. I decided to arrive early to avoid the traffic, so I left my office at two o'clock and brought along a book to read while I waited for him. Despite my planning, his flight was delayed once, and twice, and then again, so by the time he arrived, at 9:45 P.M., I had been waiting around the airport for over six hours. I'd long since finished the book I brought along, plus a couple newspapers I picked up.

The first thing I noticed as I peered down the jetway was the large scar on Neo's right eyebrow and cheek, pink against his brown skin and somehow accentuated by the old red baseball cap he wore. Because of what Kerry had told me, I was expecting to see the scar, but still it shocked me by its size and—I don't know what word to use—its freshness. But even that shock was forgotten as soon as I caught his eyes under the bill of the shabby old cap, and we both broke into smiles of recognition. His face beamed as he strode out into the waiting area. He dropped his backpack and engulfed me in a huge one-armed bear hug that lifted me off my feet. "Hey, man! You lost weight since I last saw you," he said. "You look great!"

"You too, my friend," I said. Then, not wanting to acknowledge the scar on his face, I pointed to his arm, which was bandaged in a soft cast. "How's the arm?"

"It's healing just fine," he said, and then pointed to his facial scar. "How do you like my tattoo?" he asked. "The fellows who gave it to me did it real cheap! You know how we Jamaicans love a bargain!"

Kerry had told me the story of Neo's injury right after her arrival in Maryland. One Monday morning, she and Neo went snorkeling in a bay on the island of Santa Cruz, not work this time, just a day off. While swimming, she felt something pop in her right armpit. Still underwater, she reached over with her left hand and felt a lump about the size of a golf ball. She instantly knew what it was. With surprising calmness, she swam into shore, unable to fully lower her right arm, and Neo followed her, wondering what was wrong. He caught up with her in waist-deep water. "Look," she said, pulling up the sleeve of the T-shirt she swam in. "It just popped out. It must be a lymph node."

Neo gently reached out and touched the pale lump with two fingers. It was hard. And the skin over it was cold, tight, and white, with no trace of redness or swelling, so it was not an abscess. "Oh, God, no," Neo said. They both knew too much about cancer to dismiss it or try to create a less frightening explanation.

They had reached the bay on motor scooters from the Research Center. They dried and dressed quickly and returned the scooters. They went directly to Kerry's office. Within ten minutes, they had reservations on the next flight to Quito. There was an hour wait for the bus ride to the Baltra airstrip, but after that, all connections went well, and by midnight they were in a taxi on the way to the emergency room.

Neo stayed with her until she was settled in a room in the early hours of Tuesday morning, then left, exhausted, to find a hotel nearby. Unfortunately, he decided to try to find one on foot, and after walking a few blocks, just after daybreak, he found himself lost and in a neighborhood where his black skin and large stature made him stand out. After a few minutes, he noticed that he was being followed by a group of teenaged boys who looked like they'd been up all night. When he felt a small object hit him in the back of the neck, he knew he was in trouble.

For several blocks, the boys walked a few steps behind him, whispering and occasionally laughing to one another, occasionally throwing things at him—first a bottle cap, which hit him on the back of the neck, and then an empty bottle, which sailed over his shoulder and shattered at his feet just in front of him, and then a half-full soda can, which hit him hard, and hurt, in the small of his back.

His heart started racing. He lacked confidence in his Spanish to try to talk his way out of this. He looked ahead—no open stores or police officers in sight. He thought of running, but these guys were young; they'd catch him in a minute. He thought of banging on someone's door, but really, there wasn't time for anyone to come to his aid. For some reason, the thought of yelling for help never crossed his mind at that point. So he said a quick prayer ("OK, God, here we go . . ."), turned around, and faced the gang. Three, four, five young men instantly fanned out and surrounded him.

It all happened very fast. They started shouting in Spanish, and he felt a hand going in his back pocket for his wallet. He whirled around and tried to protect his wallet, and at that instant he felt a knife slash his left forearm in a quick upstroke, and then felt it come down across his face in a vicious downstroke. He felt the sting of blood in his right eye and doubled over. The boys scattered in all directions. Blood was running down his forearm, and both hands were cupped over the right side of his face. He felt blood running—no, pouring—between his fingers. *This is serious,* he thought. He reached back with his bloody right hand to check for his wallet. His whole back pocket had been torn away, and, of course, the wallet was gone with it. He slumped to the ground, feeling an intense burning on his arm and face, and the fingers of his left hand started to go numb. He crawled over to a wall and leaned against it, raising a bloody hand and calling at the top of his lungs, "Help! Help! I've been robbed!"

His Spanish had abandoned him. He felt dizzy and thought he was about to vomit. *Going into shock,* he thought, and he was about to lie down on the sidewalk when he heard the sounds of feet scuffling around him. A few people—he never knew how many—knelt beside him, all speaking Spanish, their voices as full of love and concern as the gang's had been of hate. He tried to ask for help in English, but eventually managed to recover the one Spanish phrase he really needed: "Hospital, por favor, hospital."

He vaguely remembered hearing the sound of a siren. Some time later that Tuesday, when he woke up, he was back in the emergency room, in the same curtained area where Kerry had been a few hours earlier. His first thought was, *I'm alive.* His second, *But I'm hurt pretty bad.* And his third, *Well, no need for a hotel room now.*

That was the story behind the bandaged arm and the "tattoo" he would wear for the rest of his life on his brow and cheek—a single slash running from his forehead, mercifully sparing his eye, and continuing below his right cheekbone, pale and so prominent on his chocolate-colored skin.

He needed surgery on his forearm to repair the muscle and tendons slashed in the robbery; otherwise, he would have lost some of the use of his fingers. The plastic surgery for his face was substantial. He would be in the hospital for five days, and would be unable to get up to see Kerry in her room the whole time. Although she was more seriously ill, she was also more mobile, so she came down to see him each morning.

"What a pair we are," she said when she woke him up on Wednesday morning. Neo would have laughed, but it hurt his face even to blink an eye, much less to smile. Kerry called the owner of *La Aventura* from Neo's hospital room, explaining what happened. Neo's failure to show up for work the previous day had baffled everyone and forced the captain to set sail without a certified guide. The owner asked if Neo would be available for the next week's cruise, and Kerry said she hoped so. She spent additional hours on the phone that week working on the loss of Neo's credit cards, passport, driver's license, and naturalist certification card. As a certified naturalist, Neo was a government employee and had full health coverage, but there were so many forms to fill out, and with one arm in a cast and the other hooked to an IV, he needed Kerry's help to do so. He had come to help her, but she ended up helping him far more.

Neo's plane left Quito early on Sunday morning, a day before Kerry's scheduled departure. He would return to the islands to put Kerry's affairs in order and to complete a few more tours while his captain found a permanent replacement guide. Kerry had also given him her network passwords so that he could log on to CDRC's computer system and send that first, rather arcane, e-mail to me.

Their goodbye took place in the hospital lobby. Kerry softly placed a hand on the bandages that covered the right side of his face. She stood on tiptoe and gently kissed the other cheek. "I hope that didn't hurt," she said.

"Actually," Neo said, "I could use another one of those."

For Kerry, the week's tests had shown, along with several tumors in the lymph nodes under her arm, a tumor in her thigh, from which they had taken a biopsy. The doctors wanted her to use a cane to avoid overstressing the affected leg. As Neo's taxi drove him away to the airport, she stood on the sidewalk, smiling, waving, leaning on her cane, and—to her own surprise—she said a prayer that God would reunite them soon.

Neo always traveled light. Even returning to America, he hadn't checked any bags. There was just the small backpack he was carrying. So after our hellos (and a quick phone call to Carol to let her know we were finally on our way home), we were quickly out at my car and onto the Dulles access road, then on the Beltway, then on 270, and then at my driveway. I was eager to hear more of his travels, eager to fill in gaps left in the story as I had understood it from Kerry. But he was even more eager to hear about my life and family and ministry, and especially about Kerry's condition too, so I did most of the talking on the ride home, although I didn't bring up the problems with my leadership board.

When we stepped inside just after eleven o'clock, Carol had a whole meal waiting for us at the kitchen table. She had gone out of her way to prepare a recipe for Jamaican plantains, a Jamaican curry dish, and a splendid mango salad, all from recipes she found on the Internet. (For my contribution, I had picked up a six-pack of Pete's Wicked Ale, another favorite of Neo's. This had required me to stop in at a liquor store earlier that morning. That kind of errand is something that I, as a pastor, don't have much experience with.) Even though the meal had been waiting for hours due to Neo's delayed flight, the house smelled delicious as we entered. Neo dropped his backpack and hugged Carol, and she led us into the kitchen, where the meal was waiting, freshly warmed, in the soft glow of candlelight.

We sat down, and I asked Neo if he would say grace. The three of us held hands—our three kids were already asleep—and by the time Neo said, "Amen," he was choked up, and so was Carol, and I felt my lower lip trembling.

18

THE THRILL OF FISHING

EARLY ON SATURDAY MORNING, after a breakfast shared with the kids (Neo had met the boys over dinner one night back in 1999, and he had coached Jess in soccer, so the kids were thrilled to see him), we let him take one of our cars so he could visit Kerry by himself. He didn't return until well after dark.

I was at the kitchen table working on my sermon when he came in. Saturday nights are usually "touch-up" nights for me, going over my notes, making corrections, practicing and timing the delivery, then usually cutting sentences and paragraphs so my sermon won't run long and thus incur the wrath of the toddler Sunday school department.

I was so deep in concentration, and he was so quiet, that I didn't notice him coming in. I jumped and turned as I felt a hand on my shoulder, and he said, "So sorry to scare you, my brother! Hard at work as a servant of the Word, eh?"

He pulled up a chair by the kitchen table, turned it around backwards, and had a seat, resting his chin on his unbandaged right hand on the chair back. We talked for a half hour or so, about my sermon notes, about Kerry, about their day together. The bad news: Kerry's side effects from the chemo—not the obvious ones, like the mouth and throat sores, but the subtle ones, like her liver function tests—required that they stop treatment for at least several days. The good news: her blood counts were good enough that they were going to give her a three-day pass starting the next day, so she could come with us to the airport to pick up Kincaid when he arrived on Tuesday.

Neo expressed disappointment at not being able to come to church the next morning—he still had never attended Potomac Community Church or heard me preach—because he would be picking up Kerry at eleven o'clock.

"I don't want to disturb you any more," he said, "and besides, I need a good night's sleep."

I turned in soon myself, but first I woke up Carol to let her know about Kerry coming. "OK," she said groggily. "Hmmm. That means I give Corey's room to Kerry, and Corey will have to sleep on the couch that Trent's not using. No problem." And she was back to sleep in seconds.

After church on Sunday, we pulled into the driveway about one-thirty, just behind Neo and Kerry, and after getting her settled, we went out to the pool for a picnic lunch and a swim. This time, however, Kerry couldn't get wet, due to a catheter port that the doctors had inserted just below her clavicle. She and Carol sat at the pool's edge, dangling their feet in the water. She seemed to be feeling much better than she did when we had visited her a few days earlier.

Neo and I sat on the deck and discussed what we could do Monday to make it a special day for Kerry. We could go to downtown D.C. to see the monuments and museums, or take a drive in the mountains, or spend the day at the Inner Harbor in Baltimore, or enjoy the waterfront in Annapolis. Neo didn't seem inspired by any of the options.

"What I really wish is . . . I wish we could take Kerry on a shorter version of that hike you took me on, I guess it was almost two years ago, along the river. That was a great day, in spite of the less-than-pleasant ending, which was—"

"Which was all my fault," I interrupted, but Neo was holding up his hand in protest.

"Which was all *my* fault," he countered. "But that's behind us. It was a beautiful day in spite of . . . let's just call it the insult-and-stick incident. I wish . . ."

"Maybe we could get a wheelchair for Kerry," I offered. "The towpath is pretty smooth."

Neo shook his head. "I don't think Kerry would like that much. And the bouncing and jiggling wouldn't be the best thing for her, you know? I just wish we could get her outdoors, because all this time indoors is completely foreign to her."

"I have an idea," I said. I ran inside and made two phone calls, and came back with an offer. Carol and Kerry had seated themselves next to Neo on our back deck. "Kerry and Neo," I said, "I've got a boat reserved for tomorrow on the upper Potomac. The weather is supposed to be perfect. Are you game?" I knew this would be great in Carol's opinion, who loves nothing more than being on the water, whether it's boating, tubing, water skiing, or swimming.

Neo and Kerry loved the idea too. "That's perfect, Dan," Kerry said. "You know I'm going batty being so far from water, and being cooped up indoors every day."

We had a great evening. I love to play cards, as did Kerry, and Neo and Carol obliged us. The conversation was light and relaxed and punctuated with a lot of laughter, and Neo finished off the last Pete's Wicked Ale, assisted by Kerry, before we called it a night—early, of course, because Kerry's strength was still limited.

Monday presented us with a perfect September day. Jess promised to help her younger brothers get up and catch the school bus, freeing us to leave the house early, and she promised to keep an eye on them after school too. So by nine that morning, we had arrived at my friend's farm, near Old Town, Maryland. His boat was waiting for us at a dock. I had packed a huge thermos of hot coffee, a gallon of cider, some bottled water, and plenty of food and snacks for the day. Neo said he brought something to drink too, which he'd stored in his own pack. (I suspected it was a few more bottles of Wicked Ale.) Mist was still rising from the water as we walked out on the dock.

My friend, now a semiprofessional bass fisherman (and a semiretired former bank president), gave me a quick lesson on the two motors. On the left side was a battery-powered trolling motor for going downstream, he explained. It was silent and would help us maneuver across the current as we floated downstream. On the right side was a normal gas motor for returning upstream—noisy, but fast. He also included a few fishing poles in case we were tempted to try our luck. My friend pushed us off from the dock, and we were afloat.

Kerry and Neo loaded their gear and sat in the front, facing backwards, Neo brown and scarred but smiling in his red cap, and Kerry pale and bald and also smiling beneath a red bandana. Carol and I faced them, looking forward and downstream. Carol pulled out some sunscreen and passed it around. I sat behind the steering wheel and controls for the two motors. "This is perfect," Kerry said. "Just perfect."

I tried a few casts on the fishing pole, but not being the outdoorsy type, I gave up quickly. "The thrill of fishing," Neo said, observing my awkwardness as an angler, "is the pursuit of something that is elusive but attainable, a perpetual series of occasions for hope." Kerry commented on the eloquence of the statement, and Neo burst her bubble. "I read that on a poster in a store once. The poster was too expensive, so I just memorized the quote." We all laughed.

"Carol and Dan," Kerry said, "I told you that earlier this summer, Neo was telling me what he called 'The Story We Find Ourselves In.' Every Monday he gave me a new episode. Last time we got together—I guess it was just last month, but it seems like ages ago—our regular Monday conversation got interrupted by this . . ." Kerry lifted her arm slightly and pointed toward the place where the lump had been. "Maybe you and Neo could collaborate, Dan," she continued, "I'd love to hear how each of you would tell the next episode of the story."

Carol asked for a review, which Kerry offered. First, she said, there was creation. She recounted Neo's merging of the biblical story with the scientific story.

Carol interrupted with a question. "Neo, I remember Dan telling me that you were an evolutionist, and actually, I read something in the paper about the trouble you got in at the high school years and years ago, before I ever dreamed I'd know you personally. Do you mind if I ask why a nice man like you is so impressed with evolution? I always hear in Christian circles that evolution is overrated, you know, that there are a lot of holes in the theory."

19

STILL IN PROCESS,
STILL YOUNG,
STILL MOVING AHEAD

KERRY GAVE NEO A KNOWING GRIN, and he adjusted his red cap and answered. "This subject always gets me in trouble," he said. "But I keep walking right into it, because I think it's so important. Let me sum it up like this, Carol. If you go back to the medieval era, the world was a beautiful and integrated hierarchy.

"That word 'hierarchy' is significant, because the Greek root *arch-* means 'origin,' and the Greek root *hier-* means 'sacred.' There was a sacred origin to the universe, and it expressed that sacred origin through a sacred order. In the Middle Ages, they called it the Great Chain of Being, with everything connected and integrated, from highest to lowest. So you had the lion as the king of the beasts, down to perhaps the mouse or the spider or the worm. And you had the eagle as the king of the birds, down to the humble sparrow. And even in the inanimate world, you had the same order, with gold as the king of all minerals, down through silver and copper to maybe rock or dirt, that sort of thing. It was the same in human society: you had the pope in the religious realm and the king in the secular realm, and authority and nobility flowed downward from the highest to the lowest, through bishops and nobles down to the serf, who was at the bottom of the Great Chain. It's almost impossible for us to imagine living in a world where everything had its place, a place assigned by God."

Carol was pouring coffee for everyone, which interrupted Neo for a couple minutes. Then he continued, "OK, back to the Great Chain of Being. At the top of the chain, of course, was God, the creator and designer of the whole beautiful, balanced, ordered schema. This conceptual order was reflected even in the physical structure of the universe, in a worldview that goes all the way back to this second-century North African genius named Claudius Ptolemy."

Here, Neo became very animated, and he handed his coffee cup to Kerry so he could use both his hands (one still in a bandage) to form, out of air, spheres within spheres. "Ptolemy conceived of the universe as a series of concentric spheres. The central sphere was, of course, the earth. Above the earth was a second sphere, which contained air, and then another, a sphere of fire. In the medieval mind, these were real physical spheres, made of invisible crystal. So then there was the crystalline sphere of the moon, and above that, the sphere of some of the planets, and above that, the sun, and above that, more planets, and then the sphere of the stars. There were ten spheres in all, as I recall. Anyway, as you ascended from sphere to sphere, you rose to higher and higher levels of perfection and changelessness—the two went together in their minds. So there's a lot of change with the moon, less with the sun and the planets, and practically no change at all in the sphere of the stars."

Carol interrupted again. "What was above the stars? Heaven?" She was trying to make a joke, I think.

"Exactly," Neo replied. "No kidding, Carol. The greatest sphere of all was heaven, the home of God."

"OK, this is interesting and all, Neo, and I don't mean to be rude, but what does this have to do with evolution?" Carol asked.

"Sorry—I get carried away with this stuff. Well, this whole worldview that the church adopted and baptized from Ptolemy was nearly perfect—except, of course, when a supernova or comet would appear in the sky, as they occasionally did. That really messed things up. And the occasional retrograde motion of some planets in the sky was a problem too. And then to make matters worse, Copernicus came along, and then Galileo, with his new and improved telescope. Can you see what would happen if you suddenly tried to say that the sun was in the center, not the earth?"

"I hear the sound of crashing crystal spheres!" Carol offered, laughing.

"Exactly, exactly!" Neo said. "That's why the Office of the Inquisition tried so hard to suppress Copernicus's and Galileo's ideas. Nobody could imagine the Christian faith surviving the de-centering and deconstruction of the medieval worldview. The two were completely melded together. Even Luther and Calvin—until their dying day, they believed that Copernicus was the devil's tool."

Carol wanted to press on. "So that's in the 1500s, right? We're still 350 years away from Darwin, Neo. I think you'd better hit the fast-forward button, or we'll be in this history lesson all day. Remember: Kerry is hoping that we'll get to the next episode of the story before we float into the Atlantic."

Neo apologized and continued anyway, with almost as much animation as before. "OK, OK, I'm just trying to set the stage. Getting back to Galileo: even after he agreed, with some gentle nudging from the Office of the Inquisition, to stop talking about the sun-centered universe, he devoted the rest of his life to the exploration of what he called *mechanics,* what we would call *physics.* So through the physics of Galileo and others, during the sixteenth, seventeenth, and eighteenth centuries, the universe is becoming more and more explainable, more and more and more, by what we call physical laws—not the best term, in my opinion, but anyway, do you see what's happening?"

Even though Neo was answering Carol's question, Kerry replied, "God is getting squeezed out. Skyhooks and miracles are less and less needed to explain the universe. It's all about mechanics . . . mechanics and great amounts of time. That's the reality that hit me when I was in college and caused me to . . . to give up on faith."

"Yes," Neo continued. "That's why when Darwin comes along, his ideas are considered so dangerous. It's as if the church had already taken a stiff left jab to the stomach, and then a vicious right uppercut to the chin, and now Darwin comes along with the knockout punch, a crushing hook to the face: pure mechanics plus deep time not only explains orbits and chemical reactions, but also life, including human life. There's nothing left. The *hier-* is completely gone from the *-archy.* The sacred is gone from the origin. Now, instead of everything being derived from above, so that authority and meaning flow downward from the sacred into the physical creation . . . now, we start at the bottom, with atoms and fundamental forces like magnetism and gravity—meaningless, impersonal forces. So with Darwin, the conquest of the sacred by the mechanical becomes complete."

Carol looked puzzled, but she was even more curious now. "OK. You've successfully explained why Christians dislike evolution so much. I already knew that. But why do you want to go back to evolution? You *are* a Christian, aren't you?" She smiled at this, but she was serious.

"Carol, don't get me wrong. I don't think that evolution necessarily explains everything. Yes, I think it's a good theory, a really brilliant theory, and of course, it has its share of bugs, I'm sure. It's a long way from explaining everything. I wouldn't be surprised if there are still whole new levels of complexity to discover that are essential to the process. That's what the religious folks often bring up: an unexplained problem here, a 'black box' there. Still, the overall picture is powerfully compelling for me.

"A lot of people don't realize that the theory really arose from honest observations, from people who believed in God. They would travel around the world, especially in the South Pacific, and they'd wonder: Why does this species of bird exist on this island, but not that one? Why is this kind of butterfly on this side of the mountain different from the one on that side of the mountain? If everything had been created by God about six thousand years earlier, in the Tigris-Euphrates Valley, or if all living creatures had disseminated from Noah's ark in what we call Turkey some time later—as most biblical literalists believed—then why were plants and animals distributed in such an odd, odd way? I mean, if those stories were literally true, wouldn't you find species disseminating from Iraq or Turkey?"

Carol had never thought of that. "Good question!" she said.

"For me, Carol, we can't be faithful to God unless we're faithful to the facts, faithful to the data, if you will. And so instead of hiding from evolution, I think we'd be more faithful to God to look it right in the eye and learn from it."

"Learn what from it . . . *atheism?*" she replied. She wasn't hostile, but she was uncomfortable, a little edgy. I knew the feeling; it wasn't far from here, on the towpath to our left, where I had lost my temper with Neo about two years earlier because of a similar discomfort.

What Neo explained next was so fascinating that I could hardly sit still. In fact, I picked up the fishing rod and started casting again from the back of the boat, just out of feeling so energized, but still listening intently to Neo.

"Here's what I learn," Neo answered. "If God wants to create a universe, a real universe, not a simulation universe or a dream universe, but a real creation that really exists, where is God going to create it?"

"Huh?" Carol asked.

Kerry reached out and touched her on the knee. "Hang in there, Carol. I've heard this. This is good."

Neo said, "Bottom line: Go back before creation. If God is the only thing that exists, the only being that *is*, then God has to create some kind of neutral space, very literally, and God needs to create time, so that the universe can *be itself, become itself,* with some kind of freedom and authenticity. Otherwise, it's just a puppet universe, just a simulation. Do you see it? So if God wants to make a universe that's real, I think we would expect it to happen just as evolution says: the universe would develop, over time, writing its own story, so to speak. It's a story of becoming, of unfolding, of novelties emerging and possibilities being explored and diversity flowering. And best of all, it's not finished yet. We're still in process, still young, still moving ahead toward what we're going to be when we're all 'grown up.' And each of us, through our lives, through our choices, by cooperating with God or by withholding our cooperation, plays a part in the continuing evolution of God's creation. That's not so bad, is it?"

Neo was holding out his hands, one still bandaged, with eyes wide open and enthusiasm unbridled. "Wow," was all that Carol could manage to say for a moment. She tried again. "You're blowing my mind. So for you, evolution isn't the big enemy. It's . . . wow, you're blowing my mind."

Right about then, quite by accident, I caught a fish. I wasn't really paying attention, so I don't know how I did it. It was fun. The crazy thing jumped clear out of the water a couple of times, and Carol screamed, and Kerry laughed, and eventually Neo bent over the side of the boat and picked it up by sticking his thumb in its mouth, of all things. Then he removed the hook, estimated its length at sixteen inches, admired its beauty, and let it go. We celebrated with some cider and snacks, and enjoyed the beautiful, green, round mountains that heaved up on all sides around the ribbon of blue water that carried us gently downstream, ever so slowly toward the ocean.

20

MORE THAN EVEN ALL
THE WINDOWS CAN SHOW

AFTER THE EXCITEMENT WORE OFF, and after Neo (always the science teacher) had identified my catch as a smallmouth bass and talked about the fascinating evolution of freshwater fish, he finished his review (more quickly!) of the parts of the story that he and Kerry had gone over so far: creation, crisis, calling, conversation. (Regarding the conversation episode, Neo didn't really talk about the history; he talked about the ways God and the people communicated, through priests, prophets, poets, and philosophers. All the alliteration struck me—as it had Kerry—as a bit cheesy, but it was memorable, and Carol loved mnemonic devices, so she was thrilled.)

"Finally," Kerry said. "What's next?"

"Christ," Neo said.

"This is good, Neo," Kerry said, "because the way you talk about God really makes sense to me. But somehow, the Jesus thing seems tacked on. I mean, I respect Jesus . . . I think everyone does. But how does Jesus fit in with the story?"

"Well, if the way I'm telling the story makes sense to you," Neo responded, "that's probably because I'm telling the story from the perspective of a follower of Jesus. In other words, even though I haven't explicitly talked about Jesus yet, you've been hearing the whole story in light of Jesus. Think of it like this: during our whole trip so far today, we haven't talked about the sun at all, but we wouldn't have seen anything if it weren't for the sun."

"Still," Kerry replied, "the story seems complete to me already, just with 'Creation,' 'Crisis,' 'Calling,' and 'Communication.'"

Neo reached over with his foot and gently kicked Carol. "How would you answer that?" he asked, winking. "Why don't you pick it up from here? I've been talking too much already."

Carol looked at Kerry, whose sincere curiosity hooked Carol and pulled an answer out from her heart.

"Well, Kerry," she said, "I reckon I could give you my perspective on your question. For me, Jesus isn't tacked on at all. He's really essential. Although I don't fully get all that Neo was saying before about the universe"—and now it was her turn to gently kick Neo—"I think that the situation with Jesus might be kind of similar. If God creates a *real* universe, as Neo said, and if the people of this universe really do have the freedom to make choices, and if they make some bad choices, then we have a *real* problem."

Kerry replied, "Yes, that's what the crisis episode was about. It's a real problem. I feel it. We're disconnected from God, and from each other, and instead of helping the world become the world of God's dreams, we're turning it into a nightmare on all levels."

Carol went on. "OK. So what does God do about our wrongdoing? If God just lets it go—you know, if Cain kills Abel, and God says, 'Well, boys will be boys!'—then you have to have real questions about God's justice . . . and God's love too. Does that make sense?" Kerry's cocked head said it didn't, so Carol said, "If Cain then goes around killing a lot of other people after he kills Abel, and God says, 'I love Cain, so I'll forgive him and let it slide,' we'd have to say that God's love and mercy for Cain come at the expense of his love and mercy for Cain's other victims, not to mention their children and spouses and parents and friends."

Kerry nodded, and Carol continued. "But on the other hand, if God intervenes and punishes us for our wrongs as we deserve, then we're finished. It's all over. Because we all keep screwing up—pardon my language. So God sends Jesus into the world—"

"I'm sorry, Carol," Kerry interrupted. "I've heard this all before . . . in my childhood in Sunday school, and also whenever I happen to flip through channels and force myself to watch one of those religious broadcasts— which there are a whole lot of, you realize, if you're in the hospital and have to watch a lot of TV. So, Carol, I need to tell you, I'm really tempted to say, 'Yeah, yeah, I know all that already.' But I'm trying to keep an open mind."

Carol was quiet for a minute, very thoughtful, first looking down at her feet, then over at the mountains that surrounded us, and then back to Kerry in front of her. "Well, I believe that God sent Jesus into the world to absorb all the punishment for our sins. That's what the cross was all about. It was Jesus absorbing the punishment that all of us deserve. He became the substitute for all of us. As he suffered and died, all our wrongs were paid for, so all of us can be forgiven. OK?"

Kerry smiled. "I know that is supposed to mean something to me, and I suppose I can see it, but it raises so many questions."

"Go ahead," Carol said. "What questions?"

"For starters, if God wants to forgive us, why doesn't he just do it? How does punishing an innocent person make things better? That just sounds like one more injustice in the cosmic equation. It sounds like divine child abuse. You know?"

Carol looked for help. "I don't think I'm doing very well. Dan? Neo?"

I spoke up. "Kerry, what Carol just tried to explain is what theologians call a theory of atonement. It's a possible explanation for how Jesus' life and death play a role in the salvation of the human race."

Kerry responded, "Yes. I can see that you would need such a theory. It's just that it . . . well, Christian dogma and doctrine don't make complete sense to me. No offense, but I grew up with this stuff, and it just stopped working for me as I grew older."

"I understand," I said. "Really, what Carol explained is just one of six theories. It's called the 'substitutionary atonement' theory. To me, it's like . . ."—I gestured up toward the sky—"it's like trying to see the whole beautiful, majestic sky from one of your hospital windows."

Kerry wrinkled her forehead in a way that invited me to continue. "You can see part of the sky through your window," I went on, "and you can go to the other rooms on your floor and look through other windows too. But even after looking out all of the windows, you aren't seeing the whole sky—you aren't seeing to the end of the sky, which is infinite through each window, and is more than even all the windows can show you. I think it's the same in theology. These theories are windows, and having a theory is better than staring at a blank wall or even at a picture hanging on the wall, but theories can't give you the whole sky, you know? That's why I don't really like the words 'dogma' and 'doctrine,' which you used a second ago. I'd rather use the word 'mystery,' because even our best formulations don't give you the whole sky, just a window into it."

"Maybe if you gave me some of the other theories, it would broaden my view," she said.

"OK. I recently did some reading on all this to prepare for a sermon, so it's at least somewhat fresh in my mind. I have to begin by saying that all of these atonement theories assume that our alienation from God is a tragic predicament we can't solve ourselves. The only way we can be rescued is by God's grace. So in each theory, God graciously rescues us, forgives us; we don't earn forgiveness at all, but we receive it as a gift, by grace, through faith. OK? So each theory is an attempt to explain the role that Jesus' life, death, and resurrection play in the drama of our reconciliation with God.

The most ancient theory is often called the 'ransom' theory. This view says that we humans, through our sin, placed ourselves under the authority of Satan." I didn't notice that Kerry squirmed when I said "Satan," but Carol told me later that she did. "Jesus comes and offers himself as a ransom for us. He says to Satan, 'If I give you myself, will you set them free?' Satan agrees to the bargain, and so he takes, tortures, and kills Jesus, whose self-sacrifice sets us free. Of course, in the end, God double-crosses Satan—pardon the pun—by raising Jesus from the dead. So Satan is doubly the loser, and we're set free to live for and with God again."

"Sorry," Kerry said, "but that one makes even less sense to me than Carol's. I mean, no offense, but do you really believe in Satan? And why would God be making deals with the devil anyway?"

Now I was a bit flustered. I emphasized my belief that Satan really exists, but quickly assured Kerry that I didn't believe that Satan is a pitch-fork-carrying guy with horns on his head and dressed in red leotards. I seemed to make a little headway with her when I said that since evil is a uniquely personal trait, it can't just be an impersonal force, but has to be understood as a personal reality.

"I can see your point, I really can," Kerry said. "But wouldn't it be a little more helpful to see personal evil as analogous to a computer virus, something that attaches itself to the software of our personality and worms its way in and then . . . wow, I guess this language really works . . . it *corrupts us*? I mean, if you're saying that Satan is a personification of evil in that way, I could see that."

I shook my head and started to answer, but Neo stepped in. "Just a minute, Dan. I think Kerry might be onto something here. You know, if you go back into the most ancient parts of the Old Testament, there is no concept of Satan. That idea comes along much later. It seems to have been borrowed from the Zoroastrians, actually. Maybe it's no sin to think of Satan as a metaphor—a horribly real metaphor for a terribly real force in the universe, mind you. I think it *would* be a terrible sin to dismiss Satan as something stupid or inconsequential."

"What about the Garden of Eden?" Carol shot back. "Who tempted Eve?"

"Actually," Neo replied, "in the story itself, the tempter is never referred to as Satan, just as a snake. Later on, of course—"

I interrupted Neo, as I could see a major argument brewing between Carol and him. "I think we're getting off on a bit of a tangent. This discussion of Satan is important, but I was going through the theories of atonement, remember? We're all agreed that evil is a personal phenomenon, something very real and very, very dangerous, and maybe we can just leave it at that. So the ransom theory says that Jesus offered himself to be ravaged by evil in its most horrific, personal form, and that his self-giving somehow turns evil back on itself and frees us."

"It sounds a bit like some matter-antimatter thing in science fiction," Kerry offered, trying to be helpful. "You know, an act of absolute goodness and selflessness somehow nullifies evil and selfishness."

"Good point," I said politely and maybe a little falsely, since I really had little idea what she meant by matter-antimatter, not being a fan of science fiction myself. "What you just described may actually make a bit more sense of the 'substitutionary' theory, which Carol was explaining a minute ago. In that theory, God's merciful act of absolute goodness and selflessness in giving himself through Jesus on the cross satisfies or cancels out or absorbs God's just anger about human evil and selfishness."

Kerry just stared at me, waiting for more, and since I didn't know what else to say on that theory, I moved on. "Anyway, a third theory—and this is really the most dominant theory throughout church history—is called the 'Christus Victor' theory. In the ransom theory, the enemy is Satan, who has us as prisoners or kidnap victims, and Jesus' self-giving springs us free. In the substitutionary theory, the enemy, so to speak, is God's just wrath at our sin, and Jesus' death absorbs God's wrath. In the Christus Victor theory, our enemy is death. By entering into and overcoming death, Jesus opens the door for us to enter eternal life."

"This is helping," Kerry said. "Just knowing that it's not one simple formula. I like the idea of these windows, Dan. You said there were six?"

"Yes. OK. Next, there's the 'perfect penitent' theory. This theory acknowledges the question you raised before: 'If God wants to forgive us, why doesn't he just do so?' And the answer this theory gives is that forgiveness, for it to be legitimate and real, requires an expression of sincere repentance from the wrongdoer."

"And?" Kerry asked.

"And none of us are very good at repenting. None of us can repent sincerely or fully, because deep down, a part of us, at least, still loves to sin. Our best repentance is always ambivalent, partial, holding back. So this theory sees Jesus' acceptance of death—after all, he could have escaped any number of ways—as his enacting, on behalf of the whole human race, perfect repentance for us. He becomes a representative of all humanity, and willingly submits himself to being condemned and punished on our account, in spite of his true innocence, as a way of acting out real repentance for the human race."

"I've never heard of that one," Kerry said.

"Neither have I, and I'm a pure-bred Baptist from Atlanta!" Carol added.

I continued. "It was the view preferred by C. S. Lewis, actually—oh, sorry, Kerry, he was a well-known writer and Christian thinker in the middle of the twentieth century. He had problems with the substitutionary atonement theory for the same reason you do. Anyway, there's also what some people call the 'moral influence' theory, although I think that the name is too limiting. In this theory, the cross demonstrates Jesus' self-giving, his complete abandonment to God's will, his complete self-devotion for the sake of the world. Jesus' death completes the whole message of his life: he makes visible the self-giving love of God. When that sacrificial love touches us, we are changed internally—'constrained' is the word Paul uses for it— so that we want to stop being selfish, and we want to join God in self-giving, beginning by giving ourselves back to God, and leading us to give ourselves to our neighbors and the world too. It's as if Jesus invites us into his self-giving. He gives himself to God, for the sake of the whole world, and he invites us into his devotion, both to God and for the world."

"What's the enemy in that view?" Kerry asked.

"I guess it's our own selfishness, our own lack of love," I replied.

"I think I like that one best," Kerry said. "It reminds me of the whole idea of calling, of deciding to get back on God's side, joining God in the creative, saving process and abandoning the selfish and destructive process, you know? So maybe by coming to us in such pure, vulnerable goodness and then letting us kill him, Jesus is showing us, not just individually, but as a whole human race, how destructive our selfish ways are. Hmmm . . . But I thought you said there are six views. I've been counting on my fingers here, and that's only five."

"Maybe there were only five, then. I can't think of any more. Neo?" I asked for help.

"Well, I'm not sure what to name this, but it's one I've been thinking about," Neo said. "Let's call it the 'powerful weakness' theory, or maybe the 'foolish wisdom' theory. It hinges on exactly the word you just used, Kerry—'vulnerable.' It works like this: by becoming vulnerable on the cross, by accepting suffering *from* everyone, Jews and Romans alike, rather than visiting suffering *on* everyone, Jesus is showing God's loving heart, which wants forgiveness, not revenge, for everyone. Jesus shows us that the wisdom of God's kingdom is sacrifice, not violence. It's about accepting suffering and transforming it into reconciliation, not avenging suffering through retaliation. So through this window, the cross shows God's rejection of the human violence and dominance and oppression that have spun the world in a cycle of crisis from the story of Cain and Abel through the headlines in this morning's *Washington Post*. I don't know . . . this theory might be nonsense, but maybe there's a grain of truth in it. The cross

calls humanity to stop trying to make God's kingdom happen through coercion and force, which are always self-defeating in the end, and instead,
to welcome it through self-sacrifice and vulnerability."

Kerry replied, "Great, Neo, I think that's a very good window. What
would you say the enemy is in this theory?"

Carol stepped in. "I think it's human power, or arrogance, or pride, especially religious pride. We think we can do it all in our own way, our
timetable, our methodology, our cleverness. I reckon we just screw it all
up and make things worse."

I could tell that Neo wasn't fully listening to Carol. Instead, his eyes
were looking down into the water beside the boat, as if he were remem-
bering something. He looked distant, sad.

"What are you thinking, Neo?" I asked.

"Oh, I guess I might have one other theory of the atonement, but this
one comes more from my own life. It might be more biography than theology. Maybe it connects somehow with the ones we've already been talking about." We didn't say anything. For several seconds, Neo continued
looking down into the water, breathing slowly, brow furrowed, lips pursed.
Then he continued, first looking at each of us, then staring down at the fray-
ing bandage on his forearm the whole time he talked. There were just two
sounds: his deep, slow voice and the water lapping against the boat. "When
I was married, my wife—my ex-wife—had an affair, more than one actually. It was . . . it was beyond words . . . devastating. I was a pastor, and a
good husband, I think. I'll never forget . . ."

Carol reached over and put her hand on Neo's knee. "You don't have
to tell us this—"

"No, Carol," Neo interrupted, "I've never told this to anyone, and I
think I need to." Now he was shaking his head, his eyes looking down;
they may have been closed. "Unless you've experienced it, you never know
how *physical* betrayal feels. It's something you physically feel. You trust
someone, you think you know them, and then you find out, you find out
you've been fooled, used, taken for granted, taken advantage of. You feel
cheap, and violated, and your whole body—"

Now Kerry interrupted. She put one hand on his shoulder and leaned
forward as if trying to make eye contact with him, but he kept staring at
his bandages. "Yes," she said, "I know, Neo. Your whole world goes
empty, and your stomach burns, and your legs feel numb, and your neck
feels cold, and your lungs feel like you're breathing some poisonous gas,
and your brain is like one big fire alarm buzzing so loud you can hardly
stand it. It's exactly as you said: betrayal is something you feel in your
whole body. Believe me, Neo, I will never forget it either."

Kerry sat upright again, but kept gently rubbing his shoulder. Neo took a deep breath and resumed his story. "Anyway, we got counseling, and we talked, and she said she was sorry. She said all the right things. And I loved her, and I had made solemn vows to her. I really believed in marriage vows, and I still do. So I forgave her. And that was one of . . . no, that was *the* hardest thing I ever did. I don't know how to make that into a theory, but ever since that day, when I think of the cross, I think it's all about God's agony being made visible—you know, the pain of forgiving, the pain of absorbing the betrayal and forgoing any revenge, of risking that your heart will be hurt again, for the sake of love, at the very worst moment, when the beloved has been least worthy of forgiveness, but stands most in need of it. It's not just something legal or mental. It's not just words; it has to be embodied, and nails and thorns and sweat and tears and blood strike me as the only true language of betrayal and forgiveness."

I can't remember what happened next, because I think we all withdrew into our own thoughts for some time. Then Neo's tone of voice changed, and he said, "Anyway, we worked hard at saving our marriage, but in the end, she left, and . . . that was it."

Kerry said, "I was never given that chance, that chance to forgive. I don't know if I could have done it had I been given the chance." She reached over and let her hand dangle in the water for a few seconds, and then she said, "I wonder why forgiving hurts so much." Nobody answered.

After a while, Carol said, "I don't remember everything from my Sunday school days, but I do remember that Good Friday was my favorite holiday. It sounds morbid to say that, but it's true. Even as a little girl, I remember when we came to that moment in the Good Friday story when Jesus is so thirsty and he's hanging on the cross and he says, 'Father forgive them, for they know not what they do.' That moment always rang true with me, like that was really significant. I never thought of it as God's pain in forgiving us. I just thought that Jesus was showing us that if he could forgive us at that moment, at our ugliest, lowest point, then we should—"

At that moment, I felt like we were on the edge of something, almost getting to something that would have been a new insight into atonement for me and for all of us. But just then, I noticed that Kerry was looking over my shoulder, off in the distance. "What's that?" she asked, pointing. "It's huge."

Neo pulled off his cap, looked back to where Kerry was pointing, and said in a loud whisper, "Look! Look back there! That's not an osprey. Too big. I think . . . yes, it's a bald eagle!"

Carol and I turned and looked, and sure enough, winging majestically down the river straight toward us was a huge bald eagle. Right over our heads it flew, three wing beats and a glide, three beats and a glide, three beats and a glide, its head turning to look down at us, and then a gentle gliding arc up into a tree downstream from us. When we floated down near the bird's perch, it was up on the wing again, continuing downstream, its black body and white head soaring against the green backdrop of the mountainside, soaring over the sparkling river and then around a bend, then out of sight.

21

SOMETHING SPECIAL, SOMETHING HOLY

IT WAS ABOUT NOON BY NOW. We weren't able to get back to our conversation about atonement. We just continued floating downstream for a few minutes, each of us wrapped up in personal thoughts.

I looked at Neo and noticed how he was sweating, so I looked for a shady place to pull in for lunch. Up ahead, a stream entered the main channel of the river on the left, so I pulled into the mouth of the stream, where the current was slack. We took off our shoes, slid into the shin-deep water, and made it to shore with no mishaps. Kerry brought her cane, of course. While Carol and I spread out lunch under a huge sycamore tree, Kerry, her cane in one hand, and Neo, carefully keeping his bandaged arm dry, started skipping smooth rocks across the water. It brought back memories—memories of a tense conversation with Neo along this same stretch of river, memories of skipping rocks with Jess and Corey and Trent when they were younger, memories of doing the same with my dad as a boy. "Life is good, Lord," I prayed. "Thanks for this good day."

Just before we started eating, Neo waded back to the boat, climbed in, and brought out his backpack. He produced from inside it a bottle of wine. Kerry's eyes grew wide. "That looks just like the bottle I brought to the bay that day on Santa Cruz—"

"The day we never got around to drinking it because of that nasty lump that ruined our day," Neo broke in, smiling. "I kept it, hoping that a day like today would come."

"Well, all I've got is paper cups," Carol said. "Can we drink wine from paper cups? Remember, I'm a Baptist girl. I don't know about these things. I'm being corrupted by Episcopalians."

"And Australians," Kerry added. "Look at the label—it's Australian wine." We all laughed.

The meal was delicious. Our friend the eagle flew back overhead, moving upstream this time. I looked over at Kerry, who had moved out from under the tree into the full sunlight, near the water. She lay back on the flat rocks, her eyes closed, her hands cradling her head, her chest, flat under her T-shirt, rising and falling with slow, deep breaths, her legs extended. She may have been dozing for a few minutes. Then she slowly sat up and saw me watching her. She smiled. "I feel like a marine iguana basking on the black rocks of Fernandina," she said. "Or like a giant tortoise on the slopes of Isabela. This day is just what I needed. I feel alive again."

As Carol began cleaning up, Neo said, "Just a minute. We have wine, and we have some raisin bread there. Daniel, could we . . . would you do the honors?"

Kerry realized what Neo meant before I did. She moved to face us again. "Hold on. Let me ask a question first," she said. "How much do you have to believe in Jesus in order to take communion? I mean, I'd like to be part of this. I watched everyone do this at Aventura a bunch of times, and something inside me wanted to . . . to do it, but can I? I mean, in good faith? Look, if I have to get the whole Trinity thing, and the whole divinity thing, and all those theories . . . that's all just beyond me at this point. But I'm starting to believe the story I've been hearing from you"—now she started to cry, gently, and then harder—"and I don't have that much more time, you know? And I don't know how long it'll take to get really sure, or if I ever will, and . . . and sooner or later, I guess, I just have to . . . to take a step . . . that is, if I'm allowed, if it's permitted."

Now she was sobbing. Carol went over and knelt beside her on the stones, cradling her, rubbing her back. "Oh, Kerry . . . oh, Kerry," she kept saying.

Between sniffles and cries, Kerry said, "Look. I have tried to . . . to understand this from the outside. I've tried so hard. In the hospital, I would just lay there thinking and praying. But I don't think it's going to make sense . . . unless I try to understand from the inside. So I . . . I want to be in." And her cries poured out like a song.

The sun had moved, and now none of us were in the shadow of the tree anymore. I was too choked up to speak. Neo didn't wait for me. He got up on his knees and picked up the bottle of wine. Then he tore a chunk of raisin bread from the end of the loaf opposite the end from which Carol had so carefully cut several slices.

Then, holding the wine and bread up slightly, with his eyes open, looking up, Neo recited from memory these lines from the Book of Common Prayer: "Almighty and ever-living God, in your infinite love, You created us for yourself, but when we had fallen into sin, and become subject to evil and death, you, in your mercy, sent Jesus Christ, your only and eternal Son, to share our human nature, to live and die as one of us, to reconcile us to you, the God and Father of all. He stretched out his arms upon the cross, and offered himself, in obedience to your will, a perfect sacrifice for the whole world. We celebrate the memorial of our redemption, O Father, in this sacrifice of praise and thanksgiving. Recalling his death, resurrection, and ascension, we offer you these gifts. Sanctify them by your Holy Spirit to be for your people the Body and Blood of your Son, the holy food and drink of new and unending life in him."

Then Neo handed me the chunk of raisin bread. I said words I had said hundreds of times, but never savored as much as I did there, sitting cross-legged in the sunlight on the flat stones by the river: "On the night our Lord Jesus Christ was handed over to suffering and death, he took bread, and after he had given thanks, he broke it, and gave it to his disciples, and said, 'Take, eat, this is my body, broken for you. Do this in remembrance of me.'"

I held out the bread to Carol and Kerry, who each took a piece and held it, and then Neo did the same, and then all four of us raised our pieces of bread together, almost like we were making a toast, and then we ate them together, Kerry sniffling or crying softly the whole time.

Then Neo handed the bottle of wine to Carol, and she let go of Kerry and poured some wine into a paper cup, and she looked at it—or I should say, she looked into it—and just knelt there looking down into it for the longest time, as if it were very deep, and she were trying to see all the way to the bottom. Then, whispering, her lips quivering, pausing several times to regain her composure, she tried to recall the words she had heard so many times: "In the same way . . . after supper he took the cup, and blessed it, and gave it to his disciples, and said, 'This cup is the new . . . covenant . . . in my blood, shed . . . for the forgiveness of sins.'"

Carol seemed to forget what to say next. But then she turned, and offered the cup to Kerry, and said, "Kerry, this is for you."

And Kerry drank, and Carol, Neo, and I drank, and we stood up together on the stones in a kind of huddle or group hug, in the full September sun, with the river running by us just a few feet away, and no one spoke, again, for the longest time, Kerry still sniffling, and Carol too.

Kerry broke the silence with something none of us had expected. "I think I should be baptized," Kerry said. "I guess I was baptized as a baby, but that was so long ago, and so far away, and I left it all behind for so many years. But now, now I think this is for real, although tomorrow I may feel differently. But I think that this thing you're part of . . . I mean, this story we're part of . . . I truly believe it's real. And God is here—I know it. And this has nothing to do with me dying, or anything like that.

This has to do with me living, living for however long. So, Neo, would you? Could you? I mean, I'm not supposed to get wet, and I don't have any other clothes . . . but look, we have the river right here, and it's so perfect, and this is what I want. It really is!"

Carol stooped down and grabbed Kerry's cane. We were all in our bare feet, so we walked together across a stretch of flat stones into the shallow water. It was just two or three inches deep. Neo gulped down the rest of the wine in the cup, and he asked Kerry if she'd kneel there in the shallow water, with Carol and me on either side of her, and he filled the paper cup with water.

Neo's voice was serious. "Kerry," he said, "Do you believe in God, the Father Almighty, in Jesus Christ, God's only Son, and in the Holy Spirit, the Lord, the giver of life?"

"Neo," she said, looking up, and looking distraught, "I don't know about all the doctrines, or theories or mysteries, as Dan called them. I don't know all that stuff! That's the problem. Can I do this . . . am I crazy to even want to do this . . . if I don't have all that understanding? I want to believe. I want to believe all of it. Do I believe enough though? You have to know that, not me. That's why I asked what I asked before. How much do I have to believe?"

Carol looked first at Neo and then at me, directly in the eyes, and she was serious, something close to angry. She jabbed one finger in her other palm and said, "Look, you two, if that jailer in the book of Acts could be baptized, and if that Ethiopian official could be baptized, and if the disciples, who didn't seem to understand anything half the time could be baptized, then—for crying out loud—you'd better baptize this woman here, because her faith is real!"

Carol's intensity so surprised us that all four of us suddenly laughed, Kerry more than anyone. Or maybe we laughed because we realized how right Carol was.

Neo started again, and simply said, "Kerry, do you want to follow Jesus?"

She said, "Yes, with all my heart," and she put one hand over her heart, and with the other hand, she took off her bandana and used it to cover the catheter, just below her neck.

Neo poured the cupful of water on her bald head, and the water ran down her face and trickled back into the river. He said, "I baptize you in the name of the Father, and of the Son, and of the Holy Spirit."

Kerry stood up, and we all hugged, and she made a joke about her pants, because her backside had gotten wet, and . . . and I'll never forget what it felt like, standing there in the breeze and in the sunshine and in the water and in the company of those three people, who seemed at once so holy and so human and so wonderful.

It seemed kind of silly and anticlimactic to have to pick up our trash, but we did. Fortunately, Kerry remembered that she had stuck a camera in Neo's backpack, so we took a whole bunch of pictures to help us remember that spot and what happened there. Neo took a couple of the larger flat rocks nearby and stacked them on top of one another—a landmark, I guess, to mark this spot if we ever returned. Then we got back into the boat, and even though we still had nearly half the day left, it seemed best to throttle up the gas motor and fly back upstream at full speed.

Kerry climbed up to the front of the boat to enjoy the full effect of the wind on her face, but the wind quickly whipped the bandana off her head. Even though we turned around to retrieve it, it was too wet to wear the rest of the way back, so she wore Neo's old red cap instead. I don't remember what we talked about on the ride upstream, just that it was happy and light and not very religious. But at the same time, the conversation was very much filled with something special, something . . . I guess the best word for it is *holy*.

22

THE REVOLUTION OF GOD

"THERE'S AN OLD COUNTRY RESTAURANT back in Westminster," Neo said, as we got into the car for the drive home. "I can't remember the name of it, but I think I can get us there, if you're game. It's not too far out of the way. Lunch was good, but I could go for a country dinner and a piece of pie. In all my travels, I think pie is what I missed most about America, and this place had the best pie I ever tasted."

So we set off to Westminster to find Neo some pie. The diner we were seeking was a combination restaurant, nursery, roadside fruit stand, he said. Odd combination, but he promised that the pies would be home-made, from the freshest fruit. I started thinking about peach pie.

A few miles down the road, Carol interrupted my dreams of dessert with an unexpected question. "What is it, Kerry, that fascinates you so much about animals?"

"I don't know exactly," she said. "Maybe it's a way my childhood stays alive, through my love for the lizards and other animals that I would see back in Alice Springs. Or maybe animals are my windows, as Dan was talking about before, my windows into life and even God in a way, although I am maybe just now realizing that." It was an intriguing insight.

Dinner was good—no, much better than good: fantastic. A lot of laughter and warmth surrounded the four of us as we sat in the old-fashioned booth in the old-fashioned diner there in Westminster. And the pies were even better than Neo had led us to believe. We kept passing our plates around to sample one another's choices: warm cinnamon-apple with raisins, sweet yet tart rhubarb, pumpkin with pecans, and, of course, peach. I bought a whole pie as we left, a treat to bring home for Corey, Trent, and Jess—and yes, for myself too.

On the way home, Kerry was the one to get a bit more serious again.

"Neo, Dan and Carol gave their versions of the Christ episode of the story, but I was wondering if you'd say anything different, or more, about Christ."

I suggested that he tell her about the kingdom of God, a topic he and I had discussed once. "Too bad we aren't back at the diner. I even had some french-fry grease back there for drawing diagrams on the table," I said. It was a private joke, so Carol and Kerry looked puzzled.

Neo said that it had been a pretty intense day already, and asked if we could wait until the next day. We would all be going to the airport together in the morning to pick up Kincaid, so Neo suggested that he could offer a few more thoughts on the drive to Dulles. We had no idea how timely his words would be.

The next morning, Tuesday, we got up early—always thinking in terms of traffic—and enjoyed a quick and light breakfast together. I made sure the kids' lunches were ready, and I woke up Jess to remind her to help get the boys ready for school before she left. Feeling a little guilty for how much responsibility we had been putting on our teenager, I also told her about the pie waiting in the refrigerator. As we left, she was sitting at the kitchen table in her pajamas, eating a big slice of peach pie and drinking a glass of milk. "Drive safely, Mom," she said with her mouth half full, and with a little humor in her voice, since Carol was always saying the same thing to her, new driver that she was.

In spite of the early hour, we were all in a great mood after that unforgettable time the day before. Kerry was especially excited; she hadn't seen Kincaid since Christmas. As soon as we got in the car, Carol, who was driving this time, spoke up. "Neo, I must confess that I slept like a rock last night," she said, smiling, "but if I had been *any* less tired, I would have been awake half the night anticipating the words of wisdom you promised to share with us this morning. I'm dying to hear what else you have to say about Jesus."

Neo replied, "Carol, yesterday you and Dan emphasized Jesus' role in atonement, which is so important, so I can go in another direction, which is no less important, I'd say. That's Jesus' role as revolutionary." I guessed that Neo put it like this hoping to get a reaction out of Carol, but she didn't flinch. He continued, "Last night Dan suggested I talk about the kingdom of God, but I've thought about the term 'kingdom' a lot in my travels the last year or so. The word seems so outdated."

Kerry added, "Yeah, castles and jousting and fair maidens and the like."

"Precisely," Neo said. "For Jesus, it was a very contemporary image, but it's so different for us. So lately I've been thinking that a better term than 'kingdom of God' might be 'revolution of God.' That's what I think Jesus meant, anyway. What he was talking about was the most profound and far-reaching revolution imaginable."

Right at that moment, Carol slammed on the brakes and honked the horn. Some guy in a huge black SUV had nearly clipped our right front fender as he cut into our lane. When Carol honked, he raised his hand and offered a familiar gesticulation. (He wasn't saying hello!) Carol's Southern charm gave way to a few seconds of uncharacteristic outrage. "Did you see that? He cuts me off, and then he gives me the finger! Who does that maniac think he is?" Neo, Kerry, and I couldn't help it: we started to laugh to see Carol so completely nonplussed. In seconds, she was laughing too.

Neo eventually got us back to our conversation, "Where were we? Oh, yes. I was about to say that one of the toughest theological challenges for us Christians is to deal with a dynamic tension between the historic, eternal, individual, and global dimensions of Jesus and his mission. What we talked about yesterday was weighted to the eternal and individual side: what Jesus does for us as individuals in relation to God after this life. But the historical, global side is pretty significant in the Bible, maybe even more significant: what Jesus does for the whole world in this life, in history. In other words, yesterday we talked about Jesus as the savior of souls after this life, but we didn't talk much about Jesus as the savior of the world in this life. That's where 'revolution' comes in. As I see it, Jesus came to foment a spiritual revolution that would eventually—"

Before Neo could finish his sentence, Carol had to slam on the brakes yet again. This time we'd hit a sudden traffic jam on the Beltway. It was a good thing we had left home early. We began crawling, stop and go. I looked at my watch. It was 7:50. We had ninety minutes or so before Kincaid's flight arrived from Los Angeles. We wanted to greet him at the gate.

Neo didn't immediately pick up his previous train of thought with Carol. Instead, he turned to Kerry. "Since our time by the river yesterday, Kerry, I've been thinking about how important your question was, you know, when you asked *how much* a person has to believe in Jesus. That's a really profound question—and a difficult one."

I partially turned around so I could face Neo, who was seated behind Carol. "I've thought about the same thing, Neo. People come into my church, or any church really, and they hear statements like 'Jesus is God' and 'Jesus is the Son of God,' and they don't know whether those statements are supposed to mean the same thing or different things—"

Carol interrupted me (something we're both accustomed to). "Shoot," she said, "I grew up in church, went every week, had a perfect Sunday school attendance record from 'K' clear through to '12,' and I have the same problem. But I guess I'm just used to the ambiguity."

Kerry replied, "You're right. For people like me, it really is confusing. Whenever people say 'Jesus is God,' I wonder if they mean it the way the Greeks thought of Zeus or Hermes—you know, as some sort of a superhuman. Or else I can conjure up something that might have come from *Star Trek*, where Jesus is some kind of an emanation of God, or a holographic representation. But it's really hard for me to get my mind around it."

Neo leaned forward in his seat, with his bandaged forearm resting on the back of Carol's headrest. "Here's where I think we need to go back and reincarnate Jesus." Hearing the word 'reincarnate,' Carol shot Neo a wide-eyed glance in the rearview mirror. "I mean . . . you know, get Jesus back down to earth, from the realm of abstraction and philosophy into the flesh and blood of concrete history," Neo explained.

"Back into the story we find ourselves in." Kerry offered.

"Right. So let me try to set the stage. Kerry, do you remember when I told you the 'Conversation' episode of the story? I explained how the Israelites ended up in exile but eventually got back to Palestine."

"I forgot all the details," she said, "but, yes, I do remember the outlines of the story—north, middle, south, middle, and so on."

Neo continued, "Well, even though they were back in their homeland, they weren't free, so in their mind, the sense of exile never really ended. They were always under the domination of some Mediterranean superpower: the Persians, the Greeks, the Romans, with a couple other smaller regimes thrown in there too. And this becomes so formative in their ethos as a people. Nobody likes to be oppressed or dominated by a foreign power, but it is absolutely unacceptable when—"

Kerry anticipated, "When you fancy yourselves to be God's chosen people, and these batty idol worshipers seem to prosper as the winners while you seem to suffer as the losers."

"Exactly." Neo said. "So in the centuries before Christ, an intense expectation and anticipation builds up within the people. A deliverer is going to come, a messiah, someone like Moses and David and the prophets all wrapped up into one. And when he comes, watch out! He's going to kick Roman butt and lead the people of God to glorious victory! So—"

Carol was listening so intently that I had to interrupt Neo to remind her to take the Dulles access exit, and then we had to help her cut across several lanes of heavy traffic to avoid getting on the toll road. It was a pain, because none of the other drivers would let us into their lane. *The other drivers are especially crazy today,* I thought to myself. *It seems like everyone is on a cell phone too. Strange.*

23

BEAUTIFUL MUSIC
OF TRUTH AND GOODNESS

EVENTUALLY WE GOT ACROSS FOUR LANES of traffic and were safely, though slowly, moving along the Dulles access road. Neo continued with his story. "But here's the problem. Decades pass, but the messiah doesn't come. On several occasions, heroic groups of Jewish militants stage rebellions, hoping against hope that God will give them victory, maybe even believing that the messiah will emerge among them and give them miraculous success in spite of being so pathetically outnumbered. But no miracles come, and many of their greatest heroes are slaughtered. No deliverance. You can just imagine how the people would become more and more desperate, more and more anxious for their messiah to come.

"The people cope with their frustration and hope in four main ways. Some of them just accommodate. They give up hope, and figure that the Romans are here to stay, so they collaborate with the Romans and accept reality as it is. The tax collectors and a party called the Herodians probably are the best examples of this group. Others, known as the Zealots, say something like this: 'You know why the messiah hasn't come? Because really, we are the messiah. There is no superman coming to save us. No, we have to save ourselves. If we would stop waiting and praying and instead start acting and fighting, God would give us success. We need to grow up and face the reality that the only salvation that will come will require us to slit a few Roman throats and launch some heroic and strategic attacks.'

"On the opposite extreme, you have another group, one that figures very prominently in the Gospels—the Pharisees. They say something like this: 'No, we cannot save ourselves through military action. We're hopelessly outnumbered. The only salvation that will come will be miraculous, from God. The reason that the messiah has not come is our own fault: we are too sinful. If all of Israel would just stop sinning, if we would all obey the law of God for even just one day and become more holy and devoted, then God would send the messiah, and we would be vindicated.'"

Carol caught Neo's attention in the rearview mirror. "I never really understood that, Neo. That makes a lot of sense. No wonder the Pharisees hated prostitutes and adulterers and drunkards so much: it was their fault that the messiah wouldn't come. So when Jesus was kind to the sinners, they would think that he was actually keeping the messiah from coming."

I was a bit nervous about Carol's habit of looking in the rearview mirror while talking to Neo, so I tried to get Neo talking again. "Keep going, Neo," I said.

"OK. You have the collaborators and the Zealots and the Pharisees. And finally you have those who simply wanted to remove themselves from society and set up their little enclaves out in the desert, like the Essenes. And it's into this very dynamic political and religious milieu that Jesus comes . . . and frustrates everyone's expectations."

"What do you mean?" Kerry asked.

"Well, take the Essenes. Jesus goes out into the desert for forty days, which they would have applauded. But then he goes back into society— a big mistake in their book. And as Carol said, when Jesus eats with tax collectors—prime examples of Roman collaborators, who had probably given up hope in the messiah and were just looking out for their own interests—and when he shows mercy to adulterers and treats prostitutes with kindness, his name is mud with the Pharisees. He's doing exactly the wrong thing: the Pharisees' strategy was to increase, not reduce, the shame and isolation of 'the sinners,' believing that shame and isolation would motivate them to clean up their act and fly right and prepare the way for the messiah."

I interrupted to continue Neo's thought. "And when Jesus says to turn the other cheek, it must have infuriated the Zealots. I'll bet that some of them had hopes that Jesus would arm his disciples and mobilize the crowds that followed him. But when he talked about being peacemakers instead, they must have thought he was a wimp. So he disappointed everybody."

Kerry replied, "Everybody but God, I suppose, right? Because in a way, Jesus would have been saying that they were all missing the point. This somehow connects back with what you said about the kingdom of God being revolutionary, right, Neo? And maybe also with the 'powerful weakness' theory of the atonement that you spoke about yesterday."

"Exactly. There's King Herod, who is a Roman collaborator, and there's Caesar himself. And Jesus basically says that they aren't that big a deal. People can enter the kingdom of God whether these earthly kings are supplanted or not. The real revolution sees something bigger than politics and nations and regimes. The real revolution emerges above or beyond all that—or maybe I should say *ahead of* all that. In fact, as I said yesterday on the boat, I think Jesus shows us that if we fight fire with fire, if we use violence and coercion, then we're functioning in the kingdoms of humanity, not the kingdom of God. Violent revolution isn't revolutionary enough."

I knew what was coming next. Neo held his bandaged left arm horizontally, and then traced an imaginary line on the bandage. "Here on this line you have all the different responses to injustice and evil and violence: the Essenes here, the collaborators here, the Pharisees here, the Zealots over here. Each group wants Jesus to legitimize their point on the line. But instead"—Neo held his right hand about six inches above his left forearm and made what was, for me, a familiar circling motion—"Jesus responds on a higher level altogether. That's the revolution: moving to the higher level with Jesus."

"And because they all feel disappointed that he doesn't back their agenda," Kerry said, "they all want to kill him. Amazing. Well, either he was brilliant, and he operated on your higher level, Neo, or he was a fool."

Neo turned in his seat and faced Kerry: "Kerry, that's probably a good starting point to answer your question . . . the one about how much do you have to believe in Jesus. For starters, you need to believe that he wasn't a fool or a wimp, but that he was, as you say, brilliant. That's not the finish line, but it's a good starting line.

"For the first disciples, I have to think that this is what they understood when they talked about believing in Jesus. As time went on, their understanding expanded and deepened, but it must have begun with this sense that Jesus' way, even though it was different from everyone else's, was . . . again, brilliant. The more I think about it, the more I like your word 'brilliant.' It gets to the heart of other important words in the Gospels."

"Such as?" Kerry asked. The conversation was really theirs now, with Carol and I eavesdropping.

"Well, for example, the word 'disciple' means 'learner.' You sign on as a teacher's disciple when you think that teacher is brilliant. You want to know and do what the teacher knows and does, so you apprentice yourself to the teacher."

Kerry replied, "That sounds more like an Eastern thing, you know, with Jesus being a kind of guru or something."

"Well, remember," Neo said, "that Christianity started as an Eastern religion, or Middle Eastern anyway. The word 'guru' is pretty close to the word for a Jewish rabbi in those days—a 'master.' That's where we get the word 'Lord.' It doesn't so much mean 'master' in reference to a slave, but master in the sense of . . . in the sense of a master of martial arts, for example, or a master craftsman or a violin master."

"Except with Jesus," Kerry said, "it was more like saying he was the master of living."

"Yes, that's very good," Neo said. "A violin master is someone who can take an instrument of wood and wire and horsehair and play it so that it yields music more beautiful than anyone else can play. And for the disciples to call Jesus 'master' would mean . . . yes, it would mean that no one else could take the raw materials of life—skin and bone and blood and space and time and words and deeds and waking and sleeping and eating and walking—and elicit from them a beautiful song of truth and goodness, as Jesus did."

Carol spoke up again. "Neo, you keep doing that. You keep putting a new twist on things. I've always thought of 'Lord' as a kind of theological term for Jesus' divinity. That's really a new spin on things for me."

"That's certainly not to minimize Jesus' divinity. And really, any new spin is an old spin, I would hope, Carol," he replied. Then he turned back to Kerry. "I think that's how the first disciples understood it, that instead of following the self-seeking way of the collaborators, or the judgmental religious way of the Pharisees, or the isolationist way of the Essenes, or the violent way of the Zealots, they believed that Jesus' way was higher, and more brilliant, and . . . and the right way to launch a revolution of God. He was the master in a way that made Herod and Caesar look trivial by comparison. And when you think about it, who today is studying the teachings of Herod, or patterning their life after Caesar?"

"You didn't know my boss back at UCSB," Kerry joked. "Seriously, Neo, you've described exactly how I honestly feel about Jesus. It's when we get into the dogma about Jesus that I get a bit more nervous," she replied.

"Well, let's put the . . . I like Dan's term, 'mystery' . . . let's put the mysteries back in the context of the story, rather than trying to have them float out in space somewhere, disconnected from the narrat—"

Just then, Carol interrupted our pretty intense conversation by pointing out a rusty old Pinto in front of us, covered in bumper stickers, all of a religious nature. "'In case of the rapture, this car will self-destruct,'" Carol read. Then, "'Pray the prayer of Jabez.'"

"What's the rapture, and who's Jabez?" Kerry asked.

"Don't worry about it," Neo and I replied, in unison.

Carol read another one. "'Christians aren't perfect, just forgiven.'"

Kerry responded, "Well, I guess I agree, but I don't much like the attitude. Sounds kind of smug, you know?"

"It's the word 'just' that bugs me," Neo said.

"There's my favorite," Carol said, pointing to a large fish with the name "Jesus" inside, eating a smaller fish with the name "Darwin" inside.

She was intentionally needling Neo, but Neo wouldn't go along. "I find it disgusting and repulsive," he said with mock seriousness, "unless you want to interpret it to say that Jesus has a place even for Darwin." We laughed, except Carol, who made a face.

Kerry read, "'God is my copilot,'" and then added, "Well, it says a lot for God's humility to ride in a beastly looking jalopy like that!"

Neo said, "Besides, I think God would rather be pilot than copilot, you know?" We laughed again. I recommended that we get back to the story.

Neo continued. "OK. So we have this man Jesus, and obviously he's extraordinary—not the type to heartlessly devour Darwin, but the kind to love and redeem him, I must remind you, Carol. Now imagine you're one of Jesus' disciples, and you've quit your job and begun following him through the land. You aren't really clear what his plan is, since he isn't affiliated with any of the existing political parties or movements, but you feel that something significant is up. And you witness things that you can't explain. There are healings, and astounding episodes involving weather and food and drink. It's not just that they're astounding though; it's that each one seems pregnant with symbolism, with meaning. The biblical way of expressing it is that they're 'signs,' meaning significant and meaningful, and they're 'wonders,' meaning wonderful and astounding."

"And you really believe that those things happened?" Kerry asked. "I mean, literally? Sometimes it seems a bit far-fetched to me, like believing in Satan. I hope you don't think I'm being blasphemous, it's just that, you know, with my background and all . . ."

"I suppose there could have been some exaggeration, some legendizing—if you don't mind me inventing a word. I mean, it's possible. Human beings do this sort of thing with heroic figures, and many people who believe in Jesus feel that some of the miracle stories are fictionalized, not to be dishonest but to make a point. But if Jesus really is in some mysterious and unique way sent from God and full of God, then it's not at all impossible or even unreasonable to believe that he would precipitate some miracles. If there's ever a good time for miracles, that would be it, you know? Because miracles are just creative acts, when you think about it. Of course, miracles are problematic too, so I don't want to make too much of them. Jesus didn't."

Kerry must have recalled that earlier conversation with Neo and Glenn, when they had discussed miracles, but Carol gave Neo another sideways glance in the rearview mirror. Neo responded to her implied question. "Jesus was always telling people to keep quiet about his miracles. He seemed to be almost embarrassed by them. And I can see why, because if you do one miracle, you have a real problem. Can you see it?"

Carol was silent for a minute, and then said, "Well, if you do one, then why not two, and if two, then why not three, and if three, then why not . . . why not just remake the whole world the way you want it?"

Neo asked, "OK, and based on what we've said so far, what's wrong with that?"

Carol paused before replying. "Well, I guess that as soon as you do that, the world isn't its own story anymore. It stops being a real world and becomes a . . . a contrived world."

Kerry stepped in here, having covered this territory before. "So much comes back to that first episode—'Creation'—doesn't it?"

Neo continued without answering, interpreting her question as rhetorical. "Of course, there's one miracle that is more significant than all the others. Imagine how the disciples must have felt when Jesus was arrested and crucified."

Kerry replied, "They must have been completely gobsmacked. It's like their worst nightmare. As you're explaining this, a whole sinister pattern is emerging in my mind. The whole world is upside down. The Jewish people, who should be the most prosperous and triumphant, are at the bottom of the heap, with the idolatrous and immoral Romans over them. And then Jesus, who seems so good and right and compassionate, promises a better way, but he gets betrayed and snuffed out. So the bad guys completely and utterly win. It's tragic. It's as if Jesus ignites this glimmer of hope of something up on that higher level"—now Kerry's hand was moving in a small circle in the air, recalling Neo's earlier illustration—"and now the hope is smashed under the heel of Caesar's violence." With that, she crushed her circling hand with the other fist.

"And then comes the sign and wonder of the resurrection," Neo said, reaching over and lifting up her circling hand again.

Kerry's voice was animated as she said, "And that would mean . . . I think I'm beginning to see your point, Neo . . . that would mean that even if the worst things happen, even if the worst people remain in power and the best people are killed, don't be afraid, because God is going to triumph; and Jesus' approach, his nonviolence, his compassion, his higher perspective—it's all validated after all. God's revolution can be resisted, but never defeated."

Neo wasn't finished. "OK, Kerry, and if you believe that, then how are you going to live?"

"Well, you'll want to do right, no matter what the odds, and you'll keep loving and refusing to hate. And you'll . . . you'll trust God no matter what happens, because even though God's power seems weak—weak

enough to be betrayed and tortured and killed—it rises again and promises to win in the end."

At that point, Neo asked me something, but I didn't hear him, because
I was perplexed by something completely unrelated to our conversation.
Finally, Neo had to reach up and touch me on the shoulder. "Daniel, where
are you?"

"I'm sorry," I said. "What did you ask?"

"I asked if you think Kerry's getting it, you know, getting the gospel,
man. But what's got you so preoccupied?"

"It's the strangest thing," I answered. "Look at those cars over there.
Nearly every single driver is on a cell phone. I've never seen so many people on phones and driving at the same time. If you don't mind, I want to
flip the radio on and find out if something's going on."

24

SENT OUT TO PLAY

I PRESSED THE "ON" BUTTON on my car radio. There was nothing but static. Of course. My stupid antenna had broken off just the other day. Whatever was going on, if anything, we'd have to wait until we got to Dulles to find out about it. I expected traffic to be heavy on a Tuesday morning, but this was extraordinary. Just as we came in sight of the airport, we reached a near-standstill.

"That's odd," Kerry said. "We're this close to the airport, and I don't see any planes coming in."

"There can't be any weather problems," Carol said. "Look at this glorious sunshine." She was right. It was the second perfect September day in a row—sunny, low humidity, not too warm. Perfect.

I was having trouble concentrating. Why were all these other drivers talking on their cell phones? I couldn't shake the feeling that something was wrong. But Kerry was less anxious, and she asked Neo, "Well, are we ready to start episode six?"

Neo replied, "We could, I suppose, but there's one more thing I wanted to say about Christ, and really, it's a great segue into the next episode."

Carol was looking into the rearview mirror again. "Take your time, Neo. Even one of Kerry's Galápagos tortoises could beat this traffic."

"Well, one of the really important things Jesus did that we haven't really talked about directly was . . . was creating a community of followers. We talk a lot about Christianity and Christians, but in Jesus' day, there was no such thing as a Christian, and Christianity, as we know it, didn't exist yet. At that point, there were disciples—people who followed Jesus—and there was a way of living as disciples. Later, they got the nickname 'Christian,' which just means 'little Christ' or 'mini-messiah,' and their way of living became known as 'Christianity,' which might better be called a *messianic way of living*."

"Whatever you mean by 'messianic,' I wouldn't really think of Christianity as a way of living," Kerry said. "It seems to me to be more about a system of beliefs—you know, doctrines, dogmas, institutions, traditions, rituals, rules, that sort of thing. I know that Dan doesn't like the terms 'doctrine' and 'dogma,' but I still think that for most people, that's what Christianity brings to mind."

"That's my point, really," said Neo. "Christianity is a human creation. Theology is a human creation. Institutions are human creations. That doesn't mean they're bad. It just means they're human creations. If we root ourselves again in the story, we realize that it all starts with Jesus and this community of disciples, and we keep returning to the source, you know?"

"And you're still using 'disciple' in that more Eastern sense of the word, related to 'master,' right?" Kerry asked.

"Yes, exactly." Neo said. "Really, there were two words, two sides of a coin, to describe the early followers of Jesus. First, they were disciples, which speaks of their being called together to learn. But equally important—and this was intrinsic to the idea of being a disciple—they were also apostles, who would be sent out to practice and teach what they'd learned. That's what 'apostle' means, a person who is sent on a mission."

"So they're going to be called together to learn the violin, and then they'll be sent out to play the master's kind of music in the master's way?" Kerry asked.

"Perfect. I like your choice of the word 'play.' And they'll be sent out to gather new violinists who want to learn to play the master's way too. Plus, I imagine that the master would want all players to become composers as well," Neo said, "so there would be more and more music in his tradition."

"How much does all this still apply to Christians today?" Kerry asked. "I don't think most churchgoers in my dad's parish back in Alice Springs thought of themselves in anything close to these terms. For them, being a Christian was part of belonging to the nicer class of Australians. It meant that they spent Sunday mornings in a certain way, and that they avoided pornography and adultery and excessive alcohol—at least they were supposed to—and they shared certain, more conservative political views. And, of course, they wanted to gain more and more knowledge about the Bible, and they wanted to be prepared to go heaven when they passed on."

Neo laughed, and then he reached up and nudged my shoulder. "Daniel, brings back memories, eh? What would you say to Kerry on her definition of a Christian?"

Because I was still distracted with the traffic and cell phones in other drivers' hands, I had to ask her to repeat it, which she did. Then I said,

"Well, I think you've pretty accurately described what most people think Christianity is about. And Neo would say, and I would agree wholeheartedly, that we need to develop a new kind of Christian more along the lines of the original disciples—people who are called together, as Neo said, to learn from Jesus, and then are sent out into the world to exemplify and pass on what they learn."

"What would that look like, Dan, in today's world?" Kerry asked. "It's one thing in tunics and sandals, but it's another thing in traffic!" Before I could respond, she turned back to Neo and said, "This is more of what got you in trouble with Maricel, isn't it? She felt like you were advocating something different from the normal categories that she was used to. Maybe she felt like you were trying to be a Christian up here"—she was making a circular motion with her hand—"instead of down on the normal line?"

Neo smiled and shrugged, and then quickly got back to his original point. "I'm sure that Maricel would agree that being a Christian is at the most profound level a matter of following Jesus, of believing that he's the master at living, and apprenticing ourselves to him so that we can learn to play the music of life as he does. And of course, that brings hope for beyond this life as well as within it."

Carol said, "So Jesus brings together this community of men and women who are called out from the crowds to be disciples, and then these disciples will be sent back into the world on a mission of expressing Jesus' message of God's kingdom, and helping others become disciples who will in turn help others, and so on. I guess that's the way the revolution spreads."

Kerry replied, "That makes sense, Carol. And it spreads from country to country and generation to generation and . . . and to everyone's utter surprise, here I am! That's what I'm signing on for, isn't it—this way of living with a mission, this spiritual revolution?"

"In my experience, Kerry," Carol said, "it often feels less like you have the mission, and more like the mission has you."

"Either way, I reckon I like this," Kerry said.

Carol pulled into the parking lot. It was almost 9:00 A.M. The traffic had made us later than we wanted to be. Kincaid's plane was scheduled to arrive in about twenty minutes. We parked and walked as fast as we could, with Kerry still needing her cane.

When we entered the beautiful Dulles terminal, my earlier sense that something was wrong now intensified. People were gathered around in little groups, talking. All lines had been abandoned. We noticed that a huge crowd had gathered beyond the front check-in area. When we came to the fringe of the crowd, we could see that one of the ceiling-mounted TV screens was the center of attention. I didn't know what was happening, but my heart started pounding, really pounding.

It took a minute to realize what we were seeing. It was the New York skyline—live or prerecorded, we didn't know. One of the skyscrapers . . . was it one of the World Trade Center towers? . . . was burning and smoking. As we watched, transfixed, no one in the crowd speaking, a little dot— an airplane—angled in from the left side of the screen and disappeared into the other twin tower. Everyone gasped, and voices emerged from the loud murmur that arose from the crowd. "Did you see that?"

"Was that another one?"

"Oh, my God."

"This is unbelievable."

"Jesus Christ."

25

PLOTTING A SPIRITUAL REVOLUTION

CAROL TOOK MY HAND, and then Kerry's, and then I noticed that Kerry took Neo's as well. We just stood there watching, not speaking, searching each other's eyes when we could tear ourselves away from the screen. Then the CNN cameras switched to the Pentagon, with black, black smoke billowing up. What was going on? We didn't know how those planes had come to crash into the buildings; there was talk first of accidents, then of hijackings, but so much of the reporting was conjecture. The crowd around us had almost doubled in size, and a strange hush lingered as we everyone strained to hear the newscasters explain what was going on. Terrorists. Hijackings. Boston airport. Newark airport. Then reports of a crash in Pennsylvania. All flights were ordered to land at the nearest airport.

Then we watched the two towers fall—whether live or prerecorded we still didn't know—one tower, then the other, and the wave of smoke and dust rolling through the streets. We could hear the sounds of beeping alarms and the strangely muffled sirens through the TV speaker, the breathless reports from those at the scene. We were paralyzed, dumbstruck. After some time, maybe forty minutes or more—I can't remember—Neo caught my eye and motioned that he and Kerry were going over toward the United Airlines counter.

Carol and I waited a little longer. "Do you think it's safe to be here?" Carol asked in a whisper.

"'Safe' just became a relative term," I whispered back.

Another twenty minutes or so passed. We tore ourselves away from the screen and found Neo and Kerry. Kincaid's flight had been ordered to land in Kansas City, Missouri. I pulled out my mobile phone, and Kerry used it to try to reach Kincaid on his, but the circuits were all busy. We all agreed that we should get home.

That darn car radio! *Who knows what's happening as we drive along here, out of touch?* I thought. Carol and Kerry took turns trying to reach first our kids' schools and then Kincaid, but the phones were as useless as the radio. Then Kerry succeeded in getting through to Kincaid. There was nothing they could change or fix or even figure out at this point, but they were glad just to hear the other's voices.

That was Tuesday, September 11, a day everyone remembers with surreal clarity. The kids got home before we did; schools had let our early, and the traffic getting home was worse than the traffic had been getting to Dulles. Everyone, except me, spent the rest of the day sitting in front of the TV, switching back and forth from CNN to MSNBC to CBS to ABC to NBC. Kincaid reached us in the early afternoon to give us his hotel phone number. He was OK.

Later in the afternoon, Neo took Kerry for a walk around the neighborhood. I wondered again about the nature of their relationship. Kerry's left arm was in Neo's right (unbandaged) arm, and her right hand held her cane. Was their contact just for her physical stability and support, or was it something more? It wasn't my business, I told myself, but still I wondered.

While everyone else was watching TV or otherwise occupied, I was busy setting up a prayer meeting at Potomac Community Church. We spread the word through e-mail and a sign in front of the church: we would open the church that night for prayer. Wednesday night we did the same. Thursday evening we didn't have a prayer service, but the president had asked people to gather for prayer on Friday afternoon, so we planned a special service for noon. Neo returned Kerry to NIH on Wednesday morning, as planned, and he kept himself busy around our house, reading, watching CNN, while I was busy at the church.

He attended all three prayer meetings—the first times he had seen me "in action" in my ministry at PCC. After the Friday service, he pulled me aside and said, "You've done a great job, man. You're a good pastor. But you look tired. I'd be glad, if you'd like me to, to preach for you on Sunday. I got quite a bit of practice at Aventura."

I hate to admit this, but my first reaction was to think, *No way.* I loved Neo, and I valued his friendship and role as a spiritual mentor for me. But I worried that if he preached, he would create controversy with some of his unusual views. That felt like more stress, not less. I still hadn't told him about the tensions I felt building in the church board.

I think he anticipated my reaction, because he then added, "It's OK. Just consider it an open offer if you need a break." I assured him that I felt I could handle it, and that he had in fact already helped me with the sermon, through our conversations in recent days.

Neo returned to the airport on Friday evening to pick up Kincaid, who was lucky to get one of the first flights when they resumed after the shutdown. They went straight to the hospital and returned Friday evening, about ten o'clock. Kincaid looked pretty shaken when they walked in the door. Carol put out the last two pieces of pie and brewed some spice tea. Pretty soon Kincaid opened up. "I don't think I would have recognized Mom if I had seen her on the street," he said. "Gosh, her hair, and her face . . ." he said, staring at a piece of peach pie on his fork.

He kept thanking us for our kindness to his mom, and Carol kept assuring him that she had been a bigger blessing to us than we had been to her. "Your mom's a wonderful lady," Carol said, putting her hand on Kincaid's hand. I saw one tear ride down his face and drop from his chin onto the table.

Kincaid was a striking fellow in appearance. He was of average height, with thick blond hair that he wore in a ponytail not unlike the one his mother had when I first met her. He had a small silver stud piercing his right eyebrow, and a small blue-green stone (I think it was agate) dangled in an earring from his left ear. He also wore a dark red stone mounted in a ring on his little finger. His fingers were long—guitar player's fingers, I thought, and it turned out I was right. He was smooth-faced, with a few hairs on his chin—all the beard he could muster, I thought.

We loaned Kincaid a car on Saturday so he could have time alone with his mother. He brought her home Saturday night on a twenty-four-hour pass. Her blood counts were still below the levels needed to resume chemo, but they were rising encouragingly. Late that night, they made a call to Australia to tell Kerry's mother what was happening. She had wondered why Kerry hadn't e-mailed lately, but she had no idea that Kerry was in the hospital. Kincaid and Kerry tried to be as upbeat as possible, as Mrs. Ellison was unwell herself, and would not be able to visit.

Sunday came, and everyone came to church with us. Kincaid and Kerry sat beside Carol in the first row while I preached. Kincaid looked nervous—his church experiences so far had been very few, and he didn't know what to expect. Kerry looked tired but happy to have her son beside her with his arm around her. Because of her week's reprieve from chemo, she had a little colorless fuzz growing on her head, which was covered today in a blue bandana.

Here's part of the text of the sermon I preached that day. Neo smiled and nodded at me several times during the delivery, acknowledging, I think, that a lot of my content had come from our conversations, and that he was, in a sense, preaching with me.

○

NEVER BE THE SAME AGAIN

The world has changed, and this changing is likely the beginning of more changes that we cannot yet realize. All of us will remember for the rest of our lives where we were on Tuesday when we heard the news of the terrorist attacks, when we watched TV and saw those jets gracefully and nightmarishly flying toward the towers of the World Trade Center, saw the surreal collapse of the towers and the cloud of smoke and dust rolling through the streets of New York, saw the black smoke billowing up from the Pentagon. The world has changed. And I hope we will change too, because the tragedy of September 11 will only be intensified if we do not seize the opportunity to change for the better in response to it.

C. S. Lewis is a hero to many Christians today. Listen to what he said about sixty years ago, during World War II: "The war creates no absolutely new situation, it simply aggravates the permanent human situation so that we can no longer ignore it."

I think that those are words we need to hear today. Trent, my twelve-year-old son, was watching the news with me the other morning over breakfast, and he said, "It feels like our world has become more like the world of the Bible." How true, I thought. Trent and C. S. Lewis are right: what we are experiencing puts us in sync with the real human condition, the condition that the Bible chronicles, the condition that the gospel addresses. I would like to try to put last Tuesday's tragedy in the context of this larger story, which my friend Neil Oliver calls "The Story We Find Ourselves In."

[In the next section of the sermon, I summarized the story as we had been conversing about it to that point: creation, crisis, calling, conversation, and Christ. Then I continued with the next episode, which I decided to call "community."]

This community of people, called together by Jesus, assured of God's unconquerable love, and sent with God's good news into the whole world, was called the church. And today, more than last Sunday, and perhaps more than any Sunday in any of our lifetimes, we have the opportunity to realize what the community of faith, hope, and love is to be, and who we are to be: a community that lives to see God's dream come true for our world.

Jesus was sent into the world to express, in word and deed, the saving love of God. We, as a community of faith, are similarly sent into the world to express, in word and deed, the saving love of God. Jesus was sent here on a mission, and he said, "As the Father sent me, so I send you." We have this mission, or, as my wife put it so eloquently the other day, God's mission has us.

On September 11, we saw the worst and the best of humanity. In the hijackers, we saw the destructive hatred of human beings made visible. In the rescue workers who rushed into danger to lead others out of danger, we saw the saving love of God made visible. In the hijackers, we saw a human agenda of hatred and revenge, of in-grouping and out-grouping, of taking life and disregarding justice. In the rescue workers, we saw God's agenda of compassion and courage, of seeking to save everyone, whatever their background or social class or religion or occupation or ethnic origin. In the hijackers, we see what we can become apart from God's grace, and in the rescue workers, we see what we can become through God's grace.

Since Tuesday, I've heard many people say, "Things will never be the same." And when we say those words, I think that we feel sadness, nostalgia. We will never feel the same safety. We have lost some of our innocence. Things will never be the same—those are sad words, words of grief and loss.

And at the same time, I think that there is another way we can say those words. Along with grief and sadness, we can feel a new sense of dedication, commitment, and resolve. Because too many of us have lived with the name "church" or the name "Christian," but not with deep passion as Christ's revolutionary community of faith and mission. Christianity has been little more than a belief system for us, not a way of life. It has been an institution, not a mission for our lives. It has made us nice people with confidence of heaven after this life, but not world-changing revolutionaries with hope for justice and peace in this life. It has given us the identity of religious people, not the identity of courageous rescue workers.

To be a community of faith and mission after September 11 is no different from before, except that perhaps September 11 can awaken us from our slumber of complacency and consumerism, so that we see more clearly than before what a difference it makes if we shirk our mission or if we work our mission. A nineteenth-century British statesman, Edmund Burke, said, "All that is necessary for the forces of evil to win in this world is for enough good men to do nothing," and I speak very personally here, that September 11 has awakened me both to the reality of those forces of evil, and to the importance of my mission as a Christian, as a member of Christ's revolutionary community of faith, hope, and love.

So how do we respond? How do we live our common mission in these troubled days? Let me close by offering three responses.

First, we must remember that our mission is global. We have duties as Americans, special duties to our compatriots, to our government, to our leaders. As a nation extraordinarily gifted in so many ways, we have duties that go beyond those of other nations, since much is expected from those to whom much has been given. But those national or political duties are not our highest calling as followers of Jesus. We are Christ's missional community of faith. As members of the church of Jesus Christ, we must fulfill our national duties within the context of our larger global calling: to go into the whole world with God's saving love.

That means that we must not allow ourselves to hate anyone. We must not seek revenge. Our enemy, the gospel tells us, is not flesh and blood, not human beings. Our enemy is spiritual forces, transpersonal realities that Paul sometimes called "principalities and powers," forces of evil that hijack people and cultures much as the terrorists hijacked airplanes. If we allow ourselves to be overtaken by hatred and revenge, by fear and prejudice, then we become hijacked agents of the principalities and powers too, without realizing it. If we seek to fight fire with fire, we will all be consumed.

No, this is not a time for fighting fire with fire. On the contrary, this is a time for self-examination. The splinter in our brother's eye is acutely obvious to us at this moment: our brother's violence and hatred are easy for us to see. But what plank do we have in our own eye? What have we been missing about our own outlook? Now is a time for seeking an answer to that question.

And now is a time to ask ourselves how God can send us into the world on a mission of saving love. I'm not saying there is no place for a military mission. I imagine we will hear more about that sort of thing from our president in the days ahead. But I am saying that for us, if we discover who we are in this crisis, we will realize that the most important mission is never military; it is spiritual. It is a mission of saving love. And the violence of these days tells us more than ever that this world needs nonviolent rescue workers, sent into the whole world with God's saving love.

Second, we must take this global mission and make it local. I have been praying about what I and we can do in our own area to overcome evil with good, and I have an idea. After church today, I would like to drive over to the local mosque and assure our Muslim neighbors that we love and respect them, that we don't hold them responsible for these terrible atrocities. I saw on the news the other day that since September 11, many Muslim women are afraid to go out in public, because their dress makes them conspicuous, and they fear being singled out or harassed. I wonder if any of you women here would like to provide your names and phone numbers so that women from the mosque can call you to accompany them to the store or doctor's office or wherever. If you leave your contact information at the table in the narthex, I will bring that information with me this afternoon. It's a small thing, but I think that friendships change the world, and this would be a great way of initiating some friendships.

Third, I would like to ask you to consider making the coming months, as long as this crisis continues, a special time of reflection on our mission. It strikes me that what we're learning about terrorist cells has something to tell us about what it means to be the community of faith. Terrorist cells involve small groups of people secretly banding together, willing to give their lives for their cause, plotting how they can spread fear and violence to achieve their own ends. In much the same way, but with a completely different motivation, the church brings together cells of committed people, willing to give their lives for God's mission, plotting a spiritual revolution of love and hope and reconciliation to achieve God's dream. I don't know where this will lead, but I would like to invite our whole congregation to enter a time of reevaluation to learn who we are after September 11.

The world will never be the same again, and I hope that we will never be the same again either. I trust that God will use these days of evil and violence to inspire us as never before to be an authentic missional community of faith, hope, and love, sent into the world on a rescue mission with a message about the revolution of God—a revolution of love, not hate; joy, not terror; peace, not violence. Let's observe a few moments of silence together now, to contemplate this tragedy and its impact on our world, and to dedicate ourselves to never be the same again.

○

After the service, nearly a hundred women left their contact information. When I went to the mosque that afternoon, I found the imam and said, "I am sorry that I have never come by and introduced myself earlier. I am here today to say that I hope there won't be any problems, but if there are, you can count on me and on the people of Potomac Community Church to be there for you in any way we can. As a first step of friendship, I understand that many Muslim women are nervous about going out in public. Here are the names and phone numbers of women from my church who would be happy to accompany them anywhere they need to go."

As I handed him the list, he pulled out his glasses and silently looked down at it, and then looked up at me, his brown eyes brimming. He said, "There are no words to express what this means to us. I wish I had the vocabulary, the eloquence. Thank you, thank you." He reached out to shake my hand, but then reached around and embraced me. He was a short man, and I still recall the feeling of his face pressed hard against my chest.

26

KENYAN DOUBLE-ROAST CAFFE LATTE

WHEN I GOT HOME, Kerry was taking a nap on the couch, and Kincaid was sitting by her on the floor, stroking her hand. CNN was on the TV, but the sound was turned all the way down. He smiled at me, and quietly got up and came over to me. "Dan," he whispered, "any chance we could talk for a few minutes, in private?"

I had been hoping for a nap, but I assumed that Kincaid wanted to talk about his mother, so I whispered back, "Sure. We can sit in the living room."

"How about we go out for a cup of coffee?" he asked, and so ten minutes later we found ourselves at a nearby Starbucks. We chatted about the attacks, airline security, and what we thought would happen next. Then there was a brief pause, and I asked him what he wanted to talk with me about.

"Your lecture this morning . . . or, I guess I should call it a sermon. Anyway, it was pretty good . . . I mean, better than I expected . . . oh, crap, this is coming out all wrong. You see, I've never really gone to church, except to my grandfather's funeral. The whole time I was in the church that day, I was like, thinking, you know, wondering why people like you and my grandfather devote your lives to something that's never seemed that . . . that important or worthwhile or even good to me. But I could tell that this isn't just a . . . like . . . tradition for you. And also, my mom—she started telling me that something is going on with her, like spiritually and all, and well, I think that's good, because I understand that her relapse is pretty serious. But I guess all this is just kind of freaking me out, and I don't really have anybody in my life I can talk to about religion, so that's . . ."

"Sure, Kincaid," I said. "That makes perfect sense. Maybe—"

"One more thing," he interrupted. "I felt something this morning, you know, like God or something. And I'm not sure I believe that it was real, but I thought maybe I could tell you what I felt, and then maybe you could help me, you know, interpret it or something."

I asked him to explain, and he continued, "Well, I think it was during a prayer, and I didn't really pray. It sounds strange, but I don't know how to begin. But anyway, I just sat there quietly, and two really strong feelings, or . . . thoughts . . . ideas . . . crap, Mr. Poole, Dan, I don't know what to call them. A couple things hit me, but I'm not sure, as I said, if they were real. Anyway, first, I felt this overwhelming sense that someone knew my name. I guess that sounds kind of strange, but it was as if God was somehow—like if God really exists—God was right there around me or partly inside me or something, and he . . . or she or whatever . . . was telling me that he knew my name."

Kincaid was looking down at his hands, staring at that red stone in his ring, and I gave him some time before I invited him to continue. "The second thing, Dan, was even stronger. It was this feeling that I was loved, or accepted, or welcomed, like I was arriving at a place I had never been before, you know? And they were glad to see me in spite of . . . I don't know, in spite of something—maybe that I had never taken the time to come there before. Does this make any sense at all? What was that about, Dan, you know, in your opinion, or from your perspective? I mean, I don't expect you to read my mind or anything."

"Kincaid," I replied, "I think that was the Holy Spirit, God's Spirit, telling you some important things."

"I'm sorry, Dan. I know that has to do with the Trinity, as in 'Father, Son, and . . . ,' right? But I don't know much more beyond that."

I had finished my coffee, so I removed the plastic lid from the cardboard cup and showed the cup to Kincaid. "Let's imagine this cup is your life. Let's say that in some way you took off the lid and emptied yourself this morning. Maybe just by being there at church, you were in a sense making some space in your life for God. God's Spirit is the way God comes in to fill the empty space in your life. It sounds like God was letting you know that God is there. I think that the next move is yours."

"The next move? What do you mean?" Kincaid asked.

"Well, I think you can put the lid back on"—I snapped the lid onto the cup—"and say, 'God, I acknowledge that you're there. Thanks for making contact. Don't call me, I'll call you.' Or else you can snap the lid off"— which I did—"and say, 'God, please come into my life. Please fill the empty space inside me. I don't just want to acknowledge that you exist. I want to have you in my life.' Does that make sense?"

"Sense? Yeah, I guess so. But I don't know what to do with that. I guess I could say that, but I'm not one hundred percent sure I'd mean it. Where does doing that, like, take me?"

"Well," I said, "remember how in my sermon, or lecture, this morning, I was talking about Jesus creating this missional community? Were you following me at that point?"

"Sure. I felt like you were saying that Jesus started something and sent us, or Christians or whoever, into the world to continue what he started. You talked about saving love, and that made me think of my mom—you know, her love for wildlife and her desire to save it from extinction. So I guess you were saying that God wants to save us from extinction, so he sends Jesus, and Jesus sends us . . . or maybe I shouldn't say 'us' . . . but maybe I should. . . . I don't know. Maybe I missed the whole point."

"No, I think you got it beautifully. OK. So Jesus wants to send us—and I think you *should* include yourself in that, if you want to, but there's a problem. Jesus left a long time ago, which leaves us here on our own. How can we be sure we're really doing Jesus' thing, Jesus' mission?"

"Isn't that where the Bible is supposed to fit in?" Kincaid asked.

"Good point," I said, "That's really important. And I think that Jesus does something beyond that even. I think that Jesus says he will actually come inside us, like coffee pouring into the empty cup. His Spirit is waiting to pour in, if you'll just open up the lid and say, 'I'm ready. Please come in.' And when God's Spirit comes in, I think he does two, no, three really important things. First, I think he tries to be himself in you, while you're being yourself. In other words, he tries to live in you, so that you become a more Christlike person. I know that the word 'Christian' means a lot of different things to different people, but it's supposed to mean 'Christlike person,' and I think that's the first thing that the Holy Spirit wants to do inside you."

"So wherever I go, people wake up and smell the coffee, huh?" Kincaid said with a faint smile.

"That's a great way to put it. I like that," I said. "So first, the Spirit percolates a really strong brew of Christ inside you. And second, I think that the Spirit motivates you and guides you and empowers you to be part of the mission. I think that each person experiences this in a different way. In one person, the Holy Spirit energizes the desire to teach, and in another person, he gives an ability to care for the poor or to raise and give away money to good causes. Another person finds the Spirit motivating him to try super-difficult things. . . ."

"Like when Neo tried to get through to my mom about God and faith. I think that was a super-difficult thing, but it seems to be working. I think that Neo really has the Holy Spirit, and you and Carol do too," Kincaid said.

"That's good," I replied. "I'm glad you feel that. So I guess you could say the Holy Spirit tries to do something *in* you—make you more like Jesus—and then tries to do something *through* you by involving you in God's mission somehow and giving you some special part of the mission to do. Then the third thing is that the Holy Spirit tries to connect you with other people, so that what he does in and through one person is coordinated with what he does in and through another person, and so on. That way, it's not just a bunch of individuals working on the same cause, but it's people really united in one Spirit. And that's what the community of faith is supposed to be."

"So we get all the coffee cups together, and hopefully, they're all full of the same coffee, and together, the aroma is even stronger. That works for me," Kincaid said, with a kind of earnestness and sincerity that seemed significant to me.

I had this strange feeling that when he said, "That works for me," it was a kind of confession of faith. I spontaneously lifted my empty cup, and he tapped his half-full one against it. "To the community of faith," I said. "And to God's Spirit inside us."

"To the Kenyan double-roast caffe latte that gives us a full-bodied aroma," he said.

In the car on the way home, Kincaid said, "I hope I won't offend you, but I think I should tell you what I'm thinking." I told him to go ahead, and he continued. "Well, back at Starbucks, we were talking about the church in really positive terms—you know, being filled with God's coffee, and being on a mission of saving love, each person having something special to offer the others, and all that stuff. But, again, no offense, my impression of the church isn't all that hot. Maybe more like freeze-dried instant decaf or something."

"That doesn't offend me," I said. "I think you're right. Every church I've ever seen has had a lot of problems. That used to really bother me."

"But it doesn't any more? You got used to it?" he asked.

"Think of it like this. Let's say that today is the day you let God's Spirit come into your life. I think you'll admit that you've got some problems and faults and weaknesses, right?"

"True that," he said.

"Well," I went on, "I think that God's Spirit helps you grow, but it's a gradual process. So if we take your imperfections, and add them to mine, and your mom's, and Carol's, and Neo's, and a million other people's, then we have to face the fact that the church is in process. It has a lot of problems, but it also has God's creative power at work. So we shouldn't be surprised that the church has a lot of problems and makes a lot of mistakes. It's filled with messed-up people like us, and the percolation isn't finished yet."

"Yeah, Dan, but it would be nice if God had a little higher standards, you know? I mean, for years all I really knew about church I got from late-night cable. Sometimes me and my friends at school would just howl watching that lady with the big black wig and the costume jewelry and the fake eyelashes. It's not great PR, you know?"

I shook my head, half-laughing. "Yeah, I agree, it's pretty embarrassing. But try this: What if God looks at that lady, and sees right through her caked-on makeup and big wig, and sees a heart that is half-full of hypocrisy and who knows what else, but also sees that she really wants to help people and really wants to love God? And what if God looks at you and me the same way—a mix of sincerity and fake eyelashes and gaudy jewelry and big hair and bad makeup? In that way, her TV show is a pretty accurate mirror for all of us."

"Whew. I wish I could have you explain that to my buddies at school."

"You know, we Christians have done a lot of bad things throughout history. Sometimes we were doing the best we could, but we just didn't have a clue. Other times we were falling way below our high ideals, and we knew it. One of the best things I think we can do is just admit that—not to try to make ourselves look better, or to distance ourselves from the bad reputation. I think we say, 'Yes, that's us. We haven't done so well. But God isn't done with us yet, and the story isn't over yet. So let's pick up and keep moving in our mission.'"

"Just keep brewing. I like that, Dan," Kincaid said, and again, "That works for me." He thought for a moment. "Maybe you can help me find a church back in California when I go back. I wouldn't know where to begin to try to look."

"I'll see what I can do," I said. "But remember, the idea isn't just to find a place to attend. It's not like going to a concert or lecture."

"Oh, I know," he said. "I really liked what you said this morning. It's like a hope and love cell instead of a terrorist cell. It's something you are part of, like a team. That's what I want. I want to join something like that, not just spectate. I wish I lived here, because I'd join Potomac Community Church with you and Carol. I play guitar, you know. If I lived here, maybe I . . . maybe I could play in that band you had in the service."

"I wish you lived here too, Kincaid," I said. "That'd be great." And we were home. And Neo was standing on the front porch. He looked concerned.

27

A JUNIOR HIGH KID AT A DANCE

NEO WALKED OVER TO THE CAR. "I need to get Kerry back to the hospital," he said. "She says she's dizzy and nauseous, and her temperature is about 101. I offered to call an ambulance, but she'd rather we just drive her. Can we take your car?" Neo drove, and Kincaid, looking worried, rode in the back seat with his mom, her head resting on his lap.

As it turned out, it wasn't anything too serious. She was still somewhat immuno-compromised, and must have picked up a virus, the doctors said. They put her on prophylactic antibiotics to prevent secondary infection. Kincaid decided to spend the night at the hospital. Neo got home just after midnight. I was still up, plowing through nearly a week's worth of e-mail. I had spent the evening helping Corey with a project for a science fair. I always hated those things, but I loved the chance to be with my son, who took them very seriously.

"You made quite an impression on Kincaid," Neo told me. "He spent a long time talking to Kerry about his new understanding of the Holy Spirit and the doctrine of strong coffee." Neo chuckled and said, "Seriously, Dan, I think that what's happening to him and his mom is beautiful beyond all words."

"True that," I said, realizing how quickly I'd picked up the expression from Kincaid.

Kerry had asked Neo to catch her son up on the story—creation, crisis, calling, conversation, Christ, and, most recently, the new episode, which Neo called 'Church' and I called 'Community.' They'd been having some great talks. "He got a lot about the church from your sermon, Dan. Tonight, Kerry wanted me to go on and tell the final episode, but I just couldn't."

"Why? What is it?"

"I think I'll call it 'Consummation'—you know, eschatology, the end . . . hell, judgment, heaven, rewards, afterlife. But I just couldn't go there . . . not today."

The next evening, when Kincaid returned from the hospital with Neo, Kincaid sought me out (I was restacking some storage boxes in my garage) with another question. "Dan, can I ask you about prayer?"

"I don't think you mean prayer in the abstract, right? You're asking about praying for your mom."

"Yeah, I guess. I mean, I don't know much about praying at all, and especially for something like this. Is it OK for me to pray that God will . . . like . . . do a miracle? I mean, is that possible?"

"Anything is possible with God. But I should also say that not everyone . . . gets better."

Kincaid nodded, looking pensive. Then he teared up and said, "I don't know what to pray for. I think my mom's time is getting close."

I put my arm around his shoulder and said, "I think we should hope and pray for the best, but I also think we should prepare ourselves for the worst."

"I was thinking the same thing, basically," he said. "So I think I should pray that she'll make it, because that's what I really want. But I also think I should pray for strength, for both of us, for all of us, in case she doesn't."

I had an idea. "Kincaid, instead of talking about prayer, why don't we just pray, right now. Would that be OK?"

"Here in the garage? Well, OK, sure—but I feel kind of like a junior high kid at a dance. Like, I've never danced before, at least not in public, but maybe I should just get out on the floor and try."

I repositioned two boxes of books, we each sat on a box, and I prayed out loud. When I stopped, there was a moment of silence, and Kincaid began to pray. "Dear God, yesterday I felt like something happened between me and you. I took off the lid and let you pour yourself into me. And since then, I feel like there's a real connection between us. And I also feel like I have a special connection with Dan and Carol and Neo and my mom too, and all the people at Potomac Community Church, and everyone, really.

"I also want to thank you that . . . like I told Dan yesterday . . . that you know my name and that you love me. I realize that I haven't had much time for you in the past, but I know that's changing now. The big thing that's on my mind is my mother, God. I hope that you'll help her survive. This cancer is tough, but I believe you're tougher. But you might not want to intervene. I hope you will though. But if you don't, I'm going to need a lot of strength, and my mom is going to need a lot of courage. I sure wish you could do for her what you did for me, and let her know that you know her name too. But I think she already knows this. So I don't know exactly what to ask you for, except to tell you that I love my mom so much, and she has always been my greatest hero, and I am so thankful for her being my mom. And this is going to be really hard if we lose her. And that's all I have to say."

I reached over, placed my hand on Kincaid's shoulder, and prayed for him again. And then he prayed again, and then I did, and before we knew it, almost an hour had passed. When we finished, Kincaid said, "Wow, that was good. I needed that. I guess I can pray OK after all, and I guess church can happen in a garage, huh?"

I almost said, "True that," once again, but instead said, "Exactly. What happens when people gather on Sundays—or whenever they gather—is supposed to prepare them, give them some practice, so they can live for God throughout the week, wherever they go, including garages."

Kincaid helped me restack the rest of the boxes, and then we finished off a container of ice cream while watching CNN, and then called it a night.

The next several weeks passed with Kincaid and Neo visiting Kerry, one during the midday, the other during the evening. My kids loved having them around, because both Neo and Kincaid loved soccer, my kids' favorite sport. Many afternoons I would get back from the church and find all five of them playing soccer in the front yard, accompanied by a bunch of neighborhood kids. Some days, the group grew too large for the front yard, and so they'd move the game to an elementary school a few blocks away. It was a great sight: a tall black Jamaican with salt-and-pepper hair, a medium-sized white guy with a long blond ponytail and a pierced eyebrow, and maybe a dozen kids ranging from around Jess's age (seventeen) down to around Corey and Trent's age (twelve).

The terrorist attacks were never far from our minds, intensified by the anthrax scare in our area. And the uncertainty of Kerry's condition was also never far from our minds, although we were all relieved that she had resumed her chemo. In spite of these preoccupations, life returned to a kind of normalcy through October and into November. The only bad news came just before Halloween, when Kerry told us that Mildred had passed away. Relatives in West Virginia had taken the body home for burial, so there was no chance for any of us to pay our respects. When I told the kids about her death, they seemed pretty serious. She had made quite an impression on them.

Kerry's birthday came on November 14. She wasn't allowed to leave the hospital, so the whole extended family—Carol, Jess, Corey, Trent, and I, plus Neo and Kincaid—piled into our minivan and brought in a birthday dinner. We took over a family lounge and spread out the food—vegetarian Thai food, at Kerry's request, plus a chocolate cake (a strange combination, I know). We hung streamers and blew up balloons and tried to transform the rather sterile setting into a place for a party. We even brought along Jess's boom box, and we cranked up some Beatles music.

Kincaid brought Kerry into the room. She walked slowly, pulling an IV pole on wheels beside her. She was in jeans and a T-shirt, with a red bandana on her head and flip-flops on her feet. Corey, who was standing by me when Kerry came in, expressed my sentiments exactly when he leaned over and whispered to his twin brother, "Don't say anything about how she looks, OK? Just act like she looks OK." Trent actually looked a little scared.

Since they had seen her last, her face had puffed up and broken out in what looked to me like acne—no doubt the result of steroids that must have been part of her chemo cocktail. Her skin looked like it had a thin layer of cellophane over it, and I felt an ache in my heart as I looked at her. But I took Corey's advice, and I went over and gave her a gentle hug, and Corey and Trent followed. Jess was next, and I was impressed by how mature she seemed as she greeted Kerry and chatted with her for a few minutes. I noticed that Kerry reached over, took Jess's arm, and asked if they could both sit down. Kerry remained seated the rest of the evening. When she sat, I could see that there was a lot of empty space in the legs of her jeans. Her puffy face seemed to cover the fact that everywhere else she appeared to be wasting away.

After we distributed the paper plates and the food and drinks (Neo snuck in a Pete's Wicked Ale for Kerry, but she never touched it), we lit the candles and sang, Kerry blew out the candles, and it was all very good and natural and normal. The gifts were perfect for her: Kerry received a few CDs for the small player she kept in her room, a winter hat made of microfiber fleece (given in anticipation of getting Kerry out of the hospital and into the colder fall weather), and a set of hair brushes, combs, and clips (Jess's idea, given in hope that she would soon need them). Kerry was deeply touched and seemed genuinely happy. Then she began a little speech.

"This is a truly good day, for me," she said. "Neo, thank you for introducing me to my new family in Maryland. Kincaid, I feel that you have been given two younger brothers and a beautiful sister, and maybe a spare dad and mom too. Dan and Carol, words can never express my gratitude to you. You are everything Neo told me you would be, and more. It's so nice to get away from my room, and to have a few hours without CNN bringing so much bad news. Tonight has been a true holiday from all the terrorism and sadness in the outside world, and from the routine anxiety of hospital life. Thank you all so very much. There is one more gift—one very precious gift—that I am hoping to receive tonight."

Corey, who was sitting next to her on a loveseat, answered spontaneously, "What's that, Ms. Ellison? We'll get you anything you want."

"You're so sweet," she replied. "What I would like is something that you all already have, and it won't cost anything except some time. Neo, back in the Galápagos, you began a story that has gradually been unfolding for me. I often lie in bed at night and just run through the story in my mind: creation, crisis, calling, conversation, Christ, and church. But I know there's another episode, and with all that's been going on, you've never told me that last episode. I think I know why you haven't told it to me, but I think you'll understand if I say that I need that part of the story, and I need it tonight, on my last birthday."

Carol's eyes blinked hard when she heard the word "last," but it flowed out so naturally that no one else seemed to notice. Neo was leaning against the doorframe across the room from Kerry, and as he responded to her request, he moved toward her, and Corey got up without being asked. Neo took Corey's place and sat next to Kerry, leaning forward, his hands on his knees. He spoke directly to Kerry as if we weren't there, and all of us became eavesdroppers on a very personal conversation—welcome eavesdroppers, I'm sure. Even the boys, who I think were a little too young to know exactly what was going on, hardly moved, hardly stirred.

"Kerry, I've thought a lot about this last episode too," Neo said. "I wanted to tell it to you, but I was afraid that if I brought it up, you would feel that I was trying to . . . to prepare you for something, and that felt like it would be a betrayal of hope somehow, so I . . . I kept procrastinating. But I'm so glad you've asked for the last episode of the story we find ourselves in. Before I begin, though, I need to ask you to reorient your thinking, maybe even to reverse it."

Kerry smiled. She was used to Neo's surprises.

"Here's what I mean," Neo explained. "As scientists, we're trained to see history being pushed from behind. Causes launch effects, which become causes of new effects, creating a chain of events that started at the big bang and leads to this moment right now. Even religious people tend to see things this way, with the added proviso that God sometimes can intervene in the mechanism and change outcomes that would have otherwise unfolded. I guess you could say that for most people, God hovers over the present moment and intervenes as the chain of events that he started long ago kind of rolls on beneath him. Does that make sense?"

Kerry didn't even get a chance to answer. Corey answered for her. "Sure, Neo. That makes loads of sense." Carol and I tried to hide our smiles. That was so like Corey, to feel so into the moment and so comfortable with adults.

28

ENDING AND BEGINNING
AT THE SAME TIME

NEO CONTINUED HIS THOUGHT. "Let's assume there's a lot of truth to this model of things as being driven from behind. But let's say there's a completely different way of seeing things that's no less true. Let's say that instead of the present being pushed into the future by the past, that the past is being pushed out of the present by the future that is constantly rushing in."

Of the any number of things I'd been expecting Neo to say, this wasn't one of them. I must have shaken my head or grunted or something, because Carol nudged me and whispered, "Shhh. This isn't about you. Just listen."

Kerry said, "You need to run that by me again."

"OK," Neo said. "Instead of history being driven by the past, what if history is constantly being invited to receive the gift of the future? The image that comes to my mind is a person in a field who has a dog on a leash and lets the dog go. Another family member, who is across the field, calls the dog, and the dog runs to that person. That person's call draws the dog to leave the person with the leash. Or how about this: A father holds his little baby, who is just learning to walk, and the mother goes across the room and calls the baby to come to her, and the baby takes some steps. The baby isn't trying to walk. The baby just wants to come and receive the gift of the mother's presence that is being offered across the room.

"I guess I'm saying that God is like both of those people in one. God unleashes history in the beginning. God helps the baby to stand in the beginning. But God is also out ahead, calling history homeward across the field or across the room. God doesn't force it. Sometimes history responds, or some parts of history respond, but others resist or rebel. But God keeps calling. Everything I want to say about this last episode, I think, depends on us seeing history in this new way—not just being pushed from the past, or even engineered in the present, but being pulled, invited, called, into the future, which keeps coming to us as a gift. God is waiting to give himself to us across the field, across the room, and so we are pulled toward him by hope and desire."

This time Jess spoke up, which surprised me. "Dr. Oliver, if you want to get the whole Trinity in your analogy, you could say that first, God lets the dog off the leash, and second, God calls the dog from across the field, and third, God runs next to the dog wherever it roams in the field until it makes it across to the voice that's calling its name. You know, it's one God, but in three ways or something. Maybe that's all messed up."

"That's beautiful, Jess," Kerry said. "No one ever explained the Trinity to me any more beautifully than that." Jess met her eyes and smiled.

Then Kerry looked back at Neo. She was shaking her head slowly and thoughtfully. "I'm a little worried, Neo," she said, "because I think I can imagine what you're saying, and this idea of being beckoned from ahead instead of driven from behind goes against every single thought I've ever had in my life about how the universe works." She chuckled, and added, "You're a piece of work, Neil Edward Oliver."

Neo winked and didn't lose his rhythm. "Well, I'm glad you can imagine it, because I think this is so important. Think of the moment of creation as God standing out ahead in time, and inviting a universe to come into being. Think of the big bang not as something being pushed out of nothingness into something, but as something being invited or beckoned or called into being, welcomed into being out of nothingness. First, it's just something, something small and simple, but then it's invited to become more . . . bigger, more complex, more expansive. Can you see that—in your imagination, I mean?"

Kerry nodded her head, and I looked over, and both Corey and Trent were nodding too, as if Neo were talking to them.

"OK, then. Now think of Abraham. Instead of thinking of God pushing Abraham to do things from behind, or even instead of thinking of God being above Abraham, speaking to him in the present, think of God calling to Abraham from the future, inviting him into a future where he is blessed, and where he and his descendants become a blessing to the whole world. By believing—"

"I think I see where you're going," Kerry stepped in. "By believing in this voice from the future, Abraham will help make that future come true."

"Yes, exactly, and do you see the difference between being invited and being pushed?" Neo asked.

"Why, of course!" Kerry said. "It's the difference between being forced and being free, between being controlled and being . . . loved. It's all the difference in the world."

Neo leaned forward farther, his elbows now resting on his knees, and continued. "So God calls Abraham. And God keeps speaking to the people, inviting them into a conversation. And of course it's true to say that God is with them, but it's also true to say God is before them—not just ahead of them, as if to lead them down a path, but ahead of them in time, inviting them into a better future. This is what the prophets do, really. They speak in terms of promise, and promise is always an invitation into the future.

"And then Jesus comes, and in a sense he comes as an ambassador of the future, the future that God desires for us. And what he says matches this perfectly. He says, 'The kingdom of God is at hand.' It's just ahead. It's right in front of you, a possibility just before you, waiting for you to enter it. We're supposed to pray that it will come to us. And where do you think it comes from?"

"It comes from . . . I guess it comes from God in the future. Neo, this is fascinating," Kerry said.

"We're just getting started," Neo replied. "What are we called to do? To enter the kingdom of God . . . to come into the future of the kingdom of God. And that's a great way to understand the church. The church is a community of people who are learning to live the way everyone will live in the future, reconciled in every way. I mean . . . OK, we could drive north a couple of hours and look at the Amish. You know about the Amish? OK, we visit them in Lancaster and we say, 'How quaint, how nostalgic.' But what if the Amish are really living—not in terms of technology, that's not the point at all—what if the Amish are really living along the lines of how people will live in the future? I'm not talking about farming or driving buggies, but in terms of love and peace, of commitment and character and respect.

"And what if that's true of all genuine communities of faith? They may be out of date in a thousand ways—you know, music of the 1950s or 1760s, clothing styles that are retro by mistake, always a day late and a dollar short in terms of technology. But that's not the point. To the degree they are learning to live in love and peace and faith and hope, they are living the lifestyle of the future."

Trent came over and whispered in my ear that he had to go to the bathroom. I motioned for Corey to go with him. Neo continued, "Well, that's the last episode of our story: the episode that hasn't been written yet, but that's like a promise or a call from the future, beckoning us forward to a day when the whole universe starts working in the way God desires, when God's wishes are fulfilled, when God's dream for the universe comes true. But actually, it's not an ending, because any story that God creates can never really end. It's an ending *and* a new beginning, both at the same time."

"What do you call it?" Kerry asked.

"Let's call this episode 'Consummation'—like a wedding, like a wedding banquet and a wedding night."

"That's beautiful," she said, "because a wedding is a kind of ending and a kind of beginning, wrapped up in one. It's all about the fulfillment of some promises, and the making of new promises."

Neo replied, "Yes, yes. Now, I know that it was hard to think of history being drawn into the future, or to think of the future coming in and pushing the past out of the present, instead of thinking of the past pushing the present into the future. But what I want to ask you to think about next is even harder. Ready?"

29

EVERYTHING COMES HOME

I LOOKED AROUND THE ROOM. Every eye was focused on Neo, and Neo was looking at Kerry, oblivious to the rest of us. "OK, here goes," he began. "I want you to imagine that as the past is pushed out of the present—displaced from the present by the arrival of the future—it isn't lost or pushed into oblivion, it's retained, perfectly retained by God. It doesn't vanish into nothingness. It is saved forever, in God's memory. Can you picture that?"

Kerry at first nodded, and then shook her head slowly. "I think so. But I'm not sure. And I'm not sure where you're going. So please, keep on. Maybe it will become clearer."

"Imagine," Neo continued, "that God retains every moment, every moment of your life, and not just what would be visible to another person. Imagine that God remembers every thought and feeling, and every nuance of thought and feeling, including all the ones you weren't even aware of. And imagine that God is retaining the memory of every other person at every moment too, and not just people, but every living thing, and even the movements and states of nonliving things. Imagine that the past is never lost, not one second or one dimension or one nuance of meaning of the story anywhere. It's all remembered, all kept in God's memory.

"Now, imagine that at that point out in the future—the point from which God is calling us into the future, and the point from which God is sending each present moment with all its possibilities toward us—imagine that at that point in the future, God holds all of God's memories of all of us. When we get there, not only we will be what we are at that final moment, but also we will find all that we have ever been—all that God has remembered— and we will be reunited with all we have ever been. We won't be only the little sliver of ourselves that we are at this instant we call the present. We will be the composite of ourselves through our whole lifetime, all gathered together in God's presence, consummated, summed up, gathered in the mind and heart of God. All the momentary members of our life story, the me of a second ago, the me now, the me that I will be in a second—all these members will be re-membered, reunited, in God's memory."

Kerry leaned her head back, closed her eyes, and clapped her hands and laughed. "Neo, that's heaven! That's heaven, isn't it! I can see it, I mean, just a glimpse, but I can see what you're getting at! That's heaven! To be with God, and to be gathered together with all that I have ever been! It makes me think that now, in the present, I'm just a tiny particle, hardly real at all, just a vapor, a flicker. But then, when the me from all the moments of my life comes together, there will be something substantial, something real and solid, something with real weight."

Neo replied, "But it's even better than that. You'll be judged."

Kerry's eyes had been closed, and now she opened them wide and looked at Neo, surprised. "What? That hardly sounds—"

"I know," he broke in. "At first, it sounds terrible. But follow me. You'll be in God's presence, and the *you* that will be re-membered and re-collected, reunited and reconstituted, in God—that *you* will have passed through God's judgment. It will exist only as having been seen and known and remembered and evaluated by God. So you—not just the fragmentary *you* from any one moment, but the fully constituted *you* that emerges from every moment of your life—will be shown to you. You will see who you truly have been and have become. Every moment of your life will have been weighed and tested, and all that was false or partial or dishonest or dark will have been identified, and all that was generous and joyful and honest and true will have been identified."

Trent and Corey came back in the room at this point, and I was relieved to see them quietly take their seats, because I didn't want this moment to be disrupted. Neo was speaking more slowly than usual. "Now Kerry, remember that day on the boat when Carol was talking about Jesus, about Jesus' death? She said that Jesus' death gives us a window into God's heart, and as Jesus suffers, we see God dealing with all our wrongs, all our wickedness and evil, all our sin. Remember? So yes, all our wrongs are identified. There is no sugarcoating, no watering down, no denial. No pretending that our misdeeds didn't happen. They're faced and known by God for all they were. But what if all the guilt and regret and shame of that judgment are absorbed into God's pain, the pain Jesus made visible on the cross, so God forgives us, so none of our wrongs count for anything anymore, and—are you ready for this?—what if God, by judging our wrongs as evil and therefore worthless, actually forgets our wrongs forever because they're worthless now?

"Can you imagine what it means to say that God forgets forever? So when you leave this life, and you meet God, up ahead, up in the future, the little sliver of who you are in that moment meets the *you* from all the past moments, and the full *you* that is reconstituted there in God is fully and completely judged, and all the wrong has been named and judged, forgiven and forgotten, and there you are: full and substantial and free and pure and complete. Can you imagine *that?*"

Kerry's eyes were closed, and her hands again came together and slowly lifted to her face, and I couldn't tell whether she was crying or praying, or maybe both. "Neo, that's . . . that's too good . . . too beautiful . . . to be true," she said, just above a whisper.

Neo leaned toward her and put his arm around her. "No, Kerry, it's too good to *not* be true. And it's even better than that, because it's not just *you* that you are reunited with there. And it's not just God either. In God, you find yourself, and you find everything and everyone, everything and everyone that God has remembered, everything and everyone that have passed through God's judgment, which retains only the good and true and beautiful. Everything bad and false and ugly has been let go, forgotten, left in the past, not retained in God's memory, gone forever. The universe that God unleashed at the beginning has run free across the field of time, and now it arrives at God in the future. Everything comes home, where everything good and beautiful and true belongs."

Jess couldn't contain herself. "That's one of the most excellent things I've ever heard in my life, Dr. Oliver."

Neo leaned back in his chair now. "Why, thank you, Jess."

"I have something to say too, Dr. Oliver," Trent said. We were all surprised to hear shy Trent speak up. "I think that every animal Kerry ever loved will come running to greet her, because they're parts of God's creation too, right? And I think that they'll know then how much she loved them."

I looked over at Kerry, and she looked like she was about to melt. "You are so wise, young man," she said.

"You're right, Trent," Neo said. "It's all about love, all about love. And you know, in the last book of the Bible, John describes these wild and wonderful creatures full of eyes and wings, and I think that they represent every living thing, just as you say, all parts of God's creation, all parts of that great consummation."

Then Neo turned back to speak to Kerry. "You can think of the consummation as a love story, a romance. God creates the universe, and loves her. God calls her to him in the future, and at first, she refuses to come. But God beckons her—and this is a great way to understand Jesus—by entering time and space and by coming to her to declare his love. As Jess said,

God comes to walk beside her wherever she roams. She spurns God and rejects God. But God's love can't be defeated, and eventually, by patiently walking beside her, God wins her heart. And God continues to call her into the future, and she finally she comes to God, and God comes to her. And when they meet, because all the wrong, all the evil, all the dishonesty and ugliness and distrust are judged and gone and forgotten forever, God can take everything to himself in an embrace of boundless, uninhibited, limitless love. And that's the new beginning. That's the consummation: that embrace. Who can imagine what it will give birth to?"

Kerry leaned her head over on Neo's shoulder, and Neo took her hand. There they sat, silent and still, for a few minutes. Kincaid leaned over to me and quietly whispered in my ear. "This is kind of like your garage, you know? One of those holy moments. This is so awesome." And then he went over and put his hand on his mother's shoulder, and she slowly stood up and embraced him. Again there was silence, but it was a full silence, and no one felt the need to say anything or rush anything or disturb anything.

Finally, Kerry spoke. "I suppose I should get some rest. What a good day in my life this has been. Thanks everyone. Thanks so much. I can't imagine how this could have been a better day. Good night, everyone." I came over and helped her make her way around the room, giving hugs to everyone. Then Carol and I accompanied her out to the hallway, and she asked me to make a promise to her, which I did, and kept. Kincaid and Neo helped her walk with her IV pole back to her room.

Carol, the kids, and I went back inside and cleaned up the remnants of our meal. We dropped off the rest of the cake at the nurse's station, Kincaid joined us, and we made our way to the parking garage. Neo caught up with us just as we reached our van. The yellowish sodium light and the colorless cement walls seemed so artificial and bland after the imaginative voyage we had taken with Neo.

I put my arms around Corey and Trent's shoulders as we walked, even though they were twelve and didn't normally yield to that kind of closeness.

Corey said, "That was really interesting, Dad. They never tell us anything like that in youth group."

"Yeah," Trent added, "and they don't give us cake either."

One of Jess's CDs was in the player in the van, by a group I hadn't heard before. The kids were talking with Neo in the back seats, but Carol and I were silent in the front seat, and so I hit the "play" button. Lyrics from the first song caught my attention:

There's a farm that I know.
As a child I would go and run in its fields below.

> Near a barn on a hill stood an old windmill.
> In the afternoon sun it would glow
> With the glory of God, the glory of God,
> The glory of God shining through.
> And I pray for you that you'll see it too,
> For this life is a search for the glory of God.
> This life is a search for the glory of God.

The female singer's voice sounded so innocent and frail, and yet the hope that came through the song felt so strong and real. The next verse went like this:

> There are people I've met,
> I'll never forget, full of laughter, some young and some old.
> Sometimes on a face this mysterious grace
> Seems to smile out and shine out like gold.
> It's the glory of God, the glory of God,
> The glory of God shining through. . . .

Then came a beautiful, plaintive cello and violin duet, and then this third verse:

> There are moments that come
> Like a gift from someone who loves you but you hardly know.
> They bring a tear to the cheek, and a catch when you speak,
> And the meaning you seek seems to flow
> With the glory of God, the glory of God,
> The glory of God shining through.
> And I pray for you that you'll see it too,
> For this life is a search for the glory of God.
> This life is a search for the glory of God.

I'm not sure why that song seized me and wanted me to remember each word, but there was some resonance with Neo's story, or maybe I should say *our* story.

30

DA MIND DAT STRETCH BIG

THE NEXT DAY, THURSDAY, November 15, was my day off, and Neo and I had been planning something special: to take a walk along a stretch of the Potomac River where we had walked over two years earlier when we were first becoming friends. Hard as it may be to imagine, Neo and I had been so busy with other concerns that we hadn't found much time to just talk as friends, first because we were so focused on Kerry's needs, and then because our attention had been preoccupied with the September 11 attacks and the war that was brewing (not to mention the anthrax scare, which remained urgent local news for us). Of course, there are ways that people grow closer as friends through working and serving others together, but still, we both had been looking forward to this day devoted to walking and talking simply as two friends sharing a spiritual journey.

It was a mild day for November, sunny, perfect, with unseasonably warm temperatures expected, in the low seventies. We had a quick breakfast, and I was sure to bring a backpack filled with our lunch this time. (I had left lunch behind on our first walk together back in 1999.) On the forty-five-minute ride to the river, Neo recounted in more detail the itinerary of his year of travels between when he left the United States in the winter of 2000, and when he arrived in the Galápagos in the winter of 2001.

Back in the fall of 1999, Neo's father died suddenly, leaving Neo's mother, who suffered from Alzheimer's disease, in urgent need of live-in care in Seattle. Neo resigned from his teaching job and sold his home in Maryland to care for her, expecting that she would need constant care for a few years at least. However, her health quickly deteriorated, and she died in a matter of weeks, just before Christmas. Having left his job and sold his home, and having received an unexpected inheritance, he decided to take a once-in-a-lifetime trip around the world. He hoped to visit several missionaries he had supported for many years, and I think he also hoped to gain more clarity about what to do with the rest of his life. I know he was considering changing careers. From Seattle, he had gone to New Zealand and Australia, and from there, to Papua New Guinea. While in New Guinea, he met missionaries who had contacts in Indonesia and Cambodia. They persuaded him to add those countries to his itinerary. From Cambodia, he went to India, spending several weeks in the northeast, near Nepal, followed by several weeks in western Pakistan, near the Afghan border, visiting refugees. Those border towns were considered a backwater then, but now they were in the news every day.

Next, he visited friends who worked among refugees in Athens, Austria, and Germany. He considered going to Africa, but he was already behind his planned schedule, so he had to postpone Africa for another time. Next came an extended stay in Jamaica, where he visited some aging relatives and found two of his three childhood homes, the third having been destroyed by fire a few years earlier. It was in his homeland that he had his only bout of illness. "I was staying at a beautiful beach, in a bay with crystal-clear water and beautiful coral reefs, but all I did for two weeks was shiver with a fever, throw up, and suffer with diarrhea. Isn't that how life goes sometimes? And worst of all, there were fresh mangoes, my favorite food in all the world, fresh juicy Jamaican mangoes all around the cottage, but I was too sick to eat even one."

He planned to spend a week in the Galápagos and then to return to Seattle, and then finally to Maryland, where he planned to settle once again, but the closer he got to returning, the less ready he felt to do so. "Dan, this trip for me was like half-time in soccer. Half-time can be a crisis, whether you're winning or losing or the score is tied. If you're losing badly, you wonder if you can stand another forty-five minutes of getting banged around and humiliated. If you've got a big lead, you wonder if you can keep your passion high and sustain your concentration. It's tempting to become lazy or overconfident. And if the game is tied, you feel a mix of hope and fear that can foul you up for the second half. When I was a matter of weeks away from coming home, I realized I still hadn't figured out my second-half game plan yet, so I was unsettled about returning. That's why when the option of staying in the islands presented itself, I took it. I was procrastinating, I suppose. But at the same time, I felt that it was a gift from God to have that year to travel, and an even greater gift to extend it a bit. Then when the ministry on *La Aventura* began happening, I knew that I was in a productive place."

As Neo and I left the coastal plane and crossed Catoctin Mountain ("The front ridge of the Appalachians," Neo said), he acknowledged that Maryland really was home. "It's good, so good, to be back in Maryland," he said. (He still, after all these years, pronounced the name of the state with Jamaican music in his voice: "Mary-land"—an articulation far different from the slurred "Merrlin" one hears from natives of the "Bawmer" or "Warshuntin" area.)

We reached the river at about nine-thirty. The Chesapeake and Ohio Canal Towpath runs beside the river, on the "Merrlin" side. The green leaves that shade the path during the summer had now fallen yellow and red and brown, and as we began our trek, we both savored the swish, swish, swish, swish of dry leaves as our feet pushed through them. Their acrid scent mixed with a faint aroma of wood smoke in the moist morning air. Neo seemed to derive as much pleasure from breathing that air as I do from the scent of strong coffee.

"A lot has happened since our first walk along this path, eh, Dan?"

"Yeah, a lot has happened. And while you've covered a lot of miles and had a lot of adventures on the other side of the world, I've been on my own journey back here too. You got me thinking about things that messed me up and opened me up both at the same time. The idea of being a new kind of Christian, and helping Potomac Community Church become a new kind of church, those ideas about the postmodern transition that you infected my mind with—all of it haunted me after you left. So I've been processing a lot since you left. I'm still disturbed by a lot of the ideas you presented me with, but . . . but I'll always be grateful to you, my friend."

Neo said, "I used to tell my students a saying I picked up from my grandmother back in Jamaica: "Da mind dat stretch big to embrace da new t'ought never shrink back to da small size it were before."

I laughed. "That's good, Neo." I asked him to repeat it, partly so I'd remember the exact words and rhythm as he imitated his grandmother's voice, and partly because it was so entertaining to watch his eyes grow big and his hands stretch out wide as he imitated her manner.

"Hey, speaking of new thoughts, you were in rare form last night," I said. "You know, that whole idea of the future pushing the past out of the present, and God being in the future. That was *stretching da mind!*" (My attempt at the Jamaican accent was lame.)

"Ah, eschatological realism. I'm sure you've heard of it," Neo replied.

"I don't think so. But what you were saying reminded me of something that's become pretty controversial in the theological world here lately: 'open theism,' they call it, or 'the openness of God.' Is that what you were talking about?"

"Maybe." Neo said. "But I don't really like the way the openness-of-God argument is framed by its friends, and I like the way its opponents are attacking it even less. I prefer to frame the discussion in different terms:

the openness of the universe, not just the openness of God. What I think is really going on is this: In the modern world, the universe was a machine, right? So the highest promotion we could give to God was the position of designer and operator of the machine. But in a post-Newtonian scientific worldview—you know, a world of relativity and indeterminacy—we're already outside of the old mechanistic view of the universe. Now the universe is so much more vibrant and alive and dynamic and interesting. It's about information and emergence and possibility and novelty. What Newton called laws now seem more like language, and they seem less important than what they make possible, just as the grammar of a language is less important than the meanings it makes possible. So the new universe, or the emerging *conception* of the universe, is more poetry than machine, more story than gears and levers. In this new universe, to call God a machine operator or engineer feels like an insult, a demotion, a blasphemy even. It feels trivial and restricting. That's what they're getting at in the open theism argument, I think, and I agree with their dissatisfaction with the God-as-engineer model, but I'd just frame the whole discussion differently."

"Hmmm," was all I could muster. I wondered when he had time to keep up with all this, but then again, I had noticed a few boxes of books arriving for Neo from online booksellers since Neo had been staying with us, so I knew he was reading quite a bit, both late at night at home and when Kerry was sleeping while he sat with her at NIH.

I said, "I was really . . . really moved by what you were saying. Part of it was Kerry's situation. But part of it was the sheer beauty of what you were saying. I had tears in my eyes. So did Carol. And even the kids were blown away. They were with you."

"It really is a . . . a beautiful way to see things. You know, Dan, in the ancient world, in the world of the Bible, chaos was always at the door. People constantly had to wonder if God could possibly be stronger than the chaos, if God could achieve any order in the chaos. So naturally, people would affirm that God was powerful and orderly and in control. But something odd happens in the modern world. With Sir Isaac Newton's laws of physics, and God being seen as the powerful machine operator who perfectly controls the machine through these orderly laws, we end up with the opposite problem, the very opposite of the ancient situation. Now, instead of chaos reigning and us wondering if there's any order, order reigns supreme, and we wonder if there's any freedom. Totalitarian order is as ugly as rampant chaos, you know? And so I think that the way I talked about consummation last night was moving to all of us because it assumes that our story begins, unfolds, and consummates in freedom—

something that requires a certain dynamic mix of order and chaos, of power to control and intentional unpredictability."

"Wow. So that's what you call 'eschatological realism'?" I asked, reaching down and absent-mindedly grabbing a walking stick from the leaves at the edge of the path.

"Oh, no!" Neo said, laughing and jumping behind the tree. "Did I say something wrong?"

"No inquisitions this time, my friend," I said, and we laughed at the inside joke and gave each other a high-five.

He found a stick too, and said, "Well, this way, if we get into an argument, at least we're both similarly armed." Then Neo got a sparkle in his eye, and a wry grin appeared on his face. He raised his stick like a sword and said, "En garde, inquisitor!"

"En garde, heretic!" I said, raising my "sword" too, and bending my legs, knees pointing out, trying to look like a fencer, but probably looking more like a bowlegged cowboy. For the next couple of minutes we were clowning around, whacking sword on sword, chasing each other through the fallen leaves like a couple of kids, ducking behind trees, weaving in and out of leafless bushes, first on one side of the path, then on the other. Eventually, we both collapsed on a big flat rock down near the river, laughing, breathing hard, and then laughing some more, both of us needing the chance to let off some steam after a long run of stressful weeks.

A LITTLE SCARY AT TIMES

"THIS IS THE BEST WAY to talk theology," Neo said. "Playfully. Because we're just a couple of boys talking about matters too great and lofty for us."

Then Neo turned toward me and put his hand on my shoulder. "I've enjoyed my travels, Daniel, but I've needed this. I've needed a friend. I said it before, but I need to say it again: it's good to be home."

We rested there for a few minutes on that big flat rock, and before long, we got back to talking theology. "Neo, as I said, I was moved by what you were saying last night, but I wonder how you'd explain this eschatological realism thing in more biblical terms. I mean, is there any biblical support for what you're saying?"

"Well, Dan, for ancient people in biblical times, this wouldn't have been such a big deal, because they hadn't entered a universe where mystery had been replaced by mechanism, where everything was being pushed and determined from behind. So I think it would be natural for them to believe that nothing in this universe exists in its mature, completed, fulfilled form."

"I hear you on that, but I need some specific examples. Where in Scripture do you see this idea that the universe isn't finished yet? I keep going back to God resting on the seventh day, and to Jesus saying, 'It is finished.' I just need a couple examples."

"OK, but first I need to clarify something: creation's birth *is* finished; our universe's initial creation *is* finished; Jesus *did* finish everything necessary for our atonement. I'm not denying that in any way. But I am saying that we need to rediscover the sense that we live in a creation that's still evolving, emerging, under construction, an unfinished story. You want some biblical examples of that? OK, off the top of my head: We're all in process, Paul says in Second Corinthians, passing from 'glory to glory.' In Romans 8, he talks about how the whole universe is in childbirth, groaning in the frustration of labor, pregnant and waiting to give birth, in hope. There's unfinished business for you, Dan! Jesus uses this childbirth imagery too, in John 16. Then in Colossians, Paul talks about completing what is still lacking in the sufferings of Christ—I'm not completely sure what he means, but it's that process language again. In Philippians, he talks about God bringing to completion what has been started. The First Epistle of John says that our full identity hasn't appeared yet, and won't appear until we see God as God is. Revelation talks about all tears being wiped away by God, suggesting that the whole problem of evil and therefore the full meaning of our story can't be ascertained until . . . until the end. So in the meantime, it's all evolving, emerging, developing, and we have an important part in that process."

I wanted to put into words an idea, a suggestion actually, that had been forming in my mind for a while. This seemed like the right time. "You know, Neo, I think you'd get a lot farther with people like Carol, and me too really, if you'd *start* with those biblical passages when you talk to people about this. Because what you say is very convincing, but even more convincing when you put more Bible in. And I think you'd also get a lot farther if you'd leave the word 'evolution' out. I think you can say everything you need to say without it. I'm just worried that you'll sound too . . . "

"Liberal," he asked, saying the word, as he always did, in three distinct syllables. His voice got a bit louder now with each question. "Daniel, have you ever reflected on your exaggerated fear of that word? Might the liberals be right about one tiny thing here and there? You know, I wish I didn't have to upset good Christians with the 'e-word' . . . but what do you want me to do? Be dishonest? Hide my true thoughts?"

"Of course not, but there's so much at stake, man." I said, also quite loudly. I felt an edginess creeping into my voice, a tone I didn't like, so I took a couple of deep breaths and tried to slow down, calm down. Just a few minutes earlier we had been talking about being playful, but now I was quickly getting tense.

Neo was silent for a moment too, and then spoke with an unusually soft voice: "OK, OK. Point well taken. Maybe you're right."

I had leaned forward and was slowly scratching designs in the sand and gravel between my feet, gradually growing less agitated. Finally, I looked Neo in the eye, smiled and then winced a bit, and shook my head. "It's just that this is all so different, Neo, so different from any telling of the story I've ever heard. It's a big stretch for me, and I think it will be an even bigger stretch for so many other people. In spite of the evolution stuff, or maybe because of it, you've got this unique angle. I just don't want people to turn you off before giving you a fair hearing. I shouldn't be the only person hearing this. Thousands of people should be hearing this . . . millions. Because this is important. Inspiring. Beautiful. Big. *And*, a little scary at times."

We got up from the big flat rock and began to scramble up the bank to make our way back to the path. It was thirty yards or so up a gentle slope.

"Scary," Neo repeated. He led the way up the bank and pushed through the undergrowth. "You're right, Dan. This whole thing of deconstructing and reconstructing our understanding of our story—it *is* scary, because it's dangerous. Just think: if we're going to do the courageous thing now, as the early church leaders did in their moment, as the Reformers did in their moment, then we need to engage the best thinking and the toughest questions of our culture, with no less courage, because it's no less dangerous or difficult. And it's no less necessary either, if we're going to be faithful to Jesus and his teaching and his mission. And so we need to reenter and reengage the world, *this* world, and we need to rediscover our story here in this evol——. . . this *emerging* universe, not in some static spiritual world of concepts behind or above this one. You know?"

"I guess the only thing more dangerous and scary than doing what you're suggesting," I said, "is not doing it." Then a question formed itself slowly in my mind, and I asked, "Neo, how will you know if you're getting off track, going too far, or maybe not going far enough? Or how will you know if you're on the right track, for that matter?"

Neo started to answer, then stopped, and then said, "I hope that friends like you will consider what I say, and see how it squares up with Scripture, and common sense, and church tradition, and that internal discernment from God's Spirit. If you see anything that strikes you as wrong or bad, Dan, I hope you'll tell me." I assured him I would, and he continued, "But there's a problem: new paradigms in science can never be justified based on the criteria of the old paradigm, and I imagine that the same is true in theology. So I don't expect folks who are happy with their current version of the faith, whether carried in a system or a story, to be very interested in what I'm saying."

"I don't think you should just listen to people like me," I said. "You should pay attention to people like Kerry and Kincaid, people who are new to the story, who don't have a lot of preset categories. You should see what effects your telling of the story is having on them. And I'd say the effects are good . . . very good."

We were back on the path by this time, and we walked on for several minutes without talking. As we walked, I felt that something inside me had suddenly relaxed, that a kind of sudden advance had occurred, as if some stuck gear in an old clock gave way and the hands started moving again. Maybe I had just needed reassurance that Neo's thinking was rooted in Scripture. Anyway, for whatever reason, I stopped, playfully touched Neo's chest with my walking stick, and started thinking out loud. "Neo, I think I'm getting it. I think this is what you've been trying to help me see since . . . since I first met you. Jesus was not about creating an alternative religious world so we might escape from the world of history and science and culture and all that. He was showing how God enters our history, with all its craziness and pain and confusion, how God is *with* us in all our cultural breakthroughs and regressions, all our constructions and deconstructions and reconstructions.

"I know you've said this to me before, Neo, but for some reason, it's finally dawning on me just now: Jesus really was, and *is,* about saving more than just human souls after they die. He really *is* about saving the world—human history, creation, the whole thing, the whole process from beginning to end, as you said, from alpha to omega. So I guess what you're helping me see is that the whole idea of the incarnation of Christ is far more radical than we realize. It's not just God entering creation, and especially human history. It's God taking creation, including human history, into his heart, and declaring eternal solidarity with it. He's really with us in the . . . the process, the story, the unfolding."

Neo took my stick and his own stick, knelt down, put them on the ground, and began to arrange them in various ways. "There are so many ways we can configure these two sticks. They can be parallel, like this . . . or they can be perpendicular, like this . . . or they can intersect at an infinite number of angles to one another, like this, or this, or this. This one can cross the other up here, or down here, and vice versa. It's the same two sticks, but the number of ways they can relate to one another is almost endless. And then imagine if we had three sticks, or five, or five thousand—imagine all the ways the parts could be related.

"That's how I feel about the elements of our faith, Dan. We're not talking about jettisoning any of our material, or throwing out any of our data. We've got the Scriptures, we have our history, we have a tradition so rich in resources as a community of faith. I guess, Daniel, what I've been wrestling with all these years is the feeling that we need to reconfigure the pattern of our beliefs, maybe like an artist. I think that God gives us the material to work with, but I think that God also gives us some freedom and flexibility so that we can adjust the patterns over time. Sorry, Dan, but it's like evolution again. There are just four components in a strand of DNA: adenine, cytosine, guanine, and thymine. Those four elements can be reconfigured to give us unlimited possibilities, innovations, and vitality." Neo stood up and handed me my stick, and we continued walking.

"Reconfiguring the pattern," I said, musing. "Yes. Here's how I'd say it: what you're talking about feels like a kind of re-centering. For me, Christianity was always centered on sin—you know, solving my sin problem, forgiveness, atonement. But when you tell the story, I feel like other elements move toward the center, things like spiritual formation, mission, justice. They don't crowd out the sin issue, but everything looks so different when—as you said—you reconfigure the pattern."

After several minutes, the path took a sharp turn, paralleling a bend in the river. "Something else you said last night, really struck me," I said. "It was the way you used the word 'judgment.' Could you tell me more about that?"

We stopped to enjoy the view of some rapids in the river, just past the bend. Neo said, "Well, if God is waiting for us in the future, then God is absolutely inescapable. And that means that judgment is absolutely inescapable, because judgment means having things accurately appraised by God. To be in God's presence means to be seen and known as you really are. And that means that all of my life will one day be judged in light of God's hopes and dreams for our world and for my life in it. You like to write, Dan, so maybe you can think of it like this: God allows me to be a character in the story of creation, and every day I'm writing more and more of my story within God's story. I'm developing my character—pun intended—by the choices I make, the words I say, the things I think, the attitudes and habits I prefer. And in the end, when my story has been gathered by God into the bigger story, who I have become and what I have done will be clear—clear in God's eyes, which are perfectly gracious and just, perfectly merciful and holy. So judgment is inescapable, because every story is relative to God's big story."

"So for you, judgment doesn't just mean condemnation; it means this perfect assessment by God," I said. Neo nodded, and I invited him to go on.

Neo said, "So I can imagine God saying to someone, 'Well done! You have lived well! You helped the story advance toward my creative dreams. You fed the hungry, clothed the naked, welcomed in the lonely, visited the prisoners, shared your bread with the poor. Wherever you went, you contributed love and peace, generosity and truth, courage and sacrifice, self-control and justice, faithfulness and kindness. You enriched the story, enhanced its beauty and drama and nobility. You have become someone good and beautiful and true. Your unique, creative contributions will never be forgotten, and even the smallest act of kindness will be eternally celebrated, rewarded. After naming and forgiving and forgetting your many faults and failures, I see so much substance to your character, so much to cherish, so much of value, and it will now be set free, given a new beginning in my new creation. You have an eternal place in my story! You have been harvested from this creation, and now you will enter into the joy of the new creation!'"

"And that's heaven, as you see it?" I asked.

Neo answered my question with a question, "What do you think?"

"At first," I replied, "it sounded a little like reincarnation to me. But then again, in your story, instead of many rebirths, there's just one, and also, instead of purging ourselves of evil through suffering karma, God purges us through grace, through the suffering of Christ for us, and . . . wow . . . that's a pretty big difference. Plus, instead of ending in an unchanging state of bliss, your story never ends. It opens out into another story, a new beginning. So then again, maybe it's not that much like reincarnation after all."

"Daniel, we're looking forward to *resurrection*, not reincarnation." We started walking again.

"How would God respond to someone who hadn't done so well?" I asked, with some caution.

Neo replied, "God might say, 'Sadly, your contributions have been neutral or negative. You have added more pain and selfishness, more dishonesty and coldness, more greed and disharmony and clutter into the story. I tried in every way possible to get through to you, but you wouldn't respond to my grace. Even if I forgive and forget all the bad things you have done, is there enough of your character left for you to continue existing in my new creation? And would you even like living with me in a story you have avoided, minimized, resisted, or subverted all your life? What have you become? You've made money and enjoyed luxuries and seemed like a great success to some of your fellow characters as you pursued your own dreams and desires, but in terms of my dreams and desires, you had your chance to become a good and unforgettable character in my story, and you wasted it. You've squandered the time and space you were given. I feel regret about what you could have been, what you could have done, what you could have become, but didn't. I wish you had given me more to work with, but you haven't. Your story has been a tragedy of waste and missed opportunities.'"

I was quiet for ten or twenty paces. "And what then?" I asked. "What happens to them?"

32

WHEN WE DREAM OF THAT
KIND OF FUTURE

"WHY DO YOU ALWAYS NEED to ask that question?" Neo asked, firmly but not angrily, his "always" recalling our conversations back in 1999. "Isn't what I just described to you *enough*? Does that sound to you like trivia, like no big deal—to face the awesome, holy, living, and true God and to see what you have really done, what you have really become, to have to face that reality without denial or escape? Why isn't that enough for you, Dan?"

"Because I think that all of us are struggling with what to do with fire and brimstone and all that," I said. "Letting all that go seems like . . . like cheating at solitaire—you know, reshuffling the deck, making things easy, watering things down. It feels dangerous. But at the same time, keeping all that, the way that fundamentalists do, has got its own set of problems, you know?"

"Yes," Neo said, "it does," and he kept walking. He didn't seem disposed to add anything, or maybe he didn't have anything to add. So after a couple of minutes, I gave up waiting for him to elaborate, and I asked a different question. "Then Jesus—where does Jesus fit in with all this ambiguity about fire and brimstone?" As Neo answered me, he was at first calm, his voice unusually quiet, as it had been a few minutes before. But gradually his voice started to rise, and his hands started to map out ideas in the air as we walked, until by the end of his answer, he was waving his walking stick as if it were a huge baton and he were at the head of a big parade.

"Jesus is everywhere in this telling of the story, my friend. In the beginning, Jesus is the Word of God, is with God, and is God—as John said it—cocreating with the Father. At the end, Jesus is the judge. He is God looking at us through a human face, as one who has been here, one who

understands and sees truly and accurately, who judges both sympatheti-
cally and impartially, with unflagging mercy and unflinching honesty.
When we see the face of Jesus, we'll see the faces of the poor we neglected
and the hungry we fed, the faces of the homeless we took in and the prisoners we forgot; we'll see the face that judges and rewards. When we see
his face, it will be a familiar face—the face of one who has intersected with
every human being and invited us to leave our tragic stories of wasted
possibilities behind, to become part of this better story. That's what he did
when he walked on this earth: he invited everyone to become a part of
God's better story of grace and glory. It's what he's still doing today,
through the Holy Spirit."

"A better story of grace and glory—I like that," I said.

Neo went on. "For prostitutes, the call of Jesus was to leave their story
of men who pay money for love, and to enter the story of God, who in love
pays for us with his own life. For Pharisees, it was to leave their story of re-
ligiosity and superiority and rigidity and judgmentalism, their story that
was exclusively focused on their own narrow little sect, and instead to enter
God's broader and deeper and better story of grace and compassion and
mercy and love for all people. For Zealots like Simon, it was to leave the
political story of violence, to stop slitting Roman throats, as if that would
bring the story to its desired end, and instead to enter God's spiritual story
of peace for all people, to risk persecution for justice and to prefer suffering over causing others to suffer.

"For tax collectors like Zacchaeus or Matthew, it was to stop collabo-
rating with the Roman Empire, and profiting in the process, and instead
to collaborate with the kingdom of God, and sacrifice in the process. For
the rich—like that young ruler Jesus met—it was to abandon the hollow
story of acquisition, and instead to enter God's better story of generosity.
For farmers and shepherds, it was to realize that there's more to life than
just planting seeds of wheat or tending flocks of sheep; instead, Jesus invited them to enter into the bigger story of planting seeds of truth and
seeking lost men and women, every one of whom is loved and counted
and missed by God. For fishermen like Peter and Andrew and James and
John, it was to trade in their story of catching fish for a bigger story of fishing for men and women, inviting them into God's story of ongoing creation and redemption.

"For the middle class, who want nothing more than to create a little
social aquarium so that their biological families can experience something
they call 'family values,' it's a call to care about the families of their neighbors too, especially the poor, to see them as family too, as children of Adam
and children of God."

Neo stopped now, held out both arms, one with his walking stick, and the other open, palm up, and said, "To everyone, Jesus issues an invitation to abandon the story they will lose themselves in, and instead, to enter the story they will find themselves in."

I was deep in reflection. I found myself thinking out loud again, paraphrasing Jesus' words. "For what does it profit a person if he pursues a story of personal gain that makes his soul languish and his character miss its chance to really come to life? It would be better to lose that selfish story, to abandon that plot line, and to enter God's better story. . . ."

"That's it," Neo replied, smiling, "*that's* the story we find ourselves in." We looked at each other, and I nodded. Then we started walking again.

After a few minutes, Neo said, "This is where those theories of the atonement come together—you know, the ones you and Carol told Kerry about on our boat ride. They say something about the need to acknowledge that our story has been hijacked; and that all of us are, to some degree, passive participants or even coconspirators in the hijacking; and that our misdirected story needs to be reclaimed, saved, redeemed, and set right; and that, for this to happen, God has to step into our story and absorb an unfathomable infliction of pain, so we won't suffer it ourselves, so our story won't have a tragic end."

"Reclaimed," I echoed, "saved, redeemed. Suddenly those words seem to have more meaning for me. They describe what we need for our individual stories, and for our shared story too. And they make me look ahead and see how much is at stake . . . every day, every minute. The story is exploring ways to proceed into the future that God offers us, and either we choose a kind of mindless, easy route of consumption, competition, self-interest, greed, lust, or we try to discover a better plot line that will bring a smile to the author's face."

"Yes, yes, yes," Neo replied. "Yes."

We walked on through the fallen leaves. After some thought, I said, "Neo, do you think that a lot of people will be lost . . . I mean, in the end, like you said before, after God judges their life a tragedy, in whatever way that happens? I'm not asking *what* you think happens to them, although I do wish you would tell me that, but if you think there will be very many whose lives end in that . . . tragedy."

"I think that every Christian hopes for what God hopes for: that all will come to repentance, that all will come around and realign their lives with God's hopes and dreams for us sooner rather than later," Neo answered. "But at the same time, there's no shortage of hatred and greed and lust and laziness at work in all of us, and we need to be realistic about the power of that, the danger of that. That's why we need to find ways to help people understand the story well enough so they can see, as you said, what's at stake. We can't force anybody to change, but we have to try, through words and actions and prayer and example to show them a better possibility."

My next question came very tentatively. "What about the people . . . the people who never hear, who never hear about Jesus or any part of the story?"

"I don't think that's any of my business," Neo said calmly. "God will do what's right and just and compassionate in the end. The last thing we need is for folks like you and me to make premature pronouncements on others' eternal destiny, one way or the other, condemning or condoning. What we do need to do is what Jesus told us to do, what Jesus showed us by his own example: to identify those human actions and attitudes that spoil the story, that turn God's dream into a nightmare, that destroy and waste and pollute and degrade and profane God's sacred creation-in-process. We need to speak the truth about those human behaviors, humbly but directly, even if they occur in the heart of Jerusalem—if you know what I mean. And everywhere we go, we need to join Jesus in seeking to bring others in on God's story, helping all those whose hearts are moved to learn to live in Jesus' way, teaching them to live as Jesus taught, helping them to have complete confidence in Jesus and to identify themselves as members of his baptized community of followers. That way, when our time is finished, we'll leave a more robust legacy of people seeking God's dream, and generation after generation, the legacy will be stronger and stronger, until—"

I finished his sentence. "Until God's kingdom comes and God's will is done on earth as in heaven."

A few minutes later, I asked, "The other views of eschatology—you know, premillennialism, postmillennialism, amillennialism—they all have some predictions about a time of catastrophe near the end. How do you see all that?"

"I struggle with knowing how to read the biblical prophecies, I suppose," Neo said. "I see a dynamic tension in the Bible, emphasizing continuity and gradual progress, but also emphasizing discontinuity and crisis, and I think it's good for us to keep that dynamic tension. I don't think that we're supposed to resolve it. Biologists have the same problem. Some of them want to see evolution as being gradual, while others see punctuations, crises, even cataclysms that intervene, creating mass extinctions and at the same time accelerating change. I think that there's truth on both sides, with both hope and warning."

We walked a few more minutes without talking, and then Neo continued. "I tried to read a couple of those apocalyptic novels that became so popular here in the States after I left for my trip. I kept seeing them on the best-seller lists, so I ordered a few, but I couldn't finish them. I can affirm their intent. American consumerism is so strong. It's like a powerful sleeping pill that sends you into a coma spiritually. I'm not surprised that people need to conjure up the end of the world to wake themselves up from the narcotic of consumerism. I can appreciate that. But at the same time, I felt like they represented a kind of death wish, you know?"

My look told Neo I didn't know what he meant, so he continued. "The church in America seems so baffled by late modernity and early post-modernity that it seems to be wishing for a skyhook—as Kerry says—to come in and end history fast . . . rapture, escape from history, shortcut to heaven. It's probably similar to the way fundamentalist Muslims feel as modernity encroaches on their way of life. Suicide bombings and other acts of terrorism seem to express the same kind of death wish. Anyway, to me, those novels show that sometimes life is even more frightening to people than death, that the continuation of the world can be even scarier than the end of the world. I'm not sure that individuals feel that way exactly, but I do think that their religious systems, speaking through them, feel that way."

"So it sounds like you don't believe in some sudden apocalypse," I said.

"Then I'm not being clear," Neo replied. "I think we can hear the hoof beats of several approaching horsemen of doom—if I can use that kind of language with you, Daniel."

"Such as?" I asked.

Neo stopped, and then I stopped too and faced him. He was looking down, hardly blinking, bouncing his stick in his palm like a cop with a billy club. "The horsemen I see on the horizon are of our own making, the wages of our own sin, if you will, humanity reaping what we've sown: overpopulation, racial or ethnic or religious hatred leading to nuclear or biochemical war or some other desperate act of global terrorism that unleashes God knows what, plus good old-fashioned pollution that eventually clicks the biosphere into self-destruct mode."

Then Neo looked up, first at me, and then up to his right, at the tree-tops that lined the path. "Or maybe I should say *self-cleansing* mode, because our sin is the real threat to God's world, and if we won't separate ourselves from our sin, then maybe God's creation itself will execute judgment on us."

He continued. "Biological evolution may work very slowly most of the time, but human cultural evolution seems to accelerate at a really dangerous rate. It's like we're teenagers speeding in a hot rod on a slippery road, and if we don't wise up and learn to handle our speed wisely, we could spin out and experience what so many other species have experienced, the ultimate kind of judgment: extinction. Is that apocalyptic enough for you?"

I nodded and managed only to say, "Hmmm." For all the changes in my thinking, I still wished he'd drop the evolution and extinction language.

Neo turned, and we started walking again, and he continued. "That's one side of biblical prophecy, the apocalyptic side, that's supposed to scare the sin out of us and scare some sense into us too, and those fear tactics are very legitimate. But what's even more important to me in biblical prophecy is the other side, the hopeful side. Through the prophets, God lodges this dream in our hearts. He plants in us a dream of a time and place where the poor and hungry are fed and clothed and cared for, where justice rolls down like the river over there, where righteousness flows like a never-failing stream, where the lamb and lion lie down together in peace, where swords and spears are so useless that they are recast as plowshares and pruning hooks, where the earth is covered with the glory of the Lord as the sea is covered by water."

Neo made a gesture with his hands, as if something above him were being captured and brought into his chest. "That dream, when it lodges in our hearts, transforms us. It's a saving dream. When we dream of that kind of future, we move toward it, we are purified by it, we put aside whatever doesn't align with it, and we help make it a reality. That's the ultimate purpose of biblical prophecies, I think, first to confront us with appropriate warning and then to inspire us with hope, not to give us some sort of cosmic timetable. Anyway, you know I don't think that the future is like that, all spelled out and digitally prerecorded. I'd rather have a profound transforming dream than a facile chart of the future any day. Of course, I'm a minority, in more ways than one."

It was a good hike. We stopped for lunch at another rapids, and our conversation turned from theology to natural history. On the walk back, Neo tried to teach me how to identify common leaves and rocks (but they all looked the same to me). We came upon a tall, dead tree on which at least twenty black vultures were perching. They all took flight as we came closer. And there were more birds. Every few minutes, Neo would stop and look up at a flock of geese that passed overhead, some in a V, others in a W, others in a single-file diagonal line, their honking nearly always audible, whether near and loud or far and faint. Every flock seemed somehow important to Neo, a thing not to be missed—something about him that I still don't really understand.

As we walked back toward my car, I opened up about the changes that were happening in my church, changes that Neo had inspired in many ways, promising signs that our "modern" congregation could indeed begin to understand and engage our increasingly "postmodern" world. I shared some of the problems too, some of the criticisms, some of the people who had left for more traditional churches, fearing that I was leading people into some sort of instability, if not downright heresy. He wanted to know if I still felt like quitting. "Sometimes," I said, "but not as often. It's hard enough when other people don't believe in what you're doing, but it's even harder when you yourself don't believe in what you're doing. When you first met me, the people believed in what I was doing, but I didn't. Now, at least I do, even though I'm not so sure about everybody else—even Carol sometimes!"

We both laughed. Later, during the drive home, Neo began to open up as well, telling me about his deeper feelings for Kerry, how they began, how they strengthened, what he had hoped for, and what he didn't dare hope for. But so much of that conversation is now too painful to recount, because when we returned home, smiling and relaxed, Carol met us in the driveway, holding a cordless phone. The serious look on her face said that something was wrong. She told us before we were completely out of the car: Kerry was gone. Maybe it was the cancer that caused it, or maybe it was the chemo, but a few minutes earlier, she had died suddenly, apparently from a massive stroke.

33

TO CHRISTMAS

I HANDLED THE MEMORIAL SERVICE, which we held at Potomac Community Church on the Sunday afternoon of November 18. Around the sanctuary, Carol taped up the crayon-drawn pictures that the Sunday school children had made for Kerry, pictures that had been hanging on the walls in front of Kerry's hospital bed, cheering her until her death. Many of those young artists asked their parents to bring them to the service after learning of Kerry's death that morning in class. For most of them, this was the first time they had experienced a memorial service. In the narthex, Kincaid set up a collage of photos arranged around a pile of Kerry's favorite books. A small urn with her ashes was placed among the books. During the service, Kincaid delivered a beautiful eulogy for his mother, speaking more with pride than sadness, which helped keep him from tears, but which filled the rest of us with tears all the more. (Neo was too broken up to say anything during the whole service.) After Kincaid was seated, I gave this short homily:

> The story of Kerry Ellison, told so beautifully by her son, Kincaid, was caught up in another story in the last several months. It is a story that intersects with all of our lives. It begins with creation. This beautiful world of mountains and seas and rivers and creatures great and small—the world that Kerry loved so much and to which she devoted her life to preserve—was God's work of art, God's master creation. But we humans, who were endowed with amazing and unique capacities, plunged God's world into crisis through our selfishness and arrogance, our lust and greed, our anger and violence.
>
> So God intervened, calling on one family to become a light to all other families. God entered into a covenant with this family, inviting them into a conversation with God and about God that would span

generations. God and humanity spoke and listened to one another through priests, prophets, poets, and philosophers. This family came to know God not only as glorious creator, but also as their faithful conversation partner, companion, and friend. To this family, and through this family, in the fullness of time, came Jesus Christ, whose death and resurrection demonstrated the love and triumph of God, not through conquest, power, and violence, but through vulnerability, suffering, forgiveness, and resurrection.

Those whose hearts were won to Jesus and his message banded together into a community of faith and mission called the church, which quickly became a global movement of people devoting themselves to living life in a new way, a way that would help the world become the world God always dreamed of. Even during times of violence and evil—times like those we have experienced in recent months—these followers of Jesus were sustained by the hope that God can bring life from death and victory from defeat, and so they forged ahead with hope that ultimately, a great consummation would come, and God's love and justice and mercy and grace would prevail.

This story, in recent months, won Kerry's heart. In fact, a few days ago, when Kerry knew that her treatments weren't working, and that cancer was quickly gaining ground against her, she looked ahead to this memorial service and made me promise to tell you this story today, as I have done, in hopes that it would capture your heart as it did hers.

She wanted me to tell you the good news about God, who launched our story full of adventure, freedom, potential, and promise. Then, in the middle of the story, the heart of God was expressed in a powerful and profound way, beyond words, in flesh and blood, as one of us, walking with us, suffering with us, calling all people to engage their personal and local stories with this glorious and global one. As we look ahead to the end of the story, we see God, waiting with open arms to gather us, and to salvage or harvest from our individual histories—as from all of history—all that is good, beautiful, and true, to resurrect all that is noble from this creation to fly free in the new creation. Kerry has preceded us to the end of the story, and she has been gathered into those arms, and all that was good, beautiful, and true about her has been saved and will never be lost, but will be set free to live and grow in ways that we can hardly begin to imagine.

That was my homily. Whatever worth it had was quickly overshadowed by a surprise: a song, cowritten and performed by Kincaid and, to my complete surprise, my daughter, Jess. They had written it especially for this occasion. They came forward while I closed in prayer. Kincaid sat and played guitar, and Jess stood next to him and sang, her voice frail, tending to go sharp, the tone not very good by classical standards, but somehow all the more poignant for its quiver and frailty. The song is called "We Believe."

> We believe that You created all things
> In all their beauty and mystery.
> We believe we broke the boundaries You gave
> To keep this world in harmony.
> We believe You called a family,
> Blessing them to bless all families.
> We believe You spoke and listened through sage
> And prophet, priest, and poet.
> We believe. We believe. We believe.
> We believe You walked among us in
> Human flesh, to share our history.
> We believe You reconciled us,
> Upon a cross, brought hope from agony.
> We believe You raised Jesus
> From death to life, for our salvation.
> We believe You send us out with saving love
> For all creation.
> We believe. We believe. We believe.
> We believe Your Spirit dwells in us now
> With power for life and mission.
> We believe Your Spirit makes us one
> In purpose, hope, and vision.
> We believe You'll banish evil and fill the earth
> With holy glory.
> We believe You call all people to life
> Forever in Your story.
> We believe. We believe. We believe.

I had never heard Jess sing in public before that moment, and had never seen a line of poetry she had written. When you're a pastor, you wonder what your children will have to go through to make their faith their own; a pastor's family is not always the easiest place for that to happen. As I listened to Jess sing (I couldn't look; my eyes were holding back tears), I thought, *She's finding her own voice, finding her own faith.*

Several days later, just after Thanksgiving, I was standing in the kitchen making a cold turkey sandwich when Neo came to me with a check in his hand. "What's this? Are you finally coughing up some rent?" I joked.

"No," he replied. "It's for plane tickets for a trip that I'm hoping you'll take with me."

"Where are we going?" I asked, still not catching on to Neo's seriousness.

"I'm hoping you'll come with me to the Galápagos Islands."

"The . . . the what? Why?"

Neo leaned against the kitchen counter. "You don't know it, Daniel, but we have some unfinished business to attend to. You fulfilled your promise to Kerry by telling the story at her memorial service, but she asked me to fulfill a promise too, and it involves this check."

I gave Neo a look that asked for explanation, and he said, "That last night at the hospital, Kerry asked me to bring her ashes back to the islands. Of course, I said yes. Then she slipped me this and said it was for expenses. I stuck it in my pocket without even looking at it." He unfolded the check and showed it to me: $10,000. "It's enough for four or five of us to go. I was thinking you and Carol and Kincaid and I. With all the uncertainty, I'd like to go as soon as possible. You never know if travel will get harder, you know?"

I had turned Neo down on another occasion when he offered me a plane ticket about two years earlier, and I regretted that, so this time I said yes. Carol was less enthusiastic though, with the heightened threat of terrorism and related concerns about flying. "I don't want to leave the children home alone these days," she said. "As a mom, I couldn't enjoy the trip."

Neo had another idea: why not bring Jess? She was seventeen now, and a trip like this would be great for her. She and Kincaid had hit it off; he seemed to be the big brother she had always wished for. Then a few days later, Neo told me our party would have one more: Casey Curtis, a young woman studying to become an Episcopal priest, and a former student in Neo's youth group, had accepted Neo's invitation to join us. Over the next few weeks, Neo, Jess, and Kincaid spent hours on the Internet doing research, firming up our itinerary, applying for Jess's first passport, and getting tickets booked.

On the Saturday morning before Christmas, at about ten o'clock, I was sitting in my attic office, nursing a cup of coffee, staring out my window, and looking for last-minute inspiration for two sermons, one on Sunday, one on Christmas Eve. The inspiration was not forthcoming. Neo knocked and entered, stooping under the slanted roof, then sliding into an old leather chair that I'd inherited from my grandfather. He was wearing a clean, pressed Oxford dress shirt, fresh from the dry cleaners. Ever since his doctor had removed the bandages from his arm a few weeks earlier,

Neo seemed especially happy to be able to wear long sleeves again. I noticed a tiny patch of toilet paper stuck to his neck, where he must have nicked himself shaving, and I pointed out a bit of shaving cream behind his ear. "Are you going on a date or something?" I asked, joking.

"I wish," he said, and then got a little gleam in his eye. "Daniel, want a break?"

"Maybe later," I countered, pointing to my computer screen, which had a date and sermon title, and that's all. "What did you have in mind?"

Neo looked disappointed. "I was kind of hoping," he said, "that you'd go to see the new Tolkien movie with me. It's playing in about an hour."

There had been a lot of buzz about the movie's release in recent weeks, but I'd never read the books, and never really cared much for the fantasy genre, so had no desire to see the film. Plus, the thought of going to a movie in the morning never crossed my mind. I even considered matinees a bit strange: movies were made for evenings, not afternoons, and certainly not mornings. But it suddenly dawned on me that the gleam that had just flickered in Neo's eye was the first I'd seen since Kerry's death. So I changed my mind.

At 11:00 A.M. we sat down, just as the lights dimmed for the "coming attractions." At 2:15 P.M. we stepped out of the theater, squinting under a brilliant, cloudless sky. I couldn't talk. The film had completely captured me, and I wasn't sure why. When we got in the car, I started chattering about the film. Neo listened politely for several minutes as we navigated out of the parking lot and then pulled in at a coffee shop. We went in and sat down in some comfortable chairs, facing a huge picture window that displayed a vista of Fords and Chryslers and Hondas and an occasional BMW.

"That's the third time you've asked me why the movie affected you so much, Daniel," Neo said. "The first two times I asked you back your own question. Can I do it again?"

"It's obvious that I can't figure it out," I replied.

"Well, my friend, perhaps it was a story that you could find yourself in," he said. I cocked my head, surprised to hear him use that phrase with a subsacred story like this. "Really, Daniel, all the great literature offers entrée into the story we find ourselves in—through stories of good and evil, love and hate, pride and repentance, fear and courage. Sometimes, we become so familiar with the primal sacred story of the Bible that we need some fresh takes on it, telling us the same thing in different ways, or giving us some new vantage points to see what was always there, things we'd missed before."

"It's funny you say that," I responded, "because I remember watching the hobbits and thinking, for no apparent reason, of Mary and Joseph, and the Jews in general—that passage from Deuteronomy where God basically says that they were chosen not because they were big and powerful but because they were small and weak."

"Quite a resonance," Neo said. "I wish we had couple of those long pipes that Gandalf and Bilbo enjoyed, or at least"—he looked at his watch—"at least a pint of ale to enjoy this afternoon as the December sun gets ready to set early."

"It's an amazing story," he said. I assumed that he was talking about Tolkein's story, but then he said, "A young girl gives birth to a tiny baby in a despised little town in an oppressed little country under the heel of the greatest superpower in history. And that little baby becomes a young man who by the time he is thirty-three has undermined the superpower and injected into human culture an inextinguishable hope in the form of good news. He single-handedly releases the ring of power through the cross, and defeats the darkness that was afoot in all humanity."

I turned toward Neo. "But why," I asked, "can I get a better feel for the power of that battle of good versus evil from a fictional film than I can in . . . in the Bible itself?" I felt embarrassed to say it so bluntly, as if I were criticizing the Scriptures.

Neo smiled but didn't say anything. I thought of what he might be thinking: maybe the Bible wasn't intended to be so compelling that it would overwhelm all our creative urges; maybe it was intended to inspire those creative urges, and so had to be somewhat understated; maybe its genius was to inspire a million masterpieces rather than to be the sole, ultimate masterpiece. Neo interrupted what I imagined he might say and said, "It seems to be God's way, doesn't it, to show a greater power through weakness than could ever be shown through strength—greater power through frail people, through flawed heroes, through a young girl and a nondescript baby, and even through a cross, all conveyed through a book that really is a collection of fragments assembled over several centuries, that is uneven in style and rather appalling in content in places, and that leaves a lot of loose ends . . . a weak book in many ways."

I shook my head, smiling. Then I lifted my coffee for a toast. "To the Bible," I said, "and to the hobbits."

Neo touched his cardboard cup to mine in a silent toast and said, "Yes, and to Christmas."

At that moment I realized that I now had the inspiration I needed for my upcoming sermons.

34

LIKE A WIRE INTO THE WALL

WE WERE SCHEDULED TO DEPART January 30, 2002, a Wednesday. Casey flew into D.C. a few days earlier, joining Kincaid, Neo, Jess, and me. She was a live wire ("pistol" was Neo's word for her), and from the moment of her arrival, there was a steady flow of laughter, kidding, practical joking, and fun. She was in her mid-twenties, I guessed, beautiful, and prone to smile, with dark-coffee skin and bright eyes, and her shoulder-length hair braided with colorful beads that made a wonderful sound whenever she moved her head.

Neo convinced us to pack light. "We'll be squeezed into small cabins on a pretty small boat," he said. "Don't even think of bringing along a big suitcase. All you'll need is a pair or two of shorts, swimming trunks, a couple T-shirts, hiking shoes, maybe sandals, and lots of sunscreen for you folk of paler hue."

Before we passed through security at Baltimore/Washington International Airport, I checked Kerry's ashes, which were stored in a plastic bag, inside a box, inside my small suitcase. I was a little worried about getting them through customs in Ecuador. Given the continuing terrorism concerns about anthrax and bombs, I was apprehensive about bringing a powdery substance on the airplane. But later that day, Ecuadorian customs lived up to low expectations, and although my bags were inspected, no questions were asked about the box. (I didn't know whether to feel relieved or concerned by the lax security.)

We landed in Quito, went to a motel, and were up before daybreak the next morning, catching a cab to the airport for flights to Guayaquil and then Baltra, the airport of the Galápagos Islands. I looked down as we circled Baltra. The landscape was bleak, gray-brown, arid—far from the tropical paradise I'd expected. Once we landed, we boarded a bus and crossed Baltra, then took a ferry across a narrow channel to the north side of the island of Santa Cruz. There we boarded another bus heading south, first ascending from the arid lowlands to the lush volcanic highlands, then descending to the south side of the island toward Puerto Ayora, the main port of the islands.

Neither Jess nor I had ever been to a "third world" setting before, so we were a bit shocked by the living conditions (which actually were quite good by third world standards). We saw dirt-floor cinderblock houses, many of them apparently left half-built, with dirty, half-dressed, but obviously happy kids playing outside, laughing, chasing each other, running barefoot on the reddish volcanic gravel. Puerto Ayora itself was a bit more developed, for better or worse. We passed the Discothèque Lizard, apparently a local hangout, where a couple of drunken men lay passed out on the gravel parking lot. Then we went by a number of video stores (all out of business), and a few touristy bars and restaurants. We were greeted at the town's main waterfront intersections by large, gaudily painted, and rather bizarre statues of animals: a land iguana, a giant tortoise, and, facing the bay, a poorly proportioned seabird that may have been an albatross.

"They're for tourists to pose in front of for pictures," Neo said, striking a mock pose with his arms held out and his face exaggerating a smile, the scar on his arm matching the one on his face.

"That makes a lot of sense," Casey quipped. "Go to the prime spot in the world to see God's native wildlife in their natural setting, and have your picture taken in front of a man-made, tacky papier-mâché replica with a bad paint job."

We got off the bus and made our way down along Charles Darwin Avenue to the municipal dock, my little wheeled suitcase clicking across the cobblestones. We stopped for a few minutes to join a large crowd watching "volley," a variant of volleyball played with three-person teams. I tried to use a pay phone along the sidewalk to call Carol, but couldn't read the Spanish instructions and couldn't make it work. Neo kept looking for familiar faces in the crowd or on the street, but found none. He stopped at a pay phone in front of the Habana Bar and called Maricel. He seemed so happy when he returned to our group. "She's going to pull the old Aventura group together Sunday night when we get back," he said, "plus a few of Kerry's coworkers from the Center. We'll have a memorial service for Kerry on *La Aventura*."

At the dock, Casey pointed out a large sign:

Bienvenidos a
PUERTO AYORA
Welcome to

"That's one way to say it," she said. Then she walked around to each of us with an outstretched hand and cheerfully said, "Puerto Ayora welcome to," which got us all laughing.

Neo checked my watch: it was 3:30 P.M. He had arranged for us to be picked up at 4:00 by *panga,* which showed up promptly at 4:45, to transport us to *La Aventura,* the same boat on which Neo had worked the previous year. Our plan was to be part of a tour already in progress, our party of five joining eleven ecotourists already on board. All of us would return to Puerto Ayora late on Sunday afternoon. We would see three southern islands: Floreana, Española, and San Cristóbal.

La Aventura's Ecuadorian owner, Washington Lincoln Marti (a name Casey had fun with), was skipper this week, and he greeted Neo as an old friend, with warmth and enthusiasm. Several crew members also knew Neo, so there were smiles, laughter, hugs, handshakes, and lots of loud good Spanish (from the crew) and loud bad Spanglish (from Neo). Washington showed us around the vessel and introduced us to the other passengers, all of whom were European, except for one Japanese fellow, who had no language in common with anyone else other than the language of smiles. We enjoyed a gourmet dinner of fresh baked fish, fruit salad, and Ecuadorian corn (large, pale white kernels the size of popcorn), prepared by Miguel, the ship's chef ("cook" didn't do him justice).

After dinner, we all went up to the sundeck to watch the sunset and talk. A Dutch woman, Femke, asked me my occupation, and when I told her I was a pastor, she immediately reached out and took my arm. "Can we talk?" she asked. None of these passengers had ever attended church (aside from some baptisms as infants, and a funeral or wedding or two) or met a pastor. In a few minutes, a circle of seven or eight of us formed and an impromptu "Q&A" session began.

When the first question came, from Femke's husband, Pieter (whose English was excellent), I glanced over at Neo, who smiled and winked. "Being here in these islands," Pieter said, "with their historical connection to Charles Darwin, what do you think about evolution? Do you think it is in harmony with belief about God?"

I tried to get Neo to answer the question, but he wouldn't. So I ducked the question and answered it with one of my own. "Why do you think that's an important question?" I asked.

Pieter answered, "Well, in my country, and in all of northern Europe, really, this is one of the issues that show how Christianity has become irrelevant. People feel that Christianity requires them to go back five hundred years in time and hold a view of things that is . . . how do you say it? . . . unacceptable, incredulous . . . I mean, *incredible* today."

Neo decided to step in. "Pieter, I think that evolution is one of God's best creations. Maybe it would help if I could try to sketch out the big story that Christians believe we are part of."

"Yes," Pieter said, "I would be fascinated to be hearing this."

Neo went through the story, not specifically mentioning his episodes (creation, crisis, and so on), but just letting the story flow naturally and accommodating the questions and comments that others in the group offered. Discussion flowed. About ten o'clock, Kincaid, who had been silent up to that point, spoke up and said, "Excuse me, everybody, but I need to get some sleep. But I wanted to say something first, before I go down to my cabin." Everyone turned toward him. "Well, I'm just twenty-one, and for the last couple of years, I've been . . . well, let's just say, doing my share of partying—a lot of drinking, and some drugs too. Over the last couple of months though, I've been learning more about this story that we've been talking about. Sitting here, listening to everyone talk, I just realized that . . . that I haven't even thought about getting drunk or high for months. And I'm realizing that the reason I was messing around so much was that I didn't have any story beyond myself. You know what I mean? There was nothing bigger that I could see myself being part of, so there wasn't much more to do than try to enjoy myself. The whole world kind of shrank down to the size of . . . of my problems and feelings, or whatever. That's all. I just wanted to say that. Good night, everyone." Several heads nodded, and "Good night" went around the group in various languages.

After Kincaid left the upper deck, Neo explained the reason for our visit, and told everyone about Kincaid's mom, their friendship, and his promise to her to bring her ashes back here to the islands. "Wow," Femke said, "I feel that we on this boat have been brought into a bigger story tonight. Before you arrived, we were just here on vacation, all of us here for our own reasons, but now you have connected us in, like a wire into the wall—you know, an electrical connection. What is the way to say it? Yes, plugged into your stories. This is a very wonderful thing."

Gradually, all the passengers made their way down to their cabins, all except Neo and me. We sat on the deck chairs for a long time, looking up at the stars, talking about the evening's conversation. "It's so sad," I said, "sad and exciting at the same time. These people have such spiritual openness and interest, and need too, but the Christian faith seems like something stuck in the past, something completely irrelevant. For them, becoming a Christian makes as much sense as becoming an Aztec. We need a lot more people like you, Neo, who can help them in their spiritual search. It's like you're reinterpreting Christianity, or maybe recycling it, you know? It's been discarded like a used-up container or box or something, and you're making it useful again."

Neo looked up at the sky and asked, "How long do you suppose it will be before America is where Europe is now?" With that, he stood up and went down to the cabin that he, Kincaid, and I were sharing. I stayed on the deck for another twenty minutes or so, thinking about the evening, and praying too, and then went down to our cabin, still deep in thought. Back home, I was always worried that Neo was pushing us too far too fast. But hearing the conversation that night, I had the opposite concern. Would we go far enough, fast enough, to help dear people like these Europeans? The crew raised the anchor and started the engines for our trip to Floreana. The droning engine put me into a deep sleep.

The next morning, we were up early and, after a quick breakfast of fruit, coffee, toast, and jam, we boarded the *pangas* to tour Floreana. Clearly, this was more special for the rest of our group than for me; I hate to admit it, but I've never really appreciated animals all that much. I did enjoy the scenery. The new guide for *La Aventura*, a pretty Galápagos native named Lourdes, led us across a rugged trail to a secluded beach where dark shapes—I counted fifty, and know I missed some—floated in the turquoise water. "Sea turtles, Dad!" Jess said, running to the edge of the water. Lourdes explained that they were waiting in the shallow water until nightfall, when they'd come ashore to lay eggs.

After a few minutes, Neo opened his backpack and pulled out the box with Kerry's ashes. Our whole group—now sixteen of us—gathered around. Neo gave a little speech about Kerry's love for Floreana, and her fascination with the sea turtles, and then he opened the bag inside the box. He nodded to Kincaid, who took a few handfuls of ashes and spread them in the clear water. It wasn't a sad moment, but it was . . . sacred. I noticed that several of the Europeans were sniffling or wiping away tears, even though they'd never known Kerry and had known us only for a matter of hours.

Kincaid (who had visited the islands several times before) took Jess and Casey snorkeling for the afternoon, while Neo joined the Europeans for scuba diving. I didn't know how to do either, so I stayed on the boat, just slowing down and taking in the scenery, playing a few games of solitaire, and slathering on as much sunscreen as possible.

35

EVERYTHING WE CONSUME, WE TURN INTO . . .

THE NEXT MORNING WE ARRIVED at Española. We took another early morning hike, this one among nesting birds—red-footed boobies, I recall, and others whose names I don't recall. This was another place where Neo pulled out the box and the bag (smaller since yesterday), and again, Kincaid spread a handful of Kerry's ashes among the birds' nests. "Somehow," he said, "it seems like this is the right place for some of my mom's ashes to be, a place of birth, and a place where mothers are caring for their young."

We left Española at midday and arrived at Puerto Barquerizo Morena in the midafternoon. The town is the capital of the Galápagos province and home to a few thousand people. As we drew near the port, Jess was enthralled. "Dad, do you hear it?" she asked.

"Hear what?" I replied.

"The sound of children laughing. I don't think I've ever heard such a happy sound," she said, holding my arm.

I strained my ears, and yes, I could hear it, faintly above the boat's engine, above the calls of gulls and frigate birds (Jess identified them for me)—laughter surging and receding like the waves. The colors also struck me: vividly colored roofs and trim on the houses and shops at the waterfront—dark blue, light blue, pink, yellow, brown, orange—and brightly painted fishing boats anchored in the small harbor, each one, Jess pointed out, with a plump brown sea lion or two flopped across the deck, sleeping and oblivious to the approach of our yacht.

As we got closer, the laughter grew louder and even more delightful. Two docks jutted out into the clear waters of the bay, and from each, twenty or thirty kids, from preschoolers through teenagers, were jumping, diving, and swimming. There was plenty of good-natured horseplay, too, with kids pushing and pulling each other off the docks, kids racing each other among the fishing boats, kids challenging each other to dive to the bottom and come back with a stone or shell.

"This is like paradise, Dad," Jess said. "If I ever disappear, don't come looking here, OK? Because this is where I'll be hiding."

Paradise. The word struck me. In these islands, animals aren't afraid of humans, because humans, like the other animals around them, pose no threat; we are their fellow creatures, their friends, their protectors, interested in them for what they are, not for how we can exploit them. The word "paradise" also came to mind as we disembarked for a few hours in the town, because I noticed that Kincaid and Jess were holding hands. I hadn't realized that they had been getting closer, but I wasn't upset. "Of course," I said to myself. I was happy for both of them.

With Jess enjoying Kincaid's company, and with Neo eager to look up some friends from the town, and with Casey having disappeared somewhere, I found myself alone, so I wandered over to the Interpretive Center, just beyond the edge of town, to see what it had to offer. I felt that Neo's story, our story, was being retold by the displays in the Center. Several displays depicted the creation of the islands, arising out of the fire of volcanism, emerging from their own "big bang" in a way. Long processes were required to prepare the barren islands for the arrival and development of life, which arose gradually, through a strange combination of accidents and apparent good fortune. Against all odds, life found ways to root in the smallest niches and cracks in the volcanic rock: first plants, then insects and birds, then reptiles and a few mammals. In their isolation, six hundred miles from the coast of Ecuador, they enjoyed safety in what began as a volcanic hell and became a bountiful paradise.

Then humans arrived, and predictably, stupidly, they destroyed the paradise they discovered. First pirates and later whalers came seeking fresh water and found along with it the islands' huge tortoises, which would be quickly lugged aboard and mercilessly packed in the holds of the ships, upside down, where they could live (or better put, suffer) for up to a year without food or water—handy long-term meat storage. They were taken by the hundreds of thousands over the course of several decades, the Center's displays explained. One display showed a landscape covered by their bleached shells. I'm no "green" activist," but I was appalled. Sea turtles were taken too, mainly females that came ashore to lay their eggs. Equally destructive to the ecological balance, goats and cattle were set free on the islands, so they would reproduce and be available for food on return voyages; and along with them, rats and cats and dogs also escaped and became feral. These thoughtless introductions of nonnative species had disastrous results—evidence of human arrogance and disrespect for the fragile but beautiful (and, thank God, resilient) balances of creation's ecosystems.

Creation and crisis played out for me in a tragic tango on the walls of the Interpretive Center. There were remarkable stories of idealistic settlers who saw the islands as the perfect site for their utopian dreams to be lived out in seclusion and isolation from the corruptions of civilization. But in each case, however high their ideals, these utopian communities self-destructed in suspicion, hatred, and murder. Humans invariably brought their corruption with them, within them—ignorance, greed, arrogance, oppression, lust, distrust. I kept thinking of a book I had read in junior high school, *Lord of the Flies*. Quite a different tale from *Lord of the Rings*.

As I meandered through the Interpretive Center, taking in panel after panel of text and photographs that chronicled the tragic story of the islands, I heard the now familiar sound of Casey's beads as she bounced up and asked if I wanted any company. We began reading the panels together and relating them to the biblical story. "Here's another C-word for you, Reverend Dan," she said. "*Consumption*. We sucked up land tortoises and sea turtles for their meat and oil, butchered whales for their blubber, and bashed sea lions for their fur. Who gives a rip about the ecosystems that had taken millions of years to develop? We blew in and tried to build farms and factories to mass-produce sugar and other crops for mainland consumers. It's typical, all over the world: human consumption always dictates our agendas. It's all about consumption. Taking in food and digesting it to extract what is of value to us, leaving only . . . leaving only crap. There's no polite word for it, Reverend Dan. We consume everything we can, and everything we consume we turn into . . ." (Her word was a more colorful one than I'll repeat here.)

I couldn't really argue with her choice of words. As we walked along in silence among the displays of the Interpretive Center, I thought about how this very local story was a fractal of the global story. I thought about God's call to Abraham, about the ensuing conversation among priests, prophets, poets, and philosophers, as God invited people to become part of the solution instead of part of the problem. I thought about Jesus and his coming, his message about God's parental concern for sparrow and wildflower, his example of serving and self-giving and saving love instead of selfish consumption. I thought about Jesus' invitation to a *better* way: it's better to give than to receive, he said, better to forgive and understand than to condemn and judge, better to give and trust than to hoard and control, better to suffer violence than to inflict violence, better to serve than to be served, better to seek and rescue what is lost or threatened than to pride oneself as being safe and secure and superior, better to save than to condemn . . . better to love than anything else.

We left the Interpretive Center and sat on a bench outside, both of us feeling a little depressed. The weather seemed to sympathize, as the sky had grown cloudy and the wind was picking up, suggesting rain, but the coolness was refreshing. I shared a few of my musings with Casey, and she replied, "Yeah, beautiful words. But we didn't think Jesus' way was better. Our ways were just fine, thank you very much. So we shut up all that talk about a better way by sending Jesus straight to extinction. It seems like the bad guys always win, you know?"

Her gloomy outlook was understandable in light of the displays we had just seen. I tried to offer a few more hopeful thoughts—inspired by Neo—about how Jesus' weakness and vulnerability proved stronger than the strength and power of humanity in crisis, inspiring millions of people to continue his revolutionary mission down through the centuries and out across the globe.

"Yeah," Casey said, resistant to anything like a glib reassurance, "but remember how often we, Christ's supposed followers, totally miss the point, completely forget what he was and is about, and in his name, perpetuate the crisis and continue to turn everything into crap. Maybe that's the biggest C-word of all."

Then she softened a bit, sounding a bit less angry, but even more sad. "Reverend Dan, I was listening to one of those Christian radio shows a couple weeks ago. That famous white guy who always talks about saving America was on—I forget his name." I reminded her. "Yeah, him. He made me so mad . . . no, more than mad . . . sick. He kept talking about how we need to go back, you know, back to when they had prayer in schools and all. Is he serious? Sure, let's go back—back to when my grandmother wasn't allowed in a white church, and when my grandfather got beat up for going into the white part of town, and when my parents were forced to attend a segregated school. Yeah, those were the good old days. Prayer in the schools did a whole lot of good back then. Sure, let's go back to that."

Part of me wanted to cheer Casey up and say something hopeful; I hadn't seen this side of her before. But I resisted the urge to minimize her sadness, and instead, agreed with her. "You're right," I said. "There's a lot of crap out there." Then I gave her a good-natured pat on the back and said, "I guess that's why the world needs a new breed of pastors like you and me. We'll finally get it right."

"Yeah, right!" she said, laughing a little, and her beads added some music to her laughter. "You and me, Reverend Dan."

We got up from our bench and headed back into town, stopping at a small snack shop, which actually was the front room of a little white cottage. We were lucky to find that the young woman behind the counter, Marta, spoke pretty good English. (My only foreign languages are ancient Greek and Hebrew, arduously studied in seminary but largely forgotten since, offering little practical value in buying ice cream cones!) Marta was eager to practice her English with people who weren't in a hurry, and we were eager to learn more about life in the islands. Did she feel far removed from the rest of the world? (She used to, but not now, since they have satellite TV.) Did she ever want to leave? (She had visited Guayaquil and Quito, but always was glad to return home. "Here I feel free," she said. "Here I feel alive.") Did a lot of young people leave? ("I think about eighty percent always want to live here," she said.) What about churches on the islands?

With that question, a pained look came over her face. "We have many churches, many for such a small place," she said, "but they always arguing—you know, they fight. The Testigos sometimes knock at our door at six in the morning, telling us we go to wrong church because we are Catolicos. And the Bautistas and Pentecostales say same things." I wasn't going to ask any more, because I didn't want to hear any more about this, but she added, "But I love God, and I love my church. Do you want to see? Padre Raul is away in Guayaquil, but our church is always open." We had an hour before the *pangas* would take us back to *La Aventura*, so we said sure. Marta flipped the sign on the screen door to "Cerrado" and led Casey and me at a lively pace halfway across the little town to her church.

It was made of cinderblock, like all the larger buildings there, and had the same nondescript architecture as the stores that surrounded it, except for a wooden cross on a long wooden pole above the front entrance. When we entered, I was transfixed by what I saw.

The walls were painted with murals, and under each mural was a quote from St. Francis. "Of course," she said, "because this church we name in his honor." There were quotations—Marta translated them for us—about brother sun and sister moon, weather and wind, work and rest, and each was illustrated with colorful scenes from daily life in the islands. On the back wall was an especially moving painting. The quotation had to do with work being the prayer of our hands, and there were many brown, weathered hands pictured, one holding a fishing net, one working in a garden, one holding chalk to a blackboard, one cooking, one holding a hammer. And mixed in with all these hands was one hand holding nothing, but clearly showing a scar in the palm. I stood there a long time, just staring, thinking, unable to speak, though I wasn't sure why. No cathedral in Europe ever moved me as did that homespun mural in Puerto Barquerizo Morena. I think that Casey felt the same way.

36

NO BETTER BENEDICTION

THE NEXT DAY WAS SUNDAY, the day of our return to Santa Cruz and Puerto Ayora. We arrived on shore in the midafternoon, giving us a chance to tour the Charles Darwin Research Center. Neo and I skipped the tour (he had spent a lot of time at the Center with Kerry, and I had already had my fill of nature lore), and instead we devoted the time to preparing for Kerry's memorial service that night. Too many people were interested in coming to fit onto *La Aventura,* so Neo arranged for us to hold Kerry's memorial service on the plaza facing the water, right in front of the big papier-mâché albatross statue at the center of the waterfront. We rushed around town on foot to finalize plans for the service, tracking down people whose names I had learned from Kerry several months earlier: Humberto, Alvaro, Maricel. They greeted Neo warmly, clearly delighted to see him, but since I couldn't understand Spanish, apart from hearing Kerry's name mentioned a lot, I couldn't follow much.

The service was scheduled for 6 P.M., right about sunset. The crowd that gathered to watch "volley" began to disperse, and another crowd, almost as large, slowly formed in front of the albatross. Neo started the service, with Humberto translating, by telling the story of how he and Kerry had met. Alvaro and Maricel then sang some of the songs that Kerry had heard at the "reuniones en la Aventura." Then Neo invited people to come forward and offer a memory about or tribute to Kerry, and one after another they did so. Maricel cried so hard during her little speech that I wondered if she would be able to continue, but each time she would compose herself and go on. When she finished, she gave Neo a long, strong hug. The first person whose words were delivered in English was Glenn. He directed them to Kincaid.

"Your mother," he began, "was my true friend. I remember your first visit here, Kincaid, a couple years back . . . when you were a freshman in college, I think . . . and I took you horseback riding because your mom had a research paper she needed to finish. Remember that? Your mom just about killed me when we returned, because you fell off the horse and nearly broke your arm, and she blamed me for galloping too fast." Humberto translated into Spanish, and everyone laughed.

"It was my shoulder," Kincaid replied, with a smile, "and I still have problems with it sometimes."

As the sunset faded, the stories about Kerry continued to flow, some in Spanish, more in English now, stories of Kerry's skill as a scientist, her dedication to her work, her many kindnesses, her love for living things. The waterfront shops and the boats in the harbor provided enough light so that after the last song (one that Maricel wrote and sang especially for this occasion), the whole group walked in a silent procession out onto the municipal dock. We gathered at the end of the dock, and Neo took the remaining ashes and gave them to Kincaid. As Kincaid sprinkled some of the ashes into the water, there was complete silence among us, while in the background came the soft lapping of the waves against the dock, the sound of riggings tapping gently against the masts of the nearby sailboats, and a faint sound of happy Latino music from one of the yachts anchored in the harbor.

Then Kincaid walked over to me with the plastic bag. He held it up, gesturing that he wanted me to take the last handful of ashes. I wasn't expecting this and must have made a gesture suggesting that I wouldn't or couldn't. Kincaid leaned close and whispered in my ear, "Dan, you helped my mom so much. You helped her find God. You and Carol took her into your family. Please, this would be an honor for me, and I know that Mom would want you to have a part in this."

So I held out my two hands, cupped together, and Kincaid poured out the last of Kerry's ashes. They felt heavy, like sand, and gritty. I had never touched human ashes before. I walked over to the edge of the cement dock, and looked down into the water, black in the darkness, with lights faintly shimmering on the surface. I stood there for a brief moment, and then unbidden, a word came to my mind: *borrowed*. Borrowed? Why that word?

Before I had answered this self-posed question that had seemed to arise from nowhere, I began letting the ashes slip between my two cupped hands, slowly, like sand through an hourglass. And then, as the ashes flowed down, a realization flowed into my thoughts.

These gray, gritty particles were borrowed from the stuff of the universe. They once had been muscle, bone, tooth, hair, nerve. Before that, they had been bread, milk, fruit, vegetable. And before that, they had been soil, mineral, rock, rain. And before that, billions of years before that, they had

been part of the substance of stars. And before that, the subatomic particles that constituted these ashes had emerged from the big bang, the flash
of energy that flowered into our universe at the very beginning. Kerry had
borrowed these materials with this amazing history, and for fifty-some
years had used them (effortlessly, unconsciously) to ferment this wonderful, miraculous wine called life. They had served her well, sustaining di-
gestion, respiration, reproduction, motion, contemplation, communication,
providing a "biovehicle" in which an elusive entity called a person could
develop, emerge, and fill a name with identity.

The last of the ashes fell through my fingers, and I brushed the last particles from my palms and fingertips down into the dark water. I stood
looking down, my hands folded in front of me, thinking of the last episode of the story we find ourselves in: *consummation.* The biochemical
reactions had ceased, but that identity, that person who had emerged in syn-
ergy with those biochemical reactions, had not been lost. God had saved
Kerry, remembered her, her entire personality, not just the frail and failing Kerry of the last days of her life, but the vibrant Kerry in all her many
dimensions comprising all the moments of her life on so many levels. That
person had somehow been saved, uploaded like software, from the medium of molecules to a new medium, like music transferred from tape to
disk, or better put, like music transferred to the memory of a master mu-
sician who could let the music play again. The ashes fell between my fingers, but Kerry herself was somehow retained and preserved, saved and
cherished, in the mind of God, the heart of God. *She doesn't need these
ashes anymore.* She had become all she could in the matrix of matter, energy, and time on earth. Now, she would be created anew and set free afresh
in some other time or place, in some new, unimagined adventure, some
new story that unfolds beyond this current tale of water, ash, wave, and
wind, in a mysterious sequel to this life, both revealed and hidden in the
word "heaven."

These thoughts seemed to rise in my mind from a very deep place, res-
onating within the word "borrowed." Then, as the word "borrowed" faded
from my mind, a dark figure shot into view in the water below me. It darted
in from the right and arced out and away, and then swung back toward
me like a huge brown bullet. Then it seemed to shrink and almost disappear, only to rise and emerge with a surprise and a splash and huge, wet
eyes. "Whoa!" I said. And I must have jumped back, because immediately
the crowd of people ran forward to see what had startled me.

It was a sea lion, ready to play. *Aaar . . . aaar . . . aaar!* it bellowed, and
our whole group erupted into laughter and applause. There could have
been no better benediction.

The group gradually dispersed. Our party of five had been invited up to Maricel's home for dessert, but I remained there, sitting at the edge of the dock, dangling my legs over the water, praying, but most of the time without words. The sound of voices faded, and the quiet sounds of the night could be heard again. Maybe forty-five minutes later, Neo came and joined me, and then Kincaid came and sat beside him. Eventually, Jess and Casey joined us. No one spoke, even when Neo went to get the *panga* to bring us back to *La Aventura*.

Before Neo returned with the panga, Glenn ran up in the darkness and handed me a note scribbled on a piece of notebook paper. "Please share this with Neo," he said. The note read:

> Dan and Neo—Thanks for the memorial service tonight. We all needed that. There is this hole in our hearts here without Kerry, and you helped it heal. I wanted to tell you that I don't believe your whole story. But I am tempted to add "yet" when I say that. So maybe that's progress. In the meantime, count on me as a not-completely-convinced ally. I'll keep trying to do God's work of healing our world from the crisis you (Neo) explained to me that day at Darwin Center. With whatever little faith I have, I'll do what I can here. You two keep up the good work wherever you go, OK?—Glenn

37

IT AIN'T OVER YET

SEVERAL MONTHS LATER, on the last Saturday in September 2002, I received a letter bearing the return address of one of the board members of Potomac Community Church. I had spent the morning helping Kincaid and Neo move into the townhouse that Neo had just purchased not far from my neighborhood. Jess, now a college frosh living on campus at the nearby University of Maryland, came home from school for the weekend eager to help Kincaid, now her steady boyfriend, also enrolled at Maryland, as he settled in as Neo's housemate. When Jess and I pulled in the driveway that afternoon, Carol was sitting on the front step waiting for me. She looked odd—maybe sad, but even more, tender—and held the letter, opened, in her hand.

"I reckon you'd better sit down too to read this," she said. "I didn't realize it was personal, so I opened it accidentally. I hope you didn't mind me reading it."

"Of course not," I said, and sat down on her left to start reading, with Jess sitting on my left, reading over my shoulder.

September 25, 2002

Dear Dan,
We regret having to write this letter. While you were on vacation last month, we had several emergency Board meetings to address some complaints that have arisen over the last year or so. These complaints all relate to a subtle but real shift that we perceive has taken place in your preaching and theology. While the word "heresy" may be too strong a word, we do not want to understate the gravity of our concern.

You are loved and respected greatly by our people and our Board, which makes this letter all the more difficult to write. Effective immediately, we are placing you on paid leave and are initiating, per provisions in our bylaws, a thorough inquiry into your doctrinal fitness to continue as pastor of Potomac Community Church.

We expect this process to take one to three months, and we request that you keep this strictly confidential. We will announce to the congregation that you have been granted a sabbatical at least until the new year. During this time, we will be asking you to answer a number of questions in writing, and we will schedule several meetings with you and with those bringing complaints against you. Please do not attend the church during this time, or have unnecessary contact with church members.

Whether we are able to resolve these concerns or not, we want to be sure that the matter is handled with due diligence for your sake and the sake of the congregation.

Please be assured that no one questions your sincerity or integrity. It is clear, however, that you are changing in your thinking and theology, and we are not sure that our congregation can handle change of this depth and magnitude this fast, if at all. We hope that you will be able to reaffirm, with complete conviction and without reservation, the essential absolute and objective truths that serve as our foundation and on which our unity depends.

Prayerfully,
Marlin Magothy
Nancy Zeamer
For the Board of Directors

"Wow, Dad," Jess said. "Are you OK?"

My heart was pounding and my hands were shaking, but inwardly, I felt strangely calm. I was somewhat surprised, because Marlin and Nancy had been joking with me just the previous Sunday at church, and they gave no indication that this was coming. But in a way, I wasn't surprised, especially when I read the last lines, which contained words I had heard frequently on the lips of Nancy's husband, Gilbert: "Methods may change, but the essential absolute truths and essential foundational facts of the faith never do." I think I'd heard Gilbert say those words at least half a dozen times. (It's hard to disagree with Gil on that, but I guess it depends on who defines those truths and facts, and how and why they do so.)

I folded the letter, put it in my back pocket, and said, "Let's take a walk." The three of us spent the next hour or so wandering through the neighborhood, talking about how I should handle the situation, predicting outcomes, venting our mixed emotions, even joking a bit. When we got back home, I got out the letter and read it again, this time out loud, with Carol and Jess standing beside me in our front yard. (I was distracted for a minute when I realized that Jess was wearing Kincaid's red stone ring on a necklace. I wondered what that meant.)

I folded up the letter. "Never a dull moment," I said with a sigh, and Carol and Jess both put an arm around me.

Since receiving that letter, I've had a lot of free time—more than I've had in years, maybe since I was kid on summer vacation. With no sermons to compose, no meetings to attend (so far), no appointments to keep, no funerals to perform or meetings to chair or church problems to solve, I've said to Carol more than once, "If this is punishment, if this is persecution, keep it coming."

Carol has been less sanguine: "It ain't over yet, Dan," she says. Anyway, this involuntary "sabbatical" has given me time to write this book.

My first meeting with the Potomac Community Church board is scheduled for next week. I'm getting nervous.

Since September 3, Neo has been back teaching science at Franklin Roosevelt High School, and he tells me (always with a wink and a smile) that if I get fired from PCC, he can help me get a job on the faculty there. "But I hope it won't come to that," he says. "I hope that they'll see you're just struggling to really understand our story, and tell it straight. That's no heresy, man. That's the gospel."

The other day, Neo could tell, I think, that I'd been feeling a little anxious, a little down. He came over to the house and bounded up the stairs to my attic office, where I was rereading this manuscript, just after dinner. He handed me a present, not wrapped, but in a cardboard box. It was a framed photograph of Kerry, standing ankle-deep in the shallows along the Potomac River that day she was baptized—Carol and me on either side of her, all arm in arm: cane in hand, red bandana, bald head, and that smile.

"Beautiful," I said.

"Beyond all words," Neo said.

GROUP STUDY

MANY CLASSES AND GROUPS have used *A New Kind of Christian* for group study, and I hope that even more will use this sequel to stimulate dialogue and shared learning. No study guide is necessary if participants will do the following:

1. The group agrees on a section to read for the next meeting.
2. Each participant agrees to underline, star, highlight, annotate, or otherwise mark the text, identifying the following:

   Something I agreed with or enjoyed.

   Something I questioned or disagreed with.

   Something I'd like to discuss further.
3. At the meeting, a participant shares one of the marked passages, and why he or she felt it was noteworthy. Others respond, then the next participant shares a passage, and so on.

Various online groups provide great opportunities for dialogue too. Especially helpful is http://groups.yahoo.com/group/NKOC.

THE AUTHOR

BRIAN D. MCLAREN, born in 1956, graduated from University of Maryland with degrees in English (B.A., summa cum laude, 1978, and M.A., magna cum laude, 1981). After several years of teaching and consulting in higher education, he left academia in 1986 to become founding pastor of Cedar Ridge Community Church, an innovative, nondenominational church in the Baltimore-Washington region.

Brian has been active in networking and mentoring church planters and pastors since the mid-1980s. He is a popular speaker and lecturer for conferences, seminaries, campus groups, and retreats, nationally and internationally. His public speaking covers a broad range of topics including the spiritual search, faith and doubt, postmodernism, Biblical studies, evangelism, apologetics, global mission, leadership, pastoral survival and burnout, church growth, church planting, and the integration of faith with literature, film, music, visual arts, and ecology.

He has written four books, *More Ready Than You Realize* (Zondervan, 2002),*The Church on the Other Side: Doing Ministry in the Postmodern Matrix* (Zondervan, 2000), *Finding Faith* (Zondervan, 1999), *A New Kind of Christian* (Jossey-Bass, 2001). He has coauthored two books, *A is for Abductive* with Leonard Sweet (Zondervan, 2002) and *Adventures in Missing the Point* with Anthony Compolo (Emergent/YS, 2003), and has published articles in numerous periodicals and e-zines. He is a senior fellow in Emergent (www.emergentvillage.com) and is active on several nonprofit boards.

Brian is married to Grace, and they have four young adult children, one of whom is a cancer survivor. Brian's personal interests include wildlife, hiking, fishing, and the arts.

ABOUT LEADERSHIP NETWORK

THE MISSION OF LEADERSHIP NETWORK is to accelerate the effectiveness of the Church by identifying and connecting strategic leaders and providing them with access to resources in the form of new ideas, people, and tools. Leadership Network's focus has been on the practice and application of faith at the local congregational level. Churches and church leaders served by Leadership Network represent a wide variety of primarily Protestant faith traditions that range from mainline to evangelical to independent. All are characterized by innovation, entrepreneurial leadership, and a desire to be on the leading edge of ministry.

Established as a private foundation in 1984 by social entrepreneur Bob Buford, Leadership Network is acknowledged as an influential leader among churches and faith-based ministries and a major resource to which innovative leaders turn for networking and information.

For additional information on Leadership Network, please contact

Leadership Network
2501 Cedar Springs, Suite 200
Dallas, Texas 75201
800–765–5323
www.leadnet.org

*A New Kind of Christian: A Tale of Two
Friends on a Spiritual Journey*

A Christianity Today Award of Merit

Brian D. McLaren
$21.95 Hardcover
ISBN: 0–7879–5599–X

*Get ready to wake up your spirit and breathe
deep. McLaren's* A New Kind of Christian *is a
street-level, lived excursion into this present millennium . . . a world where ministry by control,
condescension, and smug certainty gives way to
incarnational faith.*—**Sally Morgenthaler,** president, SJM Management Co.,
Inc., and author, *Worship Evangelism*

*This is a book that heightens the depths and deepens the peaks. Like all the
best things in life, it is not to be entered into lightly, but reverently and in the
fear of a God who is waiting for the church to stop asking WWJD and start
asking WIJD–What Is Jesus Doing?*—**Leonard Sweet,** Drew University

After many years as a successful pastor, Brian McLaren has found—as more
and more Christians are finding—that none of the current streams of Christianity fully describes his own developing faith, which focuses on a more com-
prehensive understanding of the world and God's mission in it. *A New Kind
of Christian* (Jossey-Bass, 2001) gives voice to this emerging understanding
of what it means to be a Christian in our particular time in history and offers
a constructive vision of what a postmodern Christian might look like.

This inspiring and wise tale captures the new spirit of a relevant Christianity,
where traditional division and doctrinal differences must give way to a focus
on God and God's dream for this world.

BRIAN D. McLAREN is the founding pastor of Cedar Ridge Community
Church in the Washington-Baltimore area and the author of several books on
contemporary Christianity, including *The Church on the Other Side: Doing
Ministry in the Postmodern Matrix* (2000) and *The Story We Find Ourselves
In* (Jossey-Bass, 2003).

[Price subject to change]